After Oriental Despotism

After Oriental Despotism

Eurasian Growth in a Global Perspective

Alessandro Stanziani

BLOOMSBURY
LONDON · NEW DELHI · NEW YORK · SYDNEY

Bloomsbury Academic
An imprint of Bloomsbury Publishing Plc

50 Bedford Square
London
WC1B 3DP
UK

1385 Broadway
New York
NY 10018
USA

www.bloomsbury.com

Bloomsbury is a registered trade mark of Bloomsbury Publishing Plc

First published 2014

© Alessandro Stanziani, 2014

Alessandro Stanziani has asserted his right under the Copyright, Designs and Patents Act, 1988, to be identified as Author of this work.

All rights reserved. No part of this publication may be reproduced or transmitted in any form or by any means, electronic or mechanical, including photocopying, recording, or any information storage or retrieval system, without prior permission in writing from the publishers.

No responsibility for loss caused to any individual or organization acting on or refraining from action as a result of the material in this publication can be accepted by Bloomsbury or the author.

British Library Cataloguing-in-Publication Data
A catalogue record for this book is available from the British Library.

ISBN: HB: 978-1-4725-2353-2
PB: 978-1-4725-2678-6
ePDF: 978-1-4725-2265-8
ePub: 978-1-4725-3339-5

Library of Congress Cataloging-in-Publication Data
A catalog record for this book is available from the Library of Congress.

Typeset by Jones Ltd, London

Contents

Acknowledgements		vii
Introduction: The Scope and Aim		1
1	The Historical Dimension of Economic Backwardness	7
	Culture and economics	11
	Dependence, subaltern groups and the world economy	13
	The question of continuity in history	15
2	Beyond Asiatic Despotism: Territorial Power and State Construction in Eurasia	17
	Military, mercenary and peasant	22
	War and economic dynamics	24
	War and technological innovation	26
	Frontiers, territories and nomadic empires	29
3	The Power of the Steppe: The Mongol Heritage and the Expansion of Muscovy	35
	Steppe dynamics: The warrior states	36
	Military organization	39
	Administration, finances and the army	43
	Provisions in kind and wheat markets	46
	Mobilization and colonization: The frontier as a social and political experiment	50
	Military service and social order	52
	The power of the steppe	57
4	Slavery and Trade in Central Asia and Russia	61
	Introduction	61
	Kholopy: Slaves, serfs, or indentured servants?	65
	War captives at a crossroads of empires	73
	Slavery in Central Eurasia: Its estimation and overall interpretation	86

5	Neither Feudalism nor Capitalism: Agrarian Markets under Coercion	91
	The institutions of Russian serfdom	91
	Labour on Russian estates	94
	Proto-industry, trade and growth under serfdom	95
	Towards a reassessment of second serfdom in Eastern Europe	101
6	Beyond Economic Backwardness: Labour and Growth in Eurasia in the Long Nineteenth Century	107
	Growth and labour in Europe and Asia	111

Conclusion: Russia in a Globalizing World	117
Notes	124
References	157
Index	179

Acknowledgements

French CNRS (Centre National de la Rechecher Scientifique) and the French ANR (Agence Nationale de la Recherche) provided funds and grants to successfully complete this research.

This book has benefited from the support of many friends and colleagues. Jeremy Black immediately supported this book; in Paris, at the EHESS, Maurice Aymard, Gilles Postel-Vinay and Christian Lamouroux discussed at length several chapters; I also benefited from discussions with my students.

Jane Burbank (NYU) and Fred Cooper (NYU) discussed over years parts, papers and seminars linked to this book. Marcel van der Linden (IISG) always encouraged my work.

Prabhu Mohapatra (Delhi University) and Madhavan Palat – as well as the participants in the biannual meeting of Indian Labour Historians – commented on earlier drafts.

Elise Kimerling Wirtschafter (Pomona University) made comments on earlier drafts, seminars and, finally, on the whole manuscript. I fully acknowledge my debt to her valuable suggestions and comments.

Marina Mogilner and Ilia Guerasimov – friends of Ab Imperio, in Kazan, and who have just recently moved to the University of Illinois – made valuable comments at the workshop they organized in Kazan.

In Japan, I had the opportunity to present and discuss chapters of this book with Kimitaka Matsusato (Sapporo University), Kaoru Sugihara (Tokyo University) and Masashi Haneda (Tokyo University). Professor Takeo Suzuki discussed with me and organized several lectures and seminars at the Waseda University. Faculty and students helped me with extremely valuable comments.

Other friends in the USA also helped me with comments and suggestions: Brian Davis (UTSA), R. Bin Wong (UCLA), David W. Sabean (UCLA), and Kenneth Pomeranz (University of Chicago). Richard Roberts and the Stanford University provided me with a one-month invitation. Lectures at Stanford largely contributed to complete this book.

In Berlin, the Wissenschafts Kolleg provided a wonderful intellectual environment and the opportunity to discuss my work in several German universities. Andreas Eckert and Jurgen Kocka, at Re-Work (Humboldt University), debated my work at length.

In Russia, Boris Ananich and the archive personnel in both Moscow and Petersburg helped with the files, permissions and research. I strongly regret that my former mentor and friend in Russia, Viktor Petrovich Danilov, one of the greatest historians of his generation, left us before I could achieve this book.

Introduction: The Scope and Aim

Russia maintained its power, with ups and downs, for centuries, despite repeated European forecasts of its imminent fall. During the reign of Peter the Great and after the Crimean War (1853–1856), the Bolshevik revolution in 1917, the putsch in 1989 and the financial crisis in 1997, the West always believed it could see signs of Russia's impending collapse, but it never occurred.[1] What accounts for this and how can we possibly explain such a discrepancy between Western expectations and Russian performance?

From the eighteenth century to the present, comparisons between Russia and the major European countries have formed part of a wider debate about 'backwardness'. The goal has been to create a comparative scale to account for both economic growth and so-called 'blockages'. Montesquieu's 'Asiatic Despotism', Voltaire's and Diderot's perceptions of Russia and Asia, and the so-called Asiatic mode of production described by liberal, radical and Marxist historiography in the nineteenth century are well-known examples. Then, in the twentieth century, the comparative and global analysis of Eurasia found its way into discussions of backwardness and underdevelopment, decolonization, the fate of communism and the Cold War as well as arguments such as Oriental despotism and Hayek's *Road to Serfdom*. Authors as different as Kula, Wallerstein and North agree on this: in early modern times, Russia and Eastern Europe responded to the commercial, agrarian and then industrial expansion of the West by binding the peasantries to the land and its lords.[2] It is interesting that even new approaches to world history such as Pomeranz's 'great divergence', while contesting Chinese backwardness and European ethnocentrism, still consider Russia the paradigm of unfree labour and lack of markets and, as such, opposed to both the Lower Yangtzee and Britain.[3] The connections between Europe and Asia exclude Central Eurasia. What if we were to abandon both classical oppositions and the more recent ranking of 'Europe' and 'Asia' and question regional and global history through the lens of Central Eurasia?

In this book I will focus on the 'Russian case' not to confirm our preconceptions but to disclose historical possibilities, bifurcations and ultimately a new vision of modernization. Economic backwardness, Asiatic despotism, Orientalism and dependence express our perceptions of modernization over the last three centuries. Those perceptions include the identification and fear of the 'Asiatic', 'Mongol', then 'communist' and now, once again, 'yellow' and 'new Russian mafia' perils. After the collapse of the Berlin Wall and Asia's return to world prominence, after the global crisis of the Western economies, the time has come to discuss these notions and stop using history to judge or to prove the superiority of the West in terms of economic efficiency or political organization. Instead, I wish to provide a new view of Eurasian history and from that starting point, re-examine global history and modernization.

My primary aim is to avoid comparing the Russian and Inner Asian case exclusively to an ideal model of the West. I want to reconcile the differences between the historical paths specific to particular regions with their interconnections, transfers and overall dynamics. In the following pages, after a preliminary discussion (Chapter 1) of the main approaches to Oriental despotism, backwardness and dependence, we will discuss (Chapter 2) so-called Asiatic and Oriental despotism and conventional taxonomies of state formations. I will present possible state formations in Central Asia in early modern and modern times and show that Russia and the Inner Asian powers in the modern period were hardly as despotic and had more capital than Tilly and others have asserted. Whereas Europe did not adopt a modern conscription system until the Napoleonic wars, Russia – which was considered backward – was the first country to implement widespread, streamlined conscription.[4] The short-, medium- and long-term successes of Muscovy (Chapter 3) were linked to the way they combined forms of recruitment, army and social order, military supplies and overall economic organization. Compared with the West, these solutions proved to be less 'primitive' and simplistic than is usually claimed. Flexible Imperial repertoires were the most widespread political and institutional solution adopted in Eurasia over the long term.[5] Indeed, the expansion of Muscovy relied not only on military and diplomatic forces but also on trade and labour. We will study historical forms of bondage and trade in Russia and Central Asia: slavery and war captives first, then serfdom. The existence of slavery in Russia (Chapter 4) is little known outside the circle of pre-Petrine Russia specialists, despite slavery's importance not only for Russian but also for global history, e.g., the link between slavery and serfdom; the relationship between the lengthy Russian history of bondage (most prominently slavery and serfdom) and the Gulag; and last but not least, bondage as testimony to the Mongol influence on Russia or, vice versa, as a response to European world expansion. I will provide an original study of slaves, bonded people and war captives in Russia and Central Asia between the fifteenth and the nineteenth centuries. We will identify the three main areas and routes of the slave trade: the Silk Road, Central Asia and the Mediterranean; the trade of goods and slaves between Russia, Central Asia, Iran and India; the slave trade between Russia, the Crimean Khanate and the Ottoman Empire.

This innovative study of the slave trade in Eurasia has important implications for the interpretation of Russian history on the one hand, and for the global history of slavery and trade on the other. Without the Eurasian slave trade, Mediterranean and later transatlantic slavery would have been radically different. The Eurasian slave trade provided people, models and practices of enslavement to the expanding West. Thus, instead of a break between the slavery of the ancient world and colonial slavery, I will assert a continuity through the Middle Ages and early modern times on a Eurasian and then a global scale.

It would be a mistake, however, to follow this history only in the new connections between Afro-Eurasia and the Atlantic. The heritage of Eurasian slavery and state expansion was important in Russia and Inner Asia as well. New connections appeared between slavery and other forms of bondage, namely serfdom. Discussions of Russian serfdom have adopted a much more cautious attitude; they have mostly focused on its origin (the State[6] and/or the landowners[7]) and its profitability,[8] rather than on the interplay between its legal rules and economic activity. The most remarkable contributions are those of Confino, Hoch, Wirtschafter and Moon, who have effectively revisited the simplistic definition and functioning of Russian serfdom.[9] Serfdom's dynamics and rules have been questioned; it has been suggested that serfdom was never officially introduced[10] and that it was much more a set of practices than a formal system.[11] On that basis, some have argued that serfdom may have been profitable, if not everywhere in Russia, at least in many areas.[12] I have already discussed elsewhere the institutions of serfdom.[13] Here we will show (Chapter 5) that Russian serfdom was (1) an attempt to control competition between estate owners; and (2) a form of institutional extortion of peasants by landlords whose rights officially consisted in controlling marriages, second jobs and emigrations. There never was a central institutionalization of 'serfdom' in Russia, but there were local forms of bondage.[14] On the Russian estates, 'agency' problems (relationships between landlords, bailiffs and peasants) were not solved on the basis of abstract economic considerations, but they did respond to the peculiar way institutions and actors interacted. Peasants' leaders, landlords and bailiffs worked much more in coordination with, than in opposition to, each other. The attention given to supervision and its organization testifies to the role of intermediary institutions (bailiffs and village elders) and their ability to complement each other. From there, we will show that Russian local markets were increasingly incorporated into a national market during the second half of the eighteenth century; not only landlords but also their peasants firmly entered the rural agrarian markets. Peasants' activity on rural markets surpassed that of merchants and small urban traders.

This conclusion implies that there is no evidence for Kula's and Wallerstein's models. According to them, under second serfdom, Russian demesnes reduced their integration in local markets, peasants became self-sufficient and landlords extracted a surplus of grain from the peasants and then sold it mostly abroad and used the income not to invest, but only to buy luxury products. In this view, Russian and Eastern European serfdom constituted the quasi-periphery of Europe. We contest this view and show there was significant market and economic development in Russia itself in the eighteenth and early nineteenth centuries.

If this is so, then the history of global capitalism needs to be re-assessed. Capitalism could rely upon multiple cores, each based upon different social and political structures (Russia, France, Britain, and the United States). Contrary to commonly held views, I argue that neither political rights nor a free market and full property rights guarantee a higher rate of growth. The examples of nineteenth-century Russia and nowadays China testify to this fact. The link between economic growth, political equilibrium and social hierarchies has to be re-examined from a new angle. The question is not so much whether an abstract notion of the market produced a more or less efficient and egalitarian social equilibrium compared with an equally abstract old regime, but which historical forms of markets, labour, and politics have produced different outcomes in terms of both economic dynamics and social inequalities. From this perspective, the abolition of serfdom in Russia in 1861 provides a useful observatory to debate those questions. In our view, the reforms of 1861 have to be put into a broader context of multiple reforms implemented over a century and a half. The last chapter will show, contrary to the views of Gershenkron and many others, that Russia enjoyed consistent economic growth between 1861 and 1914. Thus, pauperization of the peasantry and frequent famines did not in fact take place,[15] and both agriculture and living standards grew steadily during this period.[16] Russia experienced growth rates similar to those of Germany, France, the United States, Japan, Norway, Canada and the United Kingdom. Therefore, if Gershenkron's model is not confirmed, we need to put forward an alternative explanation for the evolution of Russia compared with that of other areas.

I will argue that the answer cannot be found simply in the rate of growth, first because despite lack of democracy and freedom, the rate of growth of Russia was close to those of the main Western countries and second because historical interpretations of economic performance should not be confined to growth and efficiency but also take into consideration the distribution of wealth and social hierarchies. Russian growth was achieved by increasing, not reducing, inequalities and social tensions. Here is one of the major lessons drawn from our revisited Russian history: how long will we need to keep judging historical progress on the grounds of economic efficiency alone?

To be sure, it would be politically correct if economic efficiency, democracy and social justice would all fit together. Unfortunately this is hardly the case; we therefore need to discuss whether to give priority to economic efficiency, civil rights or social justice in our interpretation of 'modernization' and in our political philosophy views and goals.

1

The Historical Dimension of Economic Backwardness

Alexander Gershenkron is justly famous for *Economic Backwardness in Historical Perspective*. His model postulates that in backward economies, the lack of a middle class and entrepreneurs will be compensated by the state. In particular, taking the example of Germany and Russia, Gershenkron argued that the lack of bourgeoisie was compensated by the major role of the state. In latecomer countries, capital-intensive industries and large-size units, instead of agriculture and consumption units, take the lead.

Yet these two terms – the notions of backwardness and historical temporalities – are hardly compatible. In reality, economic backwardness refers to logical time, that is, a time dictated by pre-existing schemes (economic models, philosophy of history etc.). Indeed, well before Gershenkron, from the eighteenth century to today, comparisons between the Russian economy and the economies of Europe's main countries have been part of a broader debate over the notion of 'backwardness'. It involves proposing a scale of comparison to account for economic growth as well as for so-called 'obstruction' factors. The framework of comparison is created by drawing up a list of elements based on a standard Western ideal. We will not recount the history of this model[1] here but simply mention its main components. Indeed, like Max Weber, Gershenkron began by drawing up the list of Western characteristics on which his comparison would be based; he too emphasized cities, the bourgeoisie, markets and private property. Yet unlike Marx and to some extent Weber, he thought it was possible to arrive at industrialization (but not capitalism) without a bourgeoisie. In place of this component, 'backward' countries (to use the jargon of the 1960s and 1970s) such as Prussia and Russia had 'substituting factors', notably the state. This is a very clever solution to the problem raised by the need to reconcile particular features, historical specificities and general dynamics. If backwardness and diversity go together, then it is possible to conceive of alternative paths.[2]

However, contrary to appearances, Gershenkron does not compare Russia to England in specific historical contexts. Instead he opposes an ideal image of the West (and of England in particular) to an equally ideal image of nineteenth-century Russia. English economic development is associated with the early introduction of a Parliament, privatization of the commons and hence the formation of a proletariat available for agriculture and industry. In contrast, Russia is associated with market towns – and therefore with a bourgeoisie – as well as the presence of an absentee landed gentry living off serfdom.

These interpretations stemmed from the research work on England and Russia available at the time Gershenkron was writing, starting with more general works from Marx to Polanyi that stressed those characteristics in describing the English industrial revolution.[3]

Soviet and Western historiographies also concurred on the limits of the 1861 Russian reforms (abolition of serfdom), the ensuing impoverishment of the peasants and the extent of Tsarist industrialization.[4] Like these authors, Gershenkron put great trust in the economic and statistical research produced in Russia between 1870 and 1930. Though indeed these works contained a wealth of information, it is nevertheless important, as we have shown elsewhere, to understand the conditions under which it was produced. Our aim is not to invalidate turn-of-the-century Russian statistics, let alone 'correct' them in line with a given statistical history, but rather to take the empirical methods and the intellectual and political challenges of the period into account so their conclusions may be used later on.[5] In particular, the economic and social statistics produced in Russia at the turn of the century were, for the most part, the work of intellectuals, specialists and sometimes merely activists employed by the *zemstvo*, local self-government organizations.[6] These authors were quick to reveal the inadequacies of the reforms, the limits of autocracy and the impoverishment of the peasantry. Above and beyond their considerable differences, 'Marxists' and 'populists' agreed on this aspect. They selected typical cases and variables to confirm their hypotheses. Thus, Kablukov, a professor of economics and statistics at the University of Moscow in charge of statistics for the Moscow region in the early twentieth century, stated that a peasant should be classified as a *meshchane* (petit-bourgeois) as soon as he bought land for himself.[7] By definition, a peasant was someone who did not have enough land to satisfy the needs of his family.[8] These were the sources Gershenkron used in his work, which were hence doubly decontextualized: he took out of context turn-of-the-century sources, which in turn were the result of a particular empirical clarification.

At the same time, this approach completely dominated in the 1960s: a certain historical situation could fit into a more general pattern of economic development, drawing comparisons by analogy without worrying too much about the conditions in which the sources were produced. This explains how it eventually became possible to use Russian development and the debate between 'populists' and 'Marxists' from 1870 to 1914 in discussions about which type of development policies were best suited to Asia, Africa or South America during the 1960s. At that time, development policies discussed about the opportunity to give priority to agriculture or industry, small or large units. And authors found in the Russian-Soviet debate of the late nineteenth–early twentieth centuries a central reference.[9] The notion of history as a *magistra vitae* and the resulting normative temptations were at the root of these analyses, which acquired 'contemporary relevance' but lost their historical specificity. The comparisons were not so much anachronistic as a-temporal.

Such approaches were not abandoned when colonialism and the Cold War came to an end; on the contrary, those historical processes even encouraged their use. The 'transition' to capitalism in the former Soviet-bloc countries as well as in Latin America and of course China and India became the inevitable outcome of an economic model considered to be valid everywhere. Neo-institutional economics, developed in the 1970s by Douglass North among others, became the dominant paradigm in comparative economic history.[10] Instead of evoking an ideal competitive market, like liberal, neoclassical theory, neo-institutional thought took seriously the criticism of those who viewed the market economy as a particular historical construction. It incorporated institutional phenomena in the neo-liberal approach, maintaining that institutions were efficient insofar as they offered a means to cope with 'market imperfections'. Thus, the commons, which had been criticized since the eighteenth century as a source of inefficiency, were viewed as a safeguard against risk at a time when the markets were still so imperfect they prevented rapid compensation for poor harvests in one region by the surplus from other regions.[11] In this way, 'market imperfections' were the explanation for Russian peasant settlements and serfdom in Eastern Europe.[12] In other words, there is a rationale for every institution present in the history of humanity.

The only difference in relation to previous approaches was that henceforth the list of development factors was drawn up on the basis of one and only one criterion: efficiency and minimized transaction costs (i.e., a cost incurred in making an economic exchange or participating in a market). The pattern has been applied to all sorts of historical experiments, including in Russia and the USSR. Using the theory of transaction costs and the information economy, Joseph Stiglitz, a Nobel Prize winner in economics, revealed the limits of free market equilibrium along with the distortions produced by the Soviet bureaucracy and by managed economies in general.[13] Stiglitz acknowledges the imperfections of free markets, in particular in that information and prices are incomplete and do not lead, by themselves, to an efficient equilibrium as postulated by the standard neoclassical theory. At the same time, Stiglitz considers that the solution cannot be found in the plan for, as the Soviet experience shows, planners have less information (and more corruption) than the market and the outcome will be even worse than in market economies. He thus suggests that appropriate institutions can correct and help the market without suffocating it.

We may observe that, in these approaches, the same model is employed to talk about the market in nineteenth-century Africa, serfdom in Russia or fairs in Europe in the modern period: it is no accident that neo-institutional economics speaks less about capitalism than about the market economy. This approach calls into question the classifications of economic systems proposed by traditional neo-classical and Marxist literatures (capitalism, peasant economy, feudalism, etc.). Instead we find a typology of organizations that evolve strictly in relation to the institutional context. Hence, the approach cannot explain the relationship between institutional changes and forms of market organization: are institutions the result or the source of economic behaviour?

In the case of the USSR, did economic weakness cause political decline or, on the contrary, did Soviet institutions close the market and thereby bring about its inevitable collapse?

This question, which may seem innocuous to historians, was important for development policy insofar as the debate, especially in the 1990s, was focussed on knowing whether, in post-socialist countries in particular, it was first necessary to set up market institutions and a democratic political system in order to have a market, or conversely whether the market would give rise through its very development to adequate institutions.[14] The issue appears to have been resolved since then because, contrary to the politically correct arguments that always sought to link capitalism to democracy, the experiences in China and Russia in recent years confirm that this equation is by no means obvious from the standpoint of either political philosophy or historical observation.

We can therefore understand Gareth Austin's observations: the importance of markets in Africa testifies to the fact that differences from Europe are not linked to an anti-market mentality hostile to profit, but simply to institutional pressures from inside as well as outside (corruption, colonialism, etc.).[15] No doubt this reflects the author's good intentions: he is looking for a way out of the insoluble internal contradictions of a fundamental difference in the African 'mentality', for which relativist and cultural approaches are always on the lookout. In the process, however, everything pertaining to economic anthropology is swept outside the historian's vision: according to the neo-institutional approach in any case, whether it is applied to Russia in the eighteenth century, the USSR in the twentieth century, or China and Latin America, 'mentalities' have little influence on economic behaviour, which stems solely from institutional constraints.[16]

These observations may seem far removed from the historian's approach; they are probably often tautological and keep us from grasping the full complexity of historical transformations. Yet the question remains as to whether or not recourse to mentalities, to forms of 'non-optimising rationalities' and to anthropology in general can yield less mechanical comparisons.

Culture and economics

Economic history in its most economist form has been the constant target of critics who brought out the fundamental differences between societies and thus the impossibility of using a single model to explain different socio-economic dynamics in time and space.[17] Starting in the 1970s, in particular, this argument was joined to a more general one consisting in revealing the irreducible difference between history and the social sciences on the one hand, and natural sciences on the other. This approach was widely acclaimed by those who thought that proposed modalities of development had to be suited to each country. Economic and social policies should be adapted to the local 'context'.[18] Unlike general economic models, these approaches relied upon anthropology and sought to identify local conditions and features to orient development policies. This relativism, in large part anti-imperialist, but also anti-industrialist, had a twofold advantage over the approaches mentioned earlier: it avoided taking a mythical West as model and reintroduced a 'superstructure' in the objects of comparative analysis. Clifford Geertz took the lead among historians; Geertz argued that culture is public because 'meaning is', and systems of meanings are what produce culture; they are the collective property of a particular people.[19] Starting from this, many historians and social scientists talked about 'kidnapped language' and language-based or 'cultural' dependence, etc. According to this view, Western perceptions of the 'other' reduce civilization to positively valorized institutions, behaviours and accomplishments associated with the West.[20]

Along a similar line of reasoning, in Said's orientalism, these ethnocentric constructions were part of a long-term intellectual and political context: Western domination implies above all the invention of a backward Orient. Western knowledge about the East is not generated from facts or reality, but from preconceived archetypes that envision all 'Eastern' societies as fundamentally similar to one another, and fundamentally dissimilar to 'Western' societies. According to Said, this discourse establishes 'the East' as antithetical to 'the West'.[21] Wolff extended the pattern to Russia, insisting that the invention of Eastern Europe in eighteenth-century discussions in France, Prussia and England created a division between liberal, capitalist Western Europe and despotic, feudal Eastern Europe. This opposition was ultimately seen as a tool of European political and economic domination over Russia.[22]

However, this conclusion has been contested; Michael Confino in particular observed that the expression 'Eastern Europe' was not adopted in European debates until very late, towards the end of the nineteenth century, more than a century after the period discussed by Wolff. As a result, the chronology of a cultural invention hardly coincided with that of comparative economic and political dynamics.[23] This observation led to a thorough review and brought the discussion back to its starting point: how did European observers view Russia and serfdom in the eighteenth century? What were the repercussions of that view in economic, political and cultural terms? In the end, are we sure that during this period Russia was 'virtually the periphery of Europe'?

In reality, in the eighteenth century, the most commonplace images of Russia in Europe referred to two interrelated elements: despotism and serfdom. These topics were examined in connection with broader discussions of freedom and labour and hence the problem of slavery in the colonies and guilds in France, and of course in relation to the evolution of the French monarchy.[24] In 1763, Voltaire finished his history of Peter the Great and sent a copy to Catherine II.[25] In this work, as well as in his letters to Catherine, he adopted a prudent attitude towards Russian serfs, considering it premature to free them before they had been enlightened.[26]

Diderot, flattered by the attention Catherine reserved for him, asked: 'Does the serfdom of farmers have an influence on culture? Does the peasants' lack of property have any ill effects?'

He then answered tersely: 'I don't know if there is a country where farmers love the land and their homes more than in Russia. Our free provinces have almost as much grain than those that are not.'[27] At the time, Diderot believed Catherine and the French monarchy were both capable of achieving reform.

Operating on this assumption, he distinguished nations that reached the peak of civilization and began to decline from those which – being closer to nature – could civilize themselves by avoiding the evils of civilization. He put America and Russia in the latter category.[28]

His ideas changed during the 1770s on account of the weak reforms in France and Russia. Beginning in the 1780s, Diderot, like Condillac, combined his scepticism regarding enlightened despotism[29] with a more general critique of European civilization. As Condillac suggested, 'Too much communication with Europe was less likely to civilise the Russians than to pass on to them the vices of civilised nations'.[30] From this point of view, the reforms in Russia called for similar reforms in France and its colonies. The same attitude was shared by a great majority of philosophers.[31]

Though eighteenth-century thought was ultimately rather uncertain about its relationship to absolutism and (forced) labour, it would be wrong to assert that the Russians misinterpreted these approaches and transformed the liberalism and Enlightenment of Europe into reforms aimed at reconciling serfdom, the market, autocracy and reforms. Indeed, the question that arose in Russia was the same as the one that crystallized in France around slavery: should the legal status of serfs be radically abolished or merely modified? And from there, does economic condition alone, together with the free market, determine political and social status or is it part of a more complex political and moral order? No doubt the influence of more radical or even revolutionary thinking was shown, for example, by Nikolai Radishchev (after a careful reading of Raynal).[32] It is nevertheless interesting to note that the most radical Russian approaches to serfdom often included an analysis of the American experience rather than the French or European one.[33] Reciprocity, when indeed it exists, is never perfect and must be sought in three-way or even multiple comparisons. The Russian authors indeed underwent the influence of the Enlightenment, but they interpreted it through the prism of German cameralism. In any event, the invention of Eastern Europe did not take place at this time. Were there other notions in circulation that could have ensured European hegemony over Russia?

Dependence, subaltern groups and the world economy

In the wake of Gramsci,[34] the authors claiming to adhere to subaltern studies insisted first of all that language was a component of power and a factor in hierarchies, and second, that subaltern classes and colonized peoples were not necessarily passive in their interactions with the colonizers. Thus, the British exercised their power in colonial India by controlling and modifying the language, as the case of the Zamindars clearly illustrates. The Zamindars, who were income tax administrators under the Mughals, were considered landowners by the British. This 'translation' subsequently paved the way for British territorial control.

The same process could be easily discerned in other contexts, and indeed, translations, media, the circulation of legal rules and the language of international organizations have all been designated as instruments of power and domination of the 'South' by the 'North'. Notions such as market, trade, family, child, property, inheritance, peasant, worker, etc., therefore acquired specific local features that were irreducible to a more general model.[35] No doubt this approach was more nuanced and differentiated and enabled a more complex arborescence of societies and cultures than the ones we discussed earlier, resulting in both differentiation and comparison between different operating methods. From then on, dependence was decompartmentalized, along with the history of elites and dominant groups.

There are nevertheless several problematic aspects in these approaches, beginning with the interaction between elites and subaltern groups. Fred Cooper has highlighted the fact that Africans, Indians and colonized populations were far less passive than subaltern studies assert, despite their Gramscian premise. Colonized peoples had significant impact on their colonizers, whose violence and ambition did not always reflect real control over the colony.[36]

The same question arose more than once with regard to Russia: to what extent did Europe's identification of Russian autocracy and serfdom as ideal types play a part in its domination of Russia?

Similarly, to what extent does exporting a-temporal economic notions today (balanced budget, private property, privatization, etc.) by the International Monetary Fund (IMF) contribute to Russia's dependence on the West?

Let us look at the first point: the analyses cited by Wolff regarding the invention of Eastern Europe, together with those of Orientalism and subaltern studies, form a sort of complement to theories of dependence in the 1970s. Some emphasize domination through knowledge, others through the economy; in any case, 'peripheral areas' are indeed identified and world history recounts the emergence of Western capitalism dominating the rest of the world.

I will not dwell on the methodological criticisms (determinism and historical finalism, circular reasoning, etc.) levelled against these patterns by numerous authors,[37] but I will examine their empirical validity. One well-known argument borrowed from other authors by Wallerstein consisted in showing that the expansion of Western capitalism was the cause of the second serfdom in Russia: increased demand for wheat in Europe prompted Russian lords to coerce peasants into producing the amount of wheat required for export. This was said to have resulted in an international division of labour: England produced textiles using wage labour, whereas Russia sold grain by resorting to serfdom. In reality, as we will see, the situation was quite different. Russian serfdom was introduced in the fifteenth century in connection with the consolidation of Muscovite power; restrictions on peasant mobility were a factor in complex agreements and tensions between state elites and various categories of landowners. These transformations took place between the sixteenth and the seventeenth centuries, well before English industrialization, and had little to do with the West. The increase in labour service (*la corvée*) in the eighteenth century, so frequently mentioned by Wallerstein, therefore takes on a whole new meaning. According to the traditional analysis of serfdom, the rapid development of labour service was linked to a drop in commodity sales, causing the estates to fall back on their own resources and exert greater pressure on the peasants. The dynamics of Russian estates at the time does not confirm this argument. Chapter 4 will show that the economic dynamics of eighteenth-century Russia cannot be explained by an increase in serfdom in response to European growth, but on the contrary by a relaxation of the labour constraints weighing on peasants and their gradual integration, together with landowners, in trade networks. These dynamics went beyond the official rules governing 'serfdom', which were increasingly overtaken by social and economic changes. It is just as hard if not harder to find confirmation of Russia's dependence on the West as it is in the case of India or colonial Africa. Finalism and historical determinism keep us from seeing the temporal dynamics specific to the Russian context. In that sense, these questions bring us back to the continuities and breaks in comparative history.

The question of continuity in history

Gershenkron (among many others)[38] discussed the question of continuities and breaks in history. He thought it was impossible to resolve the question once and for all and that how it was viewed depended on the object under study, the historical materials used and the questions asked. His model of the factors of substitution led him to see the 1861 reforms as an incomplete break from previous periods. The problem was that, in the case of Russia, the model did not withstand epistemological challenges or empirical validation. In particular, over the last few decades, a number of works have reworked the famous argument of peasant impoverishment following the abolition of serfdom and the stagnation of the Russian economy as a whole,[39] which were at the core of Gershenkron's analysis. Historical demography, for example, has observed a significant decline in mortality, above all in relation to access to resources, and an increase in the height of conscripts.[40] Detailed analyses of the evolution of privately owned land distribution have in turn revealed a sizeable amount of land purchased by peasants (both individuals and communities).[41] Finally, careful studies of industrial[42] and proto-industrial organizations show that these sectors were far more dynamic than traditional historiography had thought.

Given what we have observed for the period prior to 1861, the elements of continuity would appear to carry the day; instead of a shift from feudalism to capitalism, from serfdom to wage labour, we find a collection of common elements (the continuation of proto-industry and of peasant communities, a long-term trend in the development of agricultural markets and of markets in general). Instead of creating a clear-cut divide, the abolition of serfdom gave a further push to a trend already under way in peasant economies, which were by no means 'immobile'. At the same time, the reforms introduced a substantial new feature: access to land ownership and the transfer of inhabited estates were no longer reserved for nobles but extended to merchants and Russian 'bourgeois'. In other words, the difference lay not in the relationships between landlords and peasants, but, as before, in the complex interaction among lords, peasants, landowners and state elites, each one a highly composite group differentiated by its income, origin and degree of social inclusion. This image of Russia is totally different from the one conveyed by traditional historiography; it is the fruit of questioning that avoids studying the country solely by the yardstick of an idealized West. In the following page, I will develop this approach for several related themes: the army and Imperial expansion; slavery and serfdom; agriculture, markets and economic growth.

2

Beyond Asiatic Despotism: Territorial Power and State Construction in Eurasia

When Karl Wittfogel published his book *Oriental Despotism*,[1] the Cold War was at its height. Using his Marxist training and Marx's notion of the Asian mode of production, the author described the USSR under Stalin as 'despotism'. From this viewpoint, he was putting the Soviet Union in the same category as earlier forms of Asian power that were said to have developed highly despotic societies by controlling hydraulic resources. Wittfogel contrasted this type of organization with slave-owning societies and feudal societies. Instead of slaves or serfs, Oriental despotic societies subjugated the entire population to the will of high-ranking bureaucrats. In the introduction to the French edition of Wittfogel's book and in other articles, Pierre Vidal-Naquet took pains to point out the similarities and differences between Wittfogel on the one hand, and Marx and Montesquieu on the other. The latter, in particular, had indeed put forward the notion of Asian despotism in his *Esprit des lois* (which we find later on in the identification of the serf (*serf de la glebe*) in Eastern Europe). Montesquieu was in fact designating both the descendants of the Mongols and absolute power in France. Criticism of one system went hand in hand with criticism of the other.

The Asian mode of production that Marx contrasted to feudalism and slavery was altogether different: as such it constituted a 'deviation' from the historical laws of economics. For decades, the Asian mode of production was hotly debated within Marxist and socialist circles. At issue was how to categorize Russia and later the USSR: was it an example of Asian despotism or a truly communist system that had succeeded 'feudalism' and then 'capitalism'? What was really at stake in Wittfogel's book was this: at the time of the Cold War, the USSR was viewed as a despotic system not only by liberals and conservatives but also by socialists and communists critical of Stalinism and the Soviet Union. For Wittfogel, as for Montesquieu and Marx before him, the analysis of Asia was actually intended as a discussion of political relationships within the 'West'. We encounter the same connection in every Western analysis of Russia; it is an aspect that should be kept in mind because it allows us first to determine the validity and origin of the main historical analyses of Russia and, second, to propose new hypotheses and original interpretations. In this process, it is important not to toss out the baby with the bathwater, for beyond the immediate political issues, the notion of Oriental despotism raised important questions. Are there methods of economic development and political and social organization that distinguish Asia from Europe? How can we account for them?

In the late seventeenth century, the French, Italian and English explorers who travelled to India and China were amazed by the vast territory, exotic customs, and, in Mughal India, the immense wealth.[2] Even at the time, they underscored the economic and military might of the Russians, who were admittedly primitive and close to the Tatars but nevertheless increasingly powerful.[3] In 1689, India, China and Russia produced 70 per cent of the world's GDP[4]; despite considerable uncertainty in the sources, the population of China was estimated at 100–130 million people and that of India at 180 million, whereas the whole of Europe had barely 100 million. These figures tell one story – that of Western wonderment – but they conceal another – how these empires were formed and operated.

The comparative history and the sociology of state construction have often taught us to think in terms of nation-states. Even if an author like Charles Tilly declares at the outset that we must avoid projecting recent constructions on the past, he cannot help doing so himself.[5] That is one of the consequences of studying the past in order to find the origins of the present. The 'myth of origins', criticized by Marc Bloch,[6] thus turns into a solid foundation for a teleological construction of history. Tilly divides states into three groups: tribute-making empires; city-states, mainly Italian; and nation-states. These three categories corresponded to different gradations of capital and coercion. City-states were distinguished by maximal capital and minimal coercive power; at the opposite extreme, again according to Tilly, in Asian empires like Russia and China, lack of capital was compensated by maximum coercion. Finally, only the European nation-states are said to have achieved the right mix of capital and coercion. This combination is said to have given birth to modern states, along with their armies as well as the industrial revolution and urbanization.

This reasoning raises two types of questions: it starts from the results and assumes the chronological antecedents were 'causes', even though there is no evidence, for example, that the growth of England was actually linked to the adoption of the Bill of Rights in 1689 or that Venice lost its power because it was unable to produce a state like France. Capitalism often developed without granting any civil rights. In the end, even the development of capitalism in nineteenth-century Europe was based on considerable restriction of civil and political rights, which were reserved for a minority of landowners. The link between democracy and capitalism is no doubt politically correct but it is not necessarily true. It is, therefore, important to look for capitalism outside current liberal, democratic countries.

Conversely, the Asian states in the modern period were hardly as despotic and had more capital than Tilly and others assert. It is true, as these authors have emphasized, that the Mongol and Turkic powers of Central Asia left their mark on major Asian states like China and Russia. Yet the Mongol and Turkic powers were far less nomadic and plundering than is usually claimed. They possessed a well-established territorial organization, tax system and conscription system that they passed on to their Eurasian successors. The empire of Chinggis Khan was among the largest if not *the* largest in history, and we now know that the Mongols were anything but mere nomadic pillagers. In short, we should not suppose that these countries were held together solely by a great deal of coercion and had no capital.[7]

For a long time, the opposition between sedentary and nomadic populations was asserted within sedentary societies: Momigliano has already underscored the importance of this opposition in Greek and Roman antiquity.[8] National historiographies typically described neighbouring populations as 'barbarians' and those who lived on the margins of territorial institutions were called 'pirates', 'nomads' and 'brigands'.[9] Why should we rely on the representations of sedentary peoples and national historiographers? When we compare each of these historiographies, we realize that the so-called nomads and pirates had often been fully integrated within territorial powers until a break occurred in the existing equilibrium, after which they were described as barbarians and plunderers.[10] It will therefore be necessary to explain the birth of nomadic states and subsequently identify their filiation within the major Eurasian empires. What is the historical link between these formations?

Nicolas di Cosmo tried to go further than Tilly by proposing a theory of state construction in Central Asia. He criticized the opposition between nomad and sedentary populations and put an emphasis on 'crisis' situations to explain the origin of territorial powers in Central Asia. Initially, political entities in Central Asia were organized into clans corresponding to extensive use of the territory. Later on, di Cosmo claimed, the depletion of resources gave rise to a crisis affecting both the economy and the legitimacy of clan chiefs, which could only be overcome by consolidating the territory and creating a tax system and a regular army. This theory goes beyond the nomad–sedentary opposition and has the virtue of introducing the Central Asian powers on the stage of world history.[11] At the same time, the author's approach ends up legitimizing a historical construction by imagining a 'crisis' at its origin: if a change occurred, that meant a crisis must have taken place. Twenty years ago, however, Reinhart Koselleck had already criticized the use of the notion of crisis: a crisis for whom and mentioned by whom?[12]

How much profit was accumulated and how many powers took hold during so-called crisis periods? The relevance of this argument applies to every period and historical configuration: no doubt it is still valid today when the media and politicians invoke a 'crisis' to gain acceptance for certain changes; it is even more valid in history. Prior to di Cosmo, famous historians like Steensgaard, Hobsbawm and many others continually spoke of a 'crisis' in the seventeenth century that would have prompted the shift from the late medieval world to the capitalist world.[13] Braudel endeavoured to criticize this supposed break, which to his mind was used not so much to account for historical dynamics than to confirm the stages of capitalism as seen by Marxists as well as the liberal vulgate. Considering crisis as a factor of change meant ignoring *la longue durée*, the persistence of structures, the slow evolution of the economy and above all of institutions.[14] And, as the political scientist Barrington Moore sensibly asked as early as the 1960s: what reasons do we have for thinking that change causes crises, whereas we take stability for granted? What about the struggles engaged to keep a way of life, a belief or an institution alive?[15]

Barrington Moore thought that in recent history much more blood had been spilt to preserve than to innovate. He was probably right. We must therefore try to integrate the moments of rupture into long-term, historical trajectories without imposing any necessity. It is always possible, with hindsight, to explain a historical phenomenon by one necessity or another. This approach prevents us from seeing the possible outcomes of a given moment as well as historical bifurcations. The formation of the Russian Empire at the expense of Lithuania, the Cossacks and the Central Asian Khanates cannot be summed up by the fact that these formations were in 'crisis' and hence had to turn into something else. The outcome cannot be explained by the supposed superiority of nation-states over nomadic powers inasmuch as these two ideal types were not found in the steppe during the period we are studying. If we cannot point to a crisis or tension between coercion and capital, how can we explain the evolutions of these territorial formations in Eurasia?

To answer that question, subaltern studies and many other historical approaches invite us to avoid thinking about non-European entities exclusively in terms of our own European categories. That is fine in theory, but in practice? Where is the boundary separating Europe from other worlds? In the case of Russia, in particular, when can we use European categories and when should we reject them? Is there a difference between the state, law, a profit-based economy and economic ethics in Russia and in Europe? Are those values homogenous throughout an area called 'Europe'?

If, as Braudel asserted, Europe encompasses the Mediterranean, then Islam is an integral part of it. On that basis, how should historians identify the values of Central Asia at the time of Islamic expansion into those regions?

In Europe, we have been accustomed by our own history of crusades, reforms and counter-reforms to view this connection as a kind of tension. The problems linked to current forms of fundamentalism incline us to adopt a similar view. We will thus be surprised to find imperial constructions in Russia, India and China during the modern period in which the coexistence of different religions and ethnic groups was the rule. Religious conflict was not used as a justification for the wars and military campaigns between Mughals and Hindu kingdoms, nor for the Russian campaigns against the Mongol Khanates or those of the Manchu against the Zunghars.[16] In all these cases, broader geopolitical considerations took precedence over more strictly religious issues. At the same time, even if the impact of this aspect was less mechanical than in the theories mentioned earlier, it nevertheless constituted a crucial element in social and economic dynamics and political and territorial organization. In Russia, while the religious factor was closely tied to the consolidation of central power, it did not play a role in imperial construction until quite late.

Thus, after Tilly's nation-states and Di Cosmo's Mongol powers, a new political actor – empire – has come to the fore in the current work of political scientists, historians and economists. Empire no longer appears to be an ancient, pre-industrial construction, but rather the institution *par excellence* of humanity's very long history.[17] This new wave is noteworthy for going beyond the framework of the nation-state and accounting for the world's complex, non-Euro-centric interactions. Has 'empire' filled the gap?

The answer is yes, provided the notion of empire is used as a heuristic device to examine historical diversities and not as a catchall idea that would only add to our confusion rather than to our understanding. This means we must grasp the characteristics of each empire and carefully differentiate them according to the period under study. When the notion of empire is historically situated, it leads us to examine fluid, mobile territorial entities in which various ethnic, religious and social groups (from the family and the clan to public administration, peasants and soldiers) interact and form a hierarchy, in keeping with different modes of integration and/or assimilation. For example, the dissemination of Islam in Africa and Eurasia was a powerful force for unifying these different parts of the world; at the same time, this influence took different shapes in different regions, depending on the role of *shar'ia* (sharia). Islamic power did not express itself in the same way in Central Asia, the Ottoman Empire and Mughal India or in Indonesia and East Africa. Thus, the relations between Muslims and Hindus, Manchu and Orthodox Russians had little in common with what one might deduce from recent tensions in India and the forms of exclusion introduced by Tsarist Russia only at the end of the nineteenth century or ethnic cleansing under Stalin and Maoist treatment of Tibetans. These tensions belong to the twentieth century; they were much weaker in the modern period.[18]

Complexity and the ability to integrate different religions and ethnic groups were common to China, Mughal India and Russia in the modern period. Ethnicity was a political project, and religion, together with an army, was its distinguishing feature. However, warrior elites were not incorporated in these empires in the same way: the political, military and social role of the Cossacks was not the same for Rajputs and Marathas in India, which in turn differed from that of the Manchu in the Qing Empire. The question is how these modes of integration interacted with imperial constructions and overall dynamics.

Military, mercenary and peasant

Here we arrive at the bedrock of our demonstration, namely the relationship between soldiers and territorial powers. The West's success in the face of the rest of the world is often explained by the military revolution constituted by the shift from medieval chivalry to cavalry charges, heavy infantry and artillery. This development is attributed to administrative centralization, the introduction of efficient taxation and of course a conscription system and a capitalist economy. Along with this evolution came the introduction of firearms, combat techniques, logistics and the organization of the army itself, which was supposedly streamlined.[19]

In reality, the main points of this demonstration should be qualified: it is not enough to mention guns; muskets have to be distinguished from rifles, repeating firearms from other types, mortars from canons, etc. In the light of these distinctions, the modernization of European armies is shown to have been a long, complex evolution and in no way a revolution. The transformation of supply techniques and logistics was also a slow process and Europe's main armies faced considerable supply problems at least until the First World War.[20]

The military revolution in the West must be qualified; however, the Eurasian empires were much less reluctant to introduce military innovations than is usually claimed. The cavalry and its role changed, along with weaponry and the infantry. The use of firearms spread across the steppe and in the Indian peninsula. Certainly to a lesser extent than in Europe, but why?

These dynamics can be explained by the conditions of field combat. For a long time, horses continued to play an important role in the steppe and Mongol techniques were efficiently passed on to the Chinese and the Russians. The superiority of European weapons and combat techniques was by no means obvious in the steppe. There was no need to wait for Vietnam or Afghanistan to realize that Western-style warfare was not very effective in other parts of the world. Whereas Europe did not adopt a modern conscription system until the Napoleonic wars, Russia, which was considered backward, was the first country to implement widespread, streamlined conscription.[21] Contrary to a common misconception, Russia's strength in the modern period did not lie in serfdom, which is said to have enabled easy, low-cost conscription, based on the power of the landowners. Serfdom, which was confined to the Russian heartland (and even then, not consistently!),[22] was in fact less a source of recruitment than a counterweight to the landowners' ambitions. On the contrary, as we will see later on, estate owners were opposed to territorial expansion, which they viewed as a threat to their power. And rightly so, for Russian expansion demanded considerable social fluidity; in the steppe, soldiers, officers and state employees were never strictly, irreversibly distinguishable. Russian expansion was carried out by settler-soldiers under state authority, which gave them relative autonomy from the landowners of central Russia. The country therefore drew its strength not from serfdom and absolutism, but, as we shall see, from its empire with relatively flexible institutions and social hierarchies in which the real centre of gravity lay in the periphery, in the steppe, rather than in Moscow and still less in Saint Petersburg. The Tsars and the Moscow elites enjoyed considerable power, but they had to negotiate constantly with the other strata of society, especially in newly conquered territories. The latter, in return, had an ongoing influence on the policies and balance of power in the 'centre'. Two factors in particular were more conducive to Russian expansion than serfdom: modern conscription and settler-soldiers in the steppe, capable of providing both armed force and wheat.

The specificities of recruitment had corresponding logistical features. The Russians gained strength without relying on overland routes – and for good reason! Their muddy, frozen roads were virtually impracticable and, in the modern period, improving them was too expensive, if not technically unfeasible. The poor development of the Russian road network was not necessarily synonymous with backwardness or the inability to invest in market infrastructures.[23] On the contrary, it reflected local climatic conditions. Hence, the Russians preferred to increase the number of production sites and bring them closer to lands acquired through expansion and occupation. Grain reserves were set up for this purpose and went hand in hand with settler-soldiers. China also introduced a system of reserves; unlike the Russians, however, the Chinese chose to overlap civilian reserves with military reserves and thus invested in roads and canals. Finally, the methods for financing these imperial projects, and armies in particular, were crucial. Russia made centralized taxation one of its flagship measures.

To summarize, the short-, medium- and long-term successes of Muscovy were linked to the way they combined forms of recruitment, army and social order, military supplies and overall economic organization.[24] Compared with the West, these solutions proved to be less 'primitive' and simplistic than is usually asserted. Russia was the most improbable power in Eurasia, very small in the beginning (the Duchy of Kiev, then Moscow), with extremely low population density and no easily exploitable resources or age-old traditions like those claimed by its neighbours. Yet Russia succeeded in expanding as much if not more than they did: first it occupied the steppe to the south and east at the expense of the Mongol powers, and later Poland, Siberia and Ukraine. These relationships are expressed both in military activity linked to economic growth and in social mixing related to Imperial construction. We will now turn to those aspects.

War and economic dynamics

Along with geopolitical and social factors, economic explanations have had the greatest influence on comparisons between the West and Eurasian empires. For decades and even today, the recurrent question in economic history is how the West achieved such success compared with China, which dates back thousands of years. The question itself is skewed: it starts from a self-satisfied position, which inevitably leads to false explanations and in reality to circular reasoning. We already know what to expect and we are simply looking for arguments to explain the West's success. Partisans and critics of the Western model share the same awe; the anti-capitalists are basically content to reverse the judgement of their opponents, while sharing their main assumptions, namely the spectacular success of the capitalist West.

There is nothing new about these attitudes but they are not the only ones possible. As early as the eighteenth century for Russia, and later, during the nineteenth century for China and India, many European travellers contrasted the civilization and economy of their own countries to Asian backwardness and barbarianism. The era of awe, which started with Marco Polo and continued into the seventeenth century, had ended, replaced by comparisons, differences and demonstrations of European progress. Naturally there were exceptions, some of them notable; numerous philosophers – Voltaire and Diderot among others – contrasted Western decadence to the possibilities of reform offered by 'virgin' or 'new' countries such as Africa or even Russia.[25] This attitude kept changing over time, however, depending in particular on how the Enlightenment was received in France, in Russia or in other 'new' countries. Their changing assessments reflected the reception given to the Enlightenment by the elites of the time.

In the late eighteenth century, these shifting attitudes ceased: henceforth, Western economic institutions, private property, centralized taxation, the market and wage labour were perceived as the foundation for progress and civilization. Anything that went against them – communal ownership, imposing limits on the market or lack of a centralized tax system – was viewed as a sign and cause of 'backwardness'.[26] The Enlightenment had projected an ideal; the ideologies of the nineteenth century had ratified it. Positivists, liberals and socialists, and later Marxists, though far removed from each other in many other respects, came together in emphasizing the economic differences between the West and the rest of the world.[27] These attitudes could not help but be reinforced during the twentieth century of extremes, the Cold War and decolonization. Economic history usually did little more than present hypotheses as if they were proofs. Tautologies took the place of explanation. On the subject of Russia, the questions always focused on why the country had never succeeded in having real cities, a middle class and private property and, finally, an efficient bureaucracy and a modern army like those in Europe.

These assertions run up against two observations: first, firearms and heavy artillery in particular were not necessarily practical in the steppe, and when they were required, the Russians made widespread use of them. Second: corruption in itself does not explain much; one could even claim that it often helped a great deal to support investment, especially in the military domain. The relevant question is why one group or another in seventeenth-century Russia opposed military innovations. Such innovations did not depend solely on their effectiveness (which in turn depended on the terrain, as we said earlier), but also on how they were linked to the underlying social fabric and economic practices. In the rural worlds that characterized the period we are studying, recruitment influenced agricultural activities and the relationships between landowners and peasants. The shift from cavalry to infantry, from archers to foot soldiers, reconfigured those relations. The resulting changes were not always welcomed by either the peasants, their lords or the military elites in place. Their resistance did not necessarily halt military innovation, but according to some historians, in Europe military innovation and technological progress supported each other, whereas in Russia (and even more in the USSR), military innovation took place at the expense of the rest of the economy.

War and technological innovation

During the decades after the Second World War, and even more during and after the war in Vietnam, most historians underscored the destruction of productive resources caused by war. This argument was used not only to study the twentieth century but also the nineteenth century and its spectacular growth, which was explained by the absence of wars. The same argument was employed to explain the disastrous wars in the sixteenth and seventeenth centuries, and even more so in the Middle Ages. In short, war was said to have an adverse effect on economic growth.[28] In contrast, since the end of the 1970s, several historians have endeavoured to highlight the benefits of war, at least in the West, where they were credited with encouraging economic development. Leaving aside the ethical aspects of these assertions, let us concentrate on the historical demonstration. In fact, there is no evidence that absence of war results in lack of innovation. What grounds do we have for saying innovation is related exclusively to war? History is replete with cases of economic development that took place without yielding any military advantage; this perception, which belongs to the twentieth century, is relatively valid for that period, but less so for other times and places. Most of the innovations in the nineteenth century, which were far from negligible, had nothing to do with war. The agricultural dynamic that began in the twelfth century and continued with great difficulty until the seventeenth and then the eighteenth century was due less to war as such than to climatic uncertainties and harvest fluctuations. In the case of Russia, historians have proposed two contradictory explanations: some think that excessive military spending kept growth in check first under the Tsars and later the USSR.[29] Others maintain that, in the face of the structural limits of Russian society and power, the army alone was consistently able to demonstrate efficiency on a par with the West.[30] It is nevertheless important to ascertain the connection between war, innovation and growth, provided we do not resort to theoretical shortcuts or commonplaces. For example, why would war be considered favourable to progress in comparisons between Europe and Russia, when it is viewed as a source of waste and backwardness in seventeenth-century Spain? A ready answer would be that in Europe war relied on efficient economic institutions, a reasonably fair tax system and a centralized state – all of which were lacking in Russia. The problem is the Russians did in fact build their empire precisely on those elements – taxation and the army. How did they do it?

There can be no real answer to these questions if we take the outcome of conflicts as our starting point: for example, there is no proof that Great Britain dominated India through its tax system and its army. To avoid this impasse, some economic historians decided to put institutions aside. They reasoned that since institutions in China, India, Russia and Europe were for the most part quite similar in the modern period, they could be safely ignored. It should be noted that this argument holds up only if one avoids taking a close look at the institutions of each country. What sultans, rajahs, the House of Lords, mandarins, the Hindu family and the extended family, Catholics and Orthodox actually had in common was a desire to 'minimize transaction costs' (i.e., the rather complicated expression economists used to indicate that, in addition to monetary costs, there were costs linked to negotiations and trade).[31]

The complexity of these social systems and the absence of instrumental rationality make such explanations mere exercises in applying economic models. The authors start with a fairly simple equation linking labour supply and demand to wages and the latter to war; it is an amusing exercise but it does not improve our understanding of military and socioeconomic mechanisms in the modern world. Why were the Russians able to set up an efficient conscription system whereas the Chinese were only partially successful? The fact that population density was higher in India than in the Russian steppe was not enough to transform peasants into soldiers. The particular relationships between landowners, military elites, the state and peasants – and therefore institutional and social aspects – played an important role in these historical trajectories.

It is no accident that some historians tried to account for the dynamics of Asian empires by downplaying the importance of military aspects and avoiding comparisons based on ideal types. This is the case of Kenneth Pomeranz, among others, who laid the groundwork for a genuine historiographical turning point – the 'great divergence'. He explained Chinese momentum using the same criteria applied to Europe: rapid demographic development, protection of private property, dynamic trade and proto-industrialization.[32] The 'great divergence' theory asserts that until the late the eighteenth century, Chinese growth was in no way inferior to Europe's and its institutions were not hostile to the market. The West was able to impose its economic and military control only because it had access to colonial resources. Conquest – not war – was what differentiated Europe from other countries. This explanation was derived partly from an argument already put forward by Marxist historians such as Hobsbawm, who claimed that Asia did not share the Western taste for conquest.[33] The same argument can be found among a constellation of authors including Jared Diamond, who also emphasizes the bellicose attitude of the West linked to metallurgical technology as well as animal husbandry and parasites, viruses and animal bacteria.[34] The advantage of these approaches is that they do not fall into the trap of the facile comparisons regarding war and economic growth we mentioned earlier; they also avoid extolling the West and, like all approaches to world history, they offer important solutions to the question of how specific features of different parts of the world were interrelated and connected to each other within a broader whole.

The problem lies in the difficulty of confirming these interpretations empirically; the environmental component and Europe's use of colonial resources correspond more to the colonizers' aims than to historical realities. Similarly, the history of Asia is punctuated with wars just as much as that of Europe. In all these cases, the subsequent imperial constructions were often unexpected historical results that need to be explained.

The explanation we are proposing here links taxation to territorial organization of the army to bring out the interrelation between colonization, supplying cities and the army and economic growth. Next, the idea that wars put a stop to trade needs to be qualified in the Eurasian context. This idea comes from a somewhat mythical representation of the medieval West, in which knights offered protection to peasants and merchants. Historians have tried very hard to show that such forms of protection were linked to strategies of accumulation. In reality, the relationship between trade and war was far more complex in the medieval West and assuredly different in Asia. As we shall see, conflicts in Asia usually took place without impeding the expansion of trade. This does not mean war should be seen as contributing to economic progress, but simply that, to understand Eurasian empires in the modern period, we must stop thinking of soldiers, peasants, colonial settlers, military officers and administrative elites as separate entities. Their overlapping accounts for imperial dynamics even more than their interaction.

On that basis, it is possible to question Tilly's schematic division between capital and coercion mentioned at the beginning of our discussion. Trade and capital played an important role in Central Asia and Russia and therefore it makes little sense to set a despotic, coercive Asia in contrast to a capitalist Europe. Capital and coercion overlapped both in Asia and in Europe. Coercion relied on capital and capital made ample use of coercion. The real question is how these elements interacted in social organization, military strategy and state construction. Russia was distinctly less coercive than is usually asserted; in Europe the solution took the form of centralizing taxation and organizing a state-run conscription system, whereas in Russia the state's monopoly on violence was not always evident. Consequently, the very notions of territory, frontier, city and state need to be re-examined.

Frontiers, territories and nomadic empires

We should avoid identifying entities called 'Russia', 'Europe' and 'China' in terms of their current borders or those in the nineteenth century. Generally speaking, the territories as well as the social and political hierarchies of these imperial areas changed over time. The core of our story concerns empires more than nation-states and frontiers more than cities and capitals. The frontiers will not be viewed as limits, but on the contrary as areas of varying scope. The frontier refers to modes of imperial expansion that applied sometimes to one region, sometimes to another, depending on the period. The centre of Russia was not always Moscow or Saint Petersburg; Kiev and Novgorod were the heart of the country at different times; the centre of power shifted with the direction of territorial expansion. In this case as well, Mongol influence was decisive, a fact ignored by Russian national and later Soviet historiography. Even when the capital was located in Moscow, the world of the steppe was the real heartland of Russian institutions and their evolution.[35] These movable frontiers call into question two key points in historical explanations: the role of territorial powers vs. nomads and the role of cities vs. the countryside. Thus, the argument linking Russia's weak economic development in the nineteenth century to that of its cities is based on the presupposition that the modern world was essentially produced by urbanization. Unlike the backward countryside, the city was believed to have 'set people free', breaking feudal bonds, stimulating growth and industrialization and bringing civilization. Such commonplaces were widespread in Europe and have been difficult to eradicate. The argument stems from a somewhat caricatured representation of European feudalism found in early twentieth-century scholarly interpretations and even today in schoolbooks in which the feudal system is associated with the protection offered by lords to peasants and artisans. This interpretation has since been considerably modified if not called into question. Trade did not disappear after the fall of the Roman Empire in the West, the 'barbarians' did not destroy everything on their way and feudalism was something other than the protection of peasants by lords.[36] Challenged by historians, the mythical image of feudalism has resurfaced in recent comparative studies due precisely to the view of history as a confrontation between ideal types: Russia vs. Europe, feudalism vs. capitalism.

This raises a twofold question: how relevant is this model to Europe itself and to what extent can it be used to study other worlds? In the last few years, many studies have qualified the role of urbanization in European development. The rural world is no longer considered synonymous with stagnation and backwardness. Quite the reverse, in fact. Peasants and landowners were more involved in market life than is commonly believed, not only in capitalist England but also in France under the *ancien régime*, and even in Central Europe, Prussia, Eastern Europe and Russia. As early as the seventeenth century, significant agricultural growth and changes in mentality were taking place everywhere.[37] Conversely, the city did not assert itself as the real centre of economic, social and cultural life until very late. Throughout nineteenth-century Europe, peasant workers successfully alternated farm life with work in urban factories.[38] The centralized factory of Smith and Marx was still relatively marginal at the time. The city and its industries were highly visible because they were new; in reality, however, they did not become dominant until the twentieth century. Prior to that date, proto-industry and agriculture continued to have considerable weight almost everywhere in Europe.[39] It was not merely by chance that social and political tensions linked to urbanization and the decline of the peasantry developed in the twentieth century rather than in the early nineteenth century.[40] The riots of peasants and workers, fascism and communism expressed a clash between different worlds, the decline of landed elites, peasants and peasant workers. When they broke out a century earlier, it was for other reasons: reactions to famine, changes in agricultural techniques or complex power relations between lords, peasants and the 'bourgeois'. It was in the interest of liberal and Marxist historiographies to frame these phenomena in terms of class struggle or the rise of the middle class. These authors anticipated, as it were, the twentieth century, but their interpretations of social phenomena and tensions at the turn of the eighteenth and nineteenth centuries were wrong.

The urban model as the engine of growth in the modern period and at the beginning of industrialization is even more beside the point when we look at non-European worlds. In this case, it is quite irrelevant to reason in terms of deficiencies compared with an ideal Europe, as certain historians have done. The absence of a middle class, private property, cities and democracy, etc., has been used to explain the backwardness of Russia, India and China.[41] We must do away with this Eurocentric approach: these other worlds deserve to be studied on the basis of their specificities and their own approach to modernity. Difference is not necessarily synonymous with backwardness. In Asia, the city, in particular, played an altogether different role from its counterpart in Europe, but that does not mean it can be singled out as the source of economic stagnation. Cities in China, India and Russia were never merely an administrative phenomenon, as a certain functionalist theory of these societies claims. Merchants were always key players, even in the distant past. And when an administration appears to have imposed its authority, in reality it was for the purpose of creating links and networks and mixing ethnic groups – in short, building an empire. Stifled growth tends to be viewed as the outcome of urban instability and slow industrialization.[42] Other historians have gone further and shown that in the case of India and Asia in general, the process of economic growth was not necessarily linked to urbanization. The engines of social, economic and even political development in these regions were deserts and oceans rather than cities. The vast expanses of the steppe forged the Chinese Empire and the Russian Empire[43]; the northern desert and the ocean guided the construction of the Mughal Empire.[44] The fact that these countries enjoyed real expansion without Western-style urbanization militates in favour of another approach: history follows diverse paths. It is only by grasping the particularities of these differences in the past that we can understand why nowadays urbanization seems to have prevailed everywhere. Once again, this phenomenon is specific to the contemporary period and we have no grounds for applying it to previous centuries.

This leads us to another aspect of the frontier, namely the relationship between sedentary and nomadic populations. We have already pointed out that historical analysis does not confirm the shared opposition to historiographies of sedentary powers. Most of the nomads of Central Asia had strong territorial institutions, and even in regions where tribal and nomadic aspects were especially pronounced, they were seamlessly incorporated into the framework of territorial units. Nomads took part in trade and strategic alliances with more sedentary groups. Over time, reciprocal acculturation between such groups became the rule in Eurasian dynamics. The problem is that nationalist historiographies minimize this impact.[45] Unlike European countries, centralization in China and Russia was seen as the formation of large, autocratic, 'agrarian' empires, incapable of mobilizing resources to achieve productive aims. According to Wong, the autocratic yoke had an even longer life in Russia than in China precisely because its expansion took place in empty territories, where there was little European presence. This made it different, for example, from India and in part from China.

These assertions merely confirm negative assumptions about Russia commonly found not only in Europe but also in China. Such a priori views bolster an idealized image of Europe or China; they do not help us to understand historical realities. Talking about the Russian occupation of 'empty' territories hints at the Han culture's scorn for the peoples of Central Asia. In reality, an occupation not only has to be achieved, it must also be maintained. Only a vacuum can maintain a vacuum and it is useless to invoke despotism and coercion to explain Russian expansion in the steppe. Instead of comparing the great Asian empires to the nomads and Kazakhs, it is necessary to examine how the latter formed alliances and were later integrated in the empires. Administrative and military management, including supplying the army and thus the involvement of lords and peasants, are all linked to different ways of integrating nomadic groups. Taken together, the frontier, peasant-settlers, social hierarchies and state construction are factors that help identify the main similarities and differences between Muscovy and later Russia and other imperial entities in Asia and Europe. The success of the West was rather late and temporary. It has spanned only two or three centuries and has already over-stimulated the Western imagination. The current strength of India, Russia and China, on the other hand, is rooted in much longer periods of time, quite apart from the stability of their territorial power. The power of Russia does not come from 'tradition' or from the 'Russian soul' (one of these days we have to stop confusing romantic notions with scientific analysis) but, on the contrary, from repeated interaction and conflicts with the populations of the steppe.

Eurasian empires cannot be fully explained by either their size or their population. Space is built up and altered over time, and even official borders (much more fragile than geographical boundaries) cannot hold by themselves. To say that Russia's strength lies in the expanse of its territory is to mistake the result for the cause. The size and maintenance of a country's borders must be explained rather than taken for granted, especially as a large size is not necessarily a source of strength; it can just as easily be the source of political and institutional weakness. This point has constantly been made with reference to China, the Byzantine Empire, and before it to the ancient empires believed to have broken apart precisely because they were too large. Size in itself is not automatically a factor of strength or weakness; what counts is how the size was achieved: empires were not enlarged and preserved in the same way in Europe, China and Russia. Relationships among lords, peasants and the army heavily influenced these processes.

Like space, population has often been invoked as an explanation, this time for Russia's weakness. It is a silly argument dating back at least to the political arithmetic of the eighteenth century, which has continued to haunt public debates ever since. Depending on the period and country, population figures have sometimes been viewed as a source of growth and sometimes as a source of poverty. In the case of Russia, both interpretations have been put forward over time. We will not go into this issue here. Instead of examining the link between population and economic growth, we will look at the connection between demographic dynamics and military organization. What is the link between population size and territorial density, on the one hand, and forms of military organization on the other? How were peasant populations mobilized? Is there a link between the labour market and the war market, between peasant-soldiers and landowner-cavalrymen?

Indeed, the relationships between institutions, the army, territory, the economy and social groups help us to understand how expansion took place. The Russian autocracy's control over landowners resulted in massive conscription, centralized military activities and constant interaction with the West, which never succeeded in forcing Russia to do anything.

This distinction has nothing to do with rigid comparisons. Indeed, the steppe, the circulation of people, goods and ideas and even imperial projects tied to the political culture in the steppe shared a common origin that gives our approach a highly circulatory dimension. Their common beginnings and components, together with these circulatory phenomena, must be added to any comparison and they account for similarities and differences across time and space. The circulation of ideas, people, goods, weapons, techniques, seeds, arts and religions constitutes an essential component of Eurasian dynamics. These aspects have already been discussed[46] and will not be dealt with here *in extenso*. We will, however, show the crucial role of the horse trade in Central Asia and Russia and of the circulation of military practices and even weapons between Russia and India, China and Russia and, in part, India and China. In addition to these elements, we will have to show the influence of religions in the transmission of ideas, trade practices,[47] and the creation of relatively stable networks linking Central Asia to India during the period under study and India to China in earlier periods. The development of markets supported Muscovite expansion at the expense of the Central Asian powers.[48]

Every empire produces its own historical sources; since it is impossible to use all of them, we will limit ourselves to examining how they were circulated and translated. I do not claim to be specialized in Turkic or Central Asian languages; I have based this discussion on Russia, my real field. This approach offers an important advantage in that a great many texts and documents in Chinese, Persian and Kazakh were translated into Russian starting in the seventeenth century. Sizeable collections of these documents have been published over time, e.g., on relations among Russians, Tatars and Chinese in the seventeenth century[49] and on trade links in Central Asia derived from sixteenth- and seventeenth-century legal documents.[50] Finally, in the local archives of Orenburg, Tashkent and Samarkand, numerous documents, published in part during the Soviet period, report on relationships between Russia and China,[51] Russia and Central Asia,[52] and Afghanistan and India.[53]

It is important to know the context in which the texts were produced, but that is not a reason to reject them outright.

3

The Power of the Steppe: The Mongol Heritage and the Expansion of Muscovy

Russia is often described as a land of despotism, corruption and serfdom and if it has any claim to great-power status, it is due to repression, centralization and large size. These arguments deserve to be examined, beginning with size: did Russia become dominant by extending its territory? If we say yes, we would be taking the effect for the cause and a readymade answer for an explanation. Large territories have to be conquered and above all held; the country was originally a tiny duchy and then a principality in the north of contemporary Russia. Over the centuries, it gradually moved into the centre, the south and the east, surrounded by much greater powers, the Safavids of Persia, the Ottoman Empire, the great Mongol Khanates, the kingdom of Poland-Lithuania and Sweden. How did Muscovy get the better of these powers?

The Russians could not rely on a large population: since the eighteenth century at least, every commentator has emphasized the great empty plains and vast spaces of Russia. In 1550, Muscovy covered about one million square kilometres for 6.5 million inhabitants. By the early eighteenth century, its territory had been considerably enlarged and the population had reached 15 million.[1] During the same period, a country like France, already smaller than Russia at the time, had about 10 million people. Thus we are hard-put to explain Russian expansion by numbers alone, even if, as we shall see, the country's military mobilization capabilities were considerable. So the question shifts to how the leaders of Muscovy were able to mobilize a substantial number of troops and, above all, achieve victory over far more solid, better-organized forces. Several authors have attributed their success to Russia's autocratic authority and serfdom: Muscovite expansion was said to be the result of its centralized power and despotism. But centralization did not come about through the sheer determination of a small group and still less of a single individual; the advent of Russian autocracy and its connection to territorial expansion demand a convincing explanation. There is nothing to suggest that an autocratic system automatically leads to wide expansion; it could just as easily produce the opposite result – history is full of examples of small, despotic kingdoms. The territorial expansion first of Muscovy and later of Russia was all the more impressive as it challenged not only the vast size of neighbouring powers but also the elites at home, who, as we shall see, opposed any form of territorial expansion, which they rightly saw as a threat to their privileges.

We have a magnificent historiographical problem here: if a majority of the elites opposed territorial expansion, how were Muscovite and then Russian officials able to mobilize the peasantry which, we are told, was bonded by serfdom? Indeed, the argument asserting that Russian expansion relied on serfdom[2] deserves close examination: how could a servile population support territorial expansion? By forcing the peasants to work the land? To serve in the army? But in that case, how could the peasants feed themselves and multiply (there was a high rate of demographic growth in the eighteenth century), guarantee food supplies to Russian elites and cities, and in addition colonize the newly conquered steppe, while at the same time providing increasing manpower for the army – with an objectively low population in relation to the territorial expanse?

Steppe dynamics: The warrior states

Indeed, Central Asia was not populated only by nomads. The dissolution of the Golden Horde, which began in 1350, produced highly unstable, relatively nomadic steppe societies like the Nogays, as well as city-states like the Khanates of Crimea, Kazan and Astrakhan. In the steppe, Turkish Kazakhs, Bashkir and Tatars also made up imposing forces, though they were often in competition with each other. Farther west, the decline first of the Golden Horde and later the Great Horde paved the way for the gradual consolidation of the Grand Duchy of Lithuania and the Polish Kingdom in the second half of the fourteenth century. It encompassed the lands all the way to the Ukraine and from there to the boundaries of the Crimean Khanate. The latter was founded by the Girei dynasty descended from Chinggis Khan. Its power was based on a federation of four tribes – the Shirin, the Baryn, the Argyn and the Kipchak. To the east, the dissolution of the Great Horde gave rise to the Khanate of Kazan, led by Ulu Muhammed, another descendant of Chinggis. The Khanates combined nomadic ways of life with sedentary structures including a real bureaucracy and taxation and military recruitment systems. These elements were not the source of their weakness, but rather the fact that the status of the khans was not hereditary and they had trouble controlling their noble and military elites.[3] These factors generated internal tensions that were to play a decisive role later on in the confrontation between the khanates and Moscow. From 1380 to 1480, the small principality of Moscow expanded mainly by annexing neighbouring principalities and republics, above all during the second half of the fifteenth century when it subjugated Yaroslavl (1471), Perm (1472), Rostov (1473), Novgorod (1478), Tver' (1485) and Viatka (1489). Muscovite forces thus reached the Volga, at the frontier of the Khanate of Kazan. The territorial conquest was pursued against the interests and hence the opposing efforts of Poland-Lithuania. At the time, the alliance between Moscow and the Crimean Khanate was founded on their mutual interest in opposing a common enemy, Poland. However, the Crimean Khanate had a further reason for joining forces with Moscow: in 1475, the Ottomans seized Caffa, then a Genoese colony in Crimea, at the frontier of the territories of Poland-Lithuania, which also covered part of today's Ukraine. In the decades from the late fifteenth to the early sixteenth century, the Crimean Khanate, Russia and the Ottoman Empire were allied against Poland-Lithuania. The alliance was advantageous for Moscow, which annexed Tver and Viatka and seized Smolensk in 1514.[4]

In this period, the steppe was surrounded by great powers: the Ottoman Empire, the Persian Safavids and Poland-Lithuania. In the steppe, the Kazan and Astrakhan Khanates (which replaced the Great Horde in 1502) were reference points. Moscow was thus the newcomer in the region and even continued to pay tribute to the khans of Astrakhan and Kazan, who considered the Muscovite prince their vassal. During the first half of the sixteenth century, the balance among these powers began to shift. In 1521, Grand Prince Vasily III annexed the principality of Ryazan, which served as a springboard towards Kazan and the southeast steppe. By incorporating Ryazan, Moscow was able to link the Oka–Volga trade route to the southern route down to the Don River and the Black Sea. The junction of these two routes was essential: for the first time, Moscow became a major actor in Central Asia and gained access to the famous 'black earth', the most fertile land in the region. The expansion aroused opposition from both the Ottomans and the Kazan Khanate. These powers began to view Moscow as a potential competitor whose expansion had to be stopped. The khan of Crimea launched several expeditions against Moscow in the 1530s and 1540s, seeking an alliance with the khan of Kazan.[5] In 1551, the new khan of Crimea,

Devlet Girei I, sent an expedition into Muscovite territory and bombarded Tula. Moscow's reaction forced him to withdraw, and Ivan IV (the Terrible), buoyed by his success, launched an attack against Kazan. The siege and ultimate conquest of Kazan in 1552 have been enshrined among the great events in Russian nationalist mythology since the sixteenth century; we are familiar with Eisenstein's cinematographic version, with the giant tower, armed with canons, advancing to the rhythm of Prokofiev. Of course the myth of Russia as liberator of the steppe and heir of Rome and Byzantium can be studied in its political and ideological dimension, but we should avoid accepting it as it stands. The seizure of Kazan was part of the geopolitical strategy of Moscow, which, after relying on its longstanding alliances with the Mongol powers, set out on to conquer the steppe and annex non-Russian populations.[6] Riding the crest of this wave, Ivan also seized Astrakhan in 1556.

These events fuelled tensions between Moscow and the Ottoman Empire and the Crimean Khanate, which demanded sovereignty over Kazan and Astrakhan. Once again, Muscovy appeared unlikely to triumph against their superior strength, but the international situation at the time worked in Russia's favour. The Ottomans were too worried about their relations with the neighbouring Hapsburgs to mobilize the forces required to stop Muscovite progress across the steppe. Without the military and financial support of the Ottomans, the khan of Crimea could not withstand Moscow's onslaught. He multiplied his raids and incursions into Muscovite territory, seeking an alliance with the Nogays, who had also come from the Great Horde. Moscow's strategy consisted in seeking Nogay support against Kazan and Astrakhan, luring them with the prospect of shared power and wealth. After the cities were taken, Moscow failed to keep its promises and the Nogays reacted by repeatedly invading Muscovite territory. Moscow nevertheless managed to control them not only militarily but also by limiting their supplies and access to pastureland. In the end, Moscow offered support to several Nogay chiefs, rallying them to its side while dividing the horde. As a result, the Nogays refused several requests from the khan of Crimea (for example in 1588–1590) to invade Muscovite territory.[7]

By the late seventeenth century, Moscow had thus become a key power, controlling the Nogays and keeping Poland-Lithuania, the Crimean Khanate and the Ottoman Empire at bay. Despite the so-called Time of Troubles – dynastic wars that ended with the Romanovs assuming power in 1613 – Moscow maintained its strength. To be sure, it suffered a bitter defeat at the hands of Poland-Lithuania during the 1630s and the Nogays and Kalmyks (a warrior people of Turkish origin, the western branch of the Oirat Mongols, whose eastern branch, the Zunghars, long opposed the Chinese) multiplied their raids into Muscovite territory. Yet the long-term trend was clear: during the seventeenth century, Moscow consolidated its power in the steppe, seized large territories from Poland-Lithuania, and strengthened its territorial and economic hold as the Crimean Khanate and the Ottoman Empire grew steadily weaker. By the end of seventeenth century, it had practically eradicated the raids by Nogays and Kalmyks. The Crimean Khanate continued to decline until it was definitively incorporated into Russia in the last quarter of the eighteenth century. Moscow eroded the power of Poland-Lithuania, which was also partitioned a century late, and succeeded in keeping the Ottoman Empire at a distance, eating away at its territories. In the space of three centuries, Moscow built the largest empire in the world along with China; together, they shared the whole of southern and central Asia. This tremendous advance can be partly explained by the diplomatic and geopolitical talents of the Moscow elites, who knew how to take advantage of divisions among their opponents. Also, Muscovite expansion was achieved through the systematic displacement and submission of more or less 'nomadic' people of the steppe. Recent valuable contributions of the historiography have helped to fill this long-standing lacuna[8] and I will not develop this point further.

At the same time, this outcome could not have been achieved without three major ingredients: trade, military and bureaucratic organization and a particular relationship between the state, the landowners and the peasants. We will discuss in detail trade and slave trade in the next chapter; here we will focus on military organization and social hierarchies in the steppe.

Military organization

One of the most widespread claims made in Russian military history and the history of the country in general is that Russia had only limited military capabilities and backward methods until the advent of Peter the Great and Western military methods. The Western military 'revolution', i.e., mass conscription and the use of light cavalry and firearms, is said to have arrived in the country only very late.[9] Russia's failure to keep pace with the West stemmed from its antiquated tax system dominated by corruption and privileges, administrative red tape and the general backwardness of the Russian people, not only peasant-soldiers but also officers.[10] Here, too, there is a broad consensus in Russia and the West that the myth is grounded in reality. From the Western standpoint, it shows that progress could be achieved in Russia and outside Europe in general only by adopting Western methods; from the Russian standpoint, the fable makes it possible to gloss over the Mongol influence and consolidate the myth of Peter the Great. These interpretations overlook the fact that even in Europe it was difficult to impose the so-called 'military revolution' before the nineteenth century.[11] These arguments are anachronistic and Eurocentric and they fail to account for the tremendous expansion of Muscovy during the centuries before Peter the Great described in the preceding pages. How could such expansion have taken place if the Russian army had been so backward? The real question is why Moscow would have adopted European weapons and military tactics in the steppe, where the rifles of the time and heavy squadron formations were totally useless against Mongol horsemen. In fact, Moscow adopted different types of weapons, soldiers and tactics, depending on the front; on the Western front with Poland-Lithuania, given the terrain and the enemy's equipment, it was more inclined to borrow European military elements, whereas in the south and the east, it resorted to Mongol tactics and weapons, duly corrected and used by far superior forces. If there was no Western-style 'military revolution' in these regions, it was because it was ill suited to conditions in the steppe.[12]

This explains why firearms were introduced only gradually, mainly in the wars conducted on the Western front, although weapons such as shells and artillery were also employed in the steppe for the siege of Mongol cities. The first infantry corps to be equipped with firearms, the *pishchal'niki*, appeared at the very beginning of the sixteenth century following Russia's defeat in Livonia in 1501. A thousand *pishchal'niki* were enrolled and financed directly by Moscow. They played an important role in taking Pskov in 1510. In the following decades, at least until the mid-1630s, the *pishchal'niki*, like other large units (notably armed cavalrymen) were recruited first among Swedish and Polish mercenaries but increasingly among the Cossacks and Tatars as time went by. They were accompanied by *strel'tsy*, a type of musketeers armed with harquebuses; they formed the first permanent army unit in Russia and were instrumental in the siege of Kazan in 1552. They were also supposed to perform police functions. Their numbers declined at the end of the sixteenth century, when Moscow chose to employ foreign mercenaries instead. Shells and artillery were introduced in the first half of the sixteenth century, but they were not widely used until the end of the century. The number of canons increased around the middle of the sixteenth century, especially with the siege of Kazan, rising from about 3,500 in 1600 to 5,000 by the end of the century.[13]

The process accelerated during the 1630s and 1640s, when firearms were massively employed by the Muscovite army thanks to the discovery of mines in the Urals.[14] From a tactical standpoint, in the sixteenth and seventeenth centuries, especially on the Western front, the Muscovite army was made up of six regiments: avant-garde, left wing, right wing, main regiment and central and rear guard. Three other regiments were added in the late sixteenth century: reconnaissance, transport and artillery. Military organization changed between the seventeenth and eighteenth centuries, with improved coordination and logistics and fewer foreign mercenaries, though the evolution was not identical on all the fronts.

On the Western front, Poland-Lithuania modernized its army in the early sixteenth century with massive use of infantry and firearms, forcing Moscow in turn to adopt firearms with the help of foreign mercenaries. The results were favourable at the start of the century (the seizure of Smolensk), mixed later on and finally unfavourable from the 1610s to the 1630s, when Moscow suffered serious defeats and lost Smolensk. The losses can be partly explained by declining interest (and financing) on the part of Sweden and the Ottoman Empire in support of Moscow against Poland-Lithuania, which was better armed and organized than its Russian adversaries.[15]

The situation would not be reversed until the 1650s and 1660s, particularly during the Thirteen Years War (1654–1667) between Russia and Poland-Lithuania. Initially, the Russians gained the upper hand due less to their tactics and weapons than to their numbers (between seven and twenty times superior to their opponents, depending on the battle or the city under siege). Moscow had a better recruitment system and funding than Poland, where the state met with resistance from the landed gentry. Problems nevertheless arose over time, particularly regarding tactics, weapons and logistics. Operations grew more complex when the Crimean Khanate and Sweden, feeling threatened by Moscow's success and the possibility it might seize Poland, Lithuania and Ukraine, decided to join the conflict. Moscow reacted by intensifying conscription and moving a large part of its garrisons and cavalry from the southern and eastern fronts to the western front, where the soldiers were equipped with heavier weapons better suited to the new context.[16]

Due to increased conscription of ill-prepared peasants, the officers employed siege tactics and defence strategies rather than attack in open terrain. They built wagons capable of transporting considerable amounts of provisions for horses and men as well as weapons over a period of several months. Naturally the convoys slowed the advance of Muscovite troops, but their solid construction made them veritable portable fortresses (*guliai gorod*). The Russians deployed one of these 'baggage trains' during the Thirteen Years War at the time of the campaign in Ukraine in 1659, with 3,000 wagons carrying 20 canons and 9.1 million kilos of food drawn and escorted by 10,000 *kholopy* (slaves) and peasants.[17] As we shall see, the sizeable mobilization of a relatively small population turned out to be a significant factor in Moscow's success.

Unlike the operations on the western front, the Muscovites adopted a totally different strategy against the Central Asian populations and the Crimean Khanate: they used light cavalry armed with bows and arrows and borrowed Mongol war tactics (sudden raids and flight). They added new elements, particularly dragoons (i.e., soldiers who travelled on horseback but fought on foot), and European shells and artillery during the sieges of cities in Central Asia and Crimea. This approach required more trenches and fortifications, entailing more coerced labour and obligatory services performed by the soldiers and the local population.[18] From a tactical standpoint, the operations were supported by increased fort construction. In the sixteenth century, the Muscovites built a line of defence known as the Abatis; it protected Moscow from Tatar invasions through the Ukraine, which was then linked to the Volga. Several fortress cities were built in these regions to reinforce the line. The fortifications were connected to each other by an intelligence service and troop rotation, stepping up the possibility of intervening to defend the nearest fort. From 1520 to 1550, these solutions were bolstered by improved fort defences in the event of a siege: sturdier construction, larger grain reserves and more troops with better weapons on site.[19]

Between 1551 and 1568, under Ivan IV (Ivan 'the Terrible'), new fortresses were built and reconnaissance services improved and augmented. The expansion continued until the end of the century. Most of the fortifications deteriorated, however, and were even abandoned during the period known as the Time of Troubles in the early seventeenth century, when Russia was torn apart by dynastic wars. Even when the period ended, the new Romanov dynasty (1613–1917) initially focused its attention on the western front, shifting men and resources to it and ultimately bringing about the fall of fortifications in the south.[20]

It was not until after 1635 that Russia once again decided to improve its defences in the region by reconstructing existing fortifications and building new defensive lines. It began by repairing the Abatis Line at the end of the 1630s. More financial resources and men were assigned to the task. The military chancellery took charge of operations, estimating it would take 27,400 workers, 3,500 draft horses and 16,900 soldiers to repair the line and defend it effectively.[21] The project was a resounding success: though only 20,000 men could be found and food supplies often ran short, within six months the line of defence was rebuilt across 600 kilometres and placed under military protection.

During the same period, tensions were growing with the Ottoman Empire and the Crimean Khanate. The Russians, realizing they were still vulnerable on that front, undertook the construction of another line of defence, the Belgorod Line, located further to the southeast. It was equipped with a wall, similar to the new lines of defence in Europe. The rest of the fortification line was completed along the Voronezh River in the 1650s. In the end, Russia erected an 800-kilometer line of defence to protect its southern and eastern flanks. It achieved its purpose: Tatar raids from Crimea were sharply reduced and Moscow could use the new fortifications as a base to launch expeditions against the Kalmiks and the Nogays and in its war against Poland-Lithuania.[22]

We have thus reached some interesting conclusions: Moscow supported its expansion by using different military tactics and techniques in the south and the west; in one region it adopted Western methods, in the other it borrowed from the Mongols. In both cases, it added new elements of its own, such as the 'portable forts' and fortification lines, using a strategy midway between Chinese defences and those of European countries. Now we must go a step further: how were these tactical and military results achieved? Thanks to an exceptionally efficient military bureaucracy? Through considerable financial and material resources?

Administration, finances and the army

Military experts and researchers are divided about the impact of centralization and military bureaucracy. Some maintain that a large army could not exist without a central organization, particularly on a countrywide scale and with modern weapons[23]; others maintain, on the contrary, that centralization results in an army bogged down by routine procedures and cumbersome red tape and hence less efficient[24] – the ideal would of course be to achieve the right balance between centralization and local autonomy. Though it is relatively easy to identify such a happy medium in theory (all it takes is a simple model of cost-benefit assessment), it is harder to put it into practice. The conditions of centralization vary according to the place and the period, the amount of available knowledge and the institutional, political and cultural constraints on organizations. These aspects must therefore be viewed in their proper historical context to avoid thinking about sixteenth-century Muscovy as if it were Prussia in the nineteenth century or the United States today. Indeed, the historians who studied this question have accused the Russian administration of being both overdeveloped and inefficient. They claim that bureaucratic excess was a feature of Russian state organization over a very long period of time. In reality, as John Le Donne, Confino and many others have noted,[25] it is anachronistic to employ the late nineteenth-century terms of Weberian analysis – rationality and efficiency – to think about the Russian administration during the modern period. We would be even farther from reality if we tried to judge the Muscovite administration of the seventeenth century by the experience we have acquired from the major growth of public administrations in the twentieth century. There was no 'state bureaucracy' functioning as a common thread directly and simplistically linking the Mongols to Muscovy and the Soviet Russia to each other.

In the period we are studying, there was often no clear-cut distinction between estate owners service cavalrymen and administrative officials in the strict sense; their roles, rights and statutes were defined in different terms than the ones we are accustomed to using. Administrative and military centralization began under Ivan III (1462–1505) when princes and cavarlrymen were obligated to serve the prince of Moscow alone, whereas previously they could offer their services to the highest bidder.[26] From a strictly administrative standpoint, real centralization and coordination was long in coming: a centralized military chancellery did not come into existence until the third quarter of the sixteenth century. In the decades that followed, this measure was soon supplemented by the creation of other chancelleries in charge of managing fortifications, supplies and armaments and remunerating service cavalrymen. Later on, tensions arose between those in favour of subordinating the chancelleries to the main military chancellery and those who wanted to decentralize tasks. The solutions changed throughout the imperial period, with periods of accelerated centralization followed by decentralization and the distribution of tasks.[27]

In reality, the area in which Moscow showed the most improvement during the seventeenth century was its reconnaissance and intelligence-gathering system. These operations were conducted primarily on the southern front where it was indispensable to have up-to-date information on the movements and location of Mongol soldiers and tribes as well as those of the Crimean Khanate and even the Ottoman Empire. The Ottoman attacks against Astrakhan in 1569–1570 and the raids of the Tatars of Crimea during the period prompted Moscow to improve its intelligence service. It increased patrols and built additional forts and fortresses closer together along its lines of defence, while attempting to coordinate and centralize the information obtained.[28] The results did not always meet their expectations: in the late sixteenth century, the Mongols and Tatars carried out surprise raids on the Russians on a number of occasions. The situation improved after 1640, when patrols were reinforced as part of an overall effort at administrative and military centralization. Administrative organization was still far from stable, and thus the process of gathering and circulating information was unreliable. This was true not only for intelligence concerning the enemy but also for information pertaining to army logistics and supplies.[29]

Muscovy and later Russia ran up against considerable problems transporting enormous quantities of wheat over very long distances, especially on the eastern front. There was undoubtedly less road construction in that part of Russia than in China during the same period; we find few if any equivalents of the 'great corridors' linking production regions to the front. Here again, this should not be interpreted as a sign of Russian backwardness or indifference, or even hostility to market and trade. It was simply due to the fact that, under local conditions and given the available techniques, building and maintaining transport routes was extremely costly. It was difficult to rely on the routes linking the centre and north of Muscovy to the steppe; in the northern half, mud and freezing temperatures made roads impracticable for much of the year. Consequently, Russian troops faced serious supply problems when they arrived in southern Ukraine. For example, in 1686, during the campaign against the Crimean Khanate, the Russians mobilized one of the largest armies of the period: 132,000 men, accompanied by 2,000 *kholopy* (bonded labourers and slaves – see next chapter),[30] servants and porters. They advanced with 100,000 horses across 300 kilometres from Samara to Crimea. The logistics chancellery estimated that, for a four-month campaign, the men would need 23,000 tons of wheat, and 9,000 tons of oats for their horses. The chancellery managed to find the resources and the wheat was brought from European Russia by oxcart and river vessels. This initial logistical success began to fall apart afterwards, when the operation dragged on. By 1680, troops numbers had risen to 200,000 men. Their commander in chief, Prince Golitsyn, had to cope with inadequate supplies and, from that point on, increasingly frequent desertions.[31] Moscow tried to stem the difficulties by pouring more and more resources into its military activities: a million roubles in 1663 alone. Historians have long emphasized Russia's deficits and debts due to military spending. In reality, in 1680, Russia allocated a million roubles to military operations, i.e., half the national budget. In the same period, England and France borrowed heavily and their expenditures far exceeded the budgets allotted to finance their wars. Great Britain devoted about 70 per cent of its national budget to military spending between 1689 and 1713. Russia's military expenditures accounted for around 50 per cent of the country's budget in 1701, but rose to 70 per cent in 1724.³² Like other European countries, Russia possessed a vast, stable army like other European countries and comparable budget deficits, despite the per capita tax introduced by Peter the Great. The system was calculated to meet army requirements and the peasants and city dwellers subject to taxation were forced to pay. Along with the per capita tax system, indirect taxation was increased and widely detested. In the early eighteenth century, it covered 50 per cent of the budget.³³ Like his predecessors, Peter drew heavily on a surreptitious form of financing, i.e., devaluation of the rouble. As the silver content of the various coins diminished, prices soared. During the Thirteen Years War, the Muscovite government began circulating copper coins alongside silver roubles. At the same time, the authorities tried to take as much silver as possible out of circulation. Prices increased (wheat prices rose from one to 24 roubles between 1656 and 1663) and merchants refused to be paid in copper, even for transactions with the state. These phenomena forced the Russian authorities to reduce the amount of money in circulation, raising the question of how to finance the military effort by other means.

Provisions in kind and wheat markets

Let us summarize: from a strictly military standpoint, we now know that different techniques were used on the various Muscovite fronts; however, this dynamic was hindered by a poorly coordinated administration and inadequate financial resources. This does not mean that monetary and fiscal resources were Moscow's weak point: their finances were by no means as catastrophic as some historians have asserted. Russia's situation was quite comparable to the one facing many European countries at the time. It was not catastrophic, but neither was it excellent. So Moscow had to finance a large number of military operations without silver: soldiers were paid in kind and officers with land and wheat. This was not unusual nor does it suggest any particular backwardness on the part of Russia. It would be a mistake to think that weapons and monetary financing were the key factors of success in the sixteenth and seventeen centuries. In fact, it is likely that in Asia, and to some extent in Europe, troop provisions, logistics and even wages were often paid for in kind when currencies were repeatedly devalued (especially in wartime) and a large portion of the troops mainly wanted food. Such practices were even more commonplace in the steppe. They were also used in China, as we saw earlier: the size of the territory and the distance between cities necessitated the transport of large quantities of food for men and horses. To a large extent, these logistical aspects determined the outcome of conflicts. China solved the problem by building roads, setting up grain reserves and, to a certain degree, through colonization. What about Russia?

In the early sixteenth century, the cavalry were still self-supporting, particularly on the southern front. Estate owners were supposed to participate in the military effort by contributing their own resources or securing them on the battlefield. Due to the rise of 'service' cavalrymen (i.e. who, in principle, did not belong to the hereditary aristocracy) and infantrymen, a different mode of functioning was gradually adopted: 'the land feeds the soldier', in other words, local resources were used to feed the local army. This method was employed especially on the southern front, where peasant-soldiers colonized the steppe and grew crops for themselves and for the cavalry. Of course, this general approach was difficult to put into practice in other regions, particularly on the western front where a tax and one tenth of the harvest was allocated to the army. These amounts often proved inadequate and other producing regions were pressed to contribute, notably during extended military campaigns.[34]

The contributions were of several different kinds: in the event of war, special levies were launched in the various regions or the army requisitioned existing grain reserves intended for the civilian population. Such interventions came under heading of the Tsars' nurturing function (*kormlenie*), which, according to some historians, lasted throughout the history of Muscovy and later of Russia and even the USSR.[35] Beginning in the sixteenth century, grain was stockpiled by provincial authorities, following the same reasoning we encountered in Qing dynasty China, even though the criteria used to calculate quantities and anticipate harvests were less sophisticated in Russia (they were not developed until the late nineteenth century). As in China, grain reserves served not only as a bulwark against poor harvests and possible unrest, but also as local banks that lent wheat to landowners as well as to peasants and institutions.[36]

Ensuring stable wheat supplies became a problem. We know that China vacillated between buying wheat directly from merchants and through intermediaries. In the case of direct procurement, it practised fixed prices, but there was always a danger of insufficient supply. When intermediaries were involved, even though some Chinese leaders had high hopes for this solution, there was always a risk that merchants would sell their foodstuffs to the highest bidder. For several centuries, China wavered between the two methods, but in general, direct procurement prevailed, especially from the eighteenth century onwards.

There was no such hesitation in Muscovy or later in Russia: the central power bought wheat from merchants only as a last resort, and even then at a fixed price set by the authorities, taking into consideration the market price, the state's budgetary constraints and the needs of the population and the army. They would not allow the army to be subjected to market fluctuations. Yet this fact did not indicate widespread hostility to the market, for, as we have shown, territorial expansion was tied to Muscovite commercial penetration. Rather than hostility, it would be better to speak of a special relationship between the market, the army and social organization. The Muscovite elites sought to stabilize policies: procurement at fixed prices worked well in relatively abundant market situations, whereas in periods of shortage during military campaigns, the army had problems securing food stocks from merchants. The supplies they obtained were therefore intended above all for the cavalry and thus the service elites. This discrimination partly reflected differences between cavalrymen and peasants (infantry); it began to disappear in the late seventeenth century when the existing order and social balance were changed by the development of the infantry and the use of firearms. Indeed, the authorities carried out exceptional levies and requisitioned grain reserves to support the army during its campaigns, but these methods could not be counted on to supply a regular army in peacetime. Initial attempts to introduce a tax in kind, and therefore ensure a stable army, were made during the first half of the seventeenth century by the musketeer chancellery, which paid merchants a fixed price rather than draw on local taxes. This solution was inspired by the fact that, at the time, the musketeers were one of the few stable corps in Muscovy; they also formed a relatively small group within the overall armed forces: 7,000–10,000 in the late sixteenth century, 33,775 in 1632, and 65,000 in 1663, when they began to decline.[37] The Chancellery's efforts were impeded, however, by the fact that the musketeers were scattered across the territory and it had to compete with the supply agencies of the other units, not to mention civilian authorities, who were also interested in procuring wheat stocks in the event of famine. The success of the tax therefore depended on individual relationships that members of the musketeer chancellery forged with producers and local administrations. It was thus particularly difficult for the musketeers to obtain wheat on the southern front.[38]

Despite this failure, the Muscovite authorities eventually succeeded in extending the system to the entire army. They were operating on the assumption that a constant tax in kind was the best solution for a regular army; restricting the method solely to the musketeers had limited its scope due to competition with the other corps. Widespread military levies began during the Thirteen Years War, but they were not expanded until later on.[39] This was due to the increase in the absolute number of infantrymen compared with the cavalry (after 1660, 80 per cent of the army was made up of new regiments and new units); more wheat was required for the army whereas the use of firearms demanded gradual professionalization and therefore stable armed forces. Like the Manchu-Qing in the same period, the Romanovs' chief concerns involved supplying the army and setting up adequate forms of taxation.

In 1663, the military chancellery opened a grain department (*khlebnyi stol*). It was based on the principle adopted by the musketeer chancellery, with some modifications. One eighth of the local harvest was intended for the army; in reality, Moscow centralized the calculation and supply operations, whereas levying the tax itself was left to the local elites who could nevertheless negotiate delivery terms and quantities. As tax collection took place at the local level, it was hoped that the local authorities would have greater control over producers. The drawback to this solution was that it could give rise to sudden scarcity. Such shortages were difficult to offset by reserves from other regions, which were frequently unavailable and in any case difficult to transport, problems that were compounded by the growing number of soldiers.

In the 1690s, Muscovite leaders decided to transform the annual tax into several seasonal taxes. The main objectives were to have a set amount of wheat reserves constantly available, reduce the cost of storage and limit speculation. The system, known as *zaprosnyi khleb* (wheat collected on demand), purported to be capable of coordinating the requirements of the various armies with local production. Until then, for example, the southern regions were supposed to produce wheat for the local troops, except in the case of war or difficulties, when other regions were called upon to compensate. Now, on the contrary, such compensations would be steady, to avoid tight markets and guarantee stable supplies,[40] which was indispensable to set up a peacetime army. One major obstacle remained, however, at the turn of the seventeenth and eighteenth centuries, when the peasants and city dwellers were already burdened by several taxes and levies: the musketeer tax, the so-called one-quarter *chetvert* tax, the one-eighth, etc. Discrepancies in taxation raised two types of problems: first, the landowners in the most severely taxed regions objected to the pressure being put on their peasants, particularly as they hardly felt concerned by Russian territorial expansion. Naturally these problems mainly affected small landowners with few peasants and were aggravated by the introduction of ever-heavier conscription. Second, in the southern regions, the distinction between groups subject to tax and those who were exempt was not the same as in the rest of Russia, mainly due to the vague differences in these regions between 'peasants' and cavalrymen. This was a further cause of the discontent of the Russian elites.[41] To clarify these aspects, it is important to understand more fully who the Russian soldiers were: the cavalrymen and infantrymen and their social origins and forms of recruitment.

Mobilization and colonization: The frontier as a social and political experiment

In terms of headcounts, the armies of the leading European countries had 40,000 men around the middle of the sixteenth century, a figure that gradually increased to about 150,000 in the 1630s. Muscovy began the Thirteen Years War (1654–1667) against Poland-Lithuania with an army of 40,000 men and ended it with 100,000. The infantry, which made up a quarter of the armed forced in 1654, grew to more than a third during the 1660s. Towards the end of the century, Russia maintained a regular army of roughly the same size, i.e., about 100,000 men, which, given its small population at the time (about 15 million), made it one of the countries with the highest percentage of conscripts (1–1.5 per cent). Finally, by the mid-eighteenth century, both Russia and France had 1.3 per cent of their populations in uniform, ahead of England (1 per cent), but well behind Prussia (4.2 per cent).[42]

Before instituting widespread conscription under Peter the Great, Russia resorted like other countries to mercenaries and armed populations like the Cossacks. Mercenaries were used above all on the western front and less in the wars against the Mongols, e.g., in the war to seize Smolensk in 1632–1633 and the Thirteen Years War, when the Russians engaged Swedish and German military units. In every instance, the use of mercenaries led to disagreements within the Russian military and political elites; some favoured this solution, because they considered the foreign soldiers better equipped and trained than their Russian counterparts; others had doubts about their loyalty. The former objected that even Russian peasants and some officers deserted when resources were scarce.[43]

In 1663, during the Thirteen Years War, there were 54,448 foreigners among the officer ranks, i.e., 79 per cent of the forces on the ground. During the 1660s, of 227 high-ranking offers (colonels, lieutenant-colonels, majors), barely 18 were Russians, whereas they accounted for 648 of the 1,922 captains and lieutenants. Finally, Russians made up the majority of non-commissioned officers and of course almost all the soldiers.[44] The Russians paid their foreign officers well above the standards of the time. Colonels received between 250 and 400 roubles per month. About one third of the army's monetary expenditures in 1663 (around a million roubles) went to officers' pay. Problems arose with the mercenaries during prolonged campaigns when inflation was compounded by supply shortages. Furthermore, as conditions were harsher for Russian troops, discontent grew within the army. The Thirteen Years War gradually led to the elimination of mercenaries; the length of the conflict drove some of them to desert and Moscow's dissatisfaction with their attitude did the rest. At every defeat, several Muscovite leaders emphasized the negative role of the mercenaries. With the expanded use of firearms and infantrymen, Russia was prompted to introduce conscription, which was initially attempted in 1652 and again in 1658, and finally definitively established by Peter the Great.

It was not enough to eliminate mercenaries in the strict sense to claim the Russian state had a monopoly on violence. Unlike Europe, the army market in Asia also included real ethnic and warrior groups that were by no means merely mercenaries: they had their own organizations and resources. Though indeed they sold their services to the highest bidder, they were also directly concerned by geopolitical dynamics. This was the case of the famous Don Cossacks.

The Cossacks posed a classic problem: they were relatively autonomous and effective warriors; Moscow wanted to be able to use them without incorporating them from the outset into its own elites. It also thought it could deploy them against its neighbours and deny any responsibility for the attack when the latter protested. This strategy was notably adopted after the Cossack incursions against the Ottoman Empire, the Crimean Khanate and Poland-Lithuania. In other words, Moscow was forced to negotiate a monopoly on violence. To achieve it, it had to allow the Cossacks relative freedom, which could always backfire if the latter decided to launch raids on their own initiative. This happened frequently, as the Cossacks were well organized and their numbers were constantly growing: their ranks were swelled by Tatar populations, together with peasants and soldiers fleeing the central regions of Muscovy and Ukraine and even ordinary criminals. These groups defined themselves as free Cossacks, i.e., they refused to be subject to Muscovite taxation or conscription. At the same time, due to their varied origins and forms of organization, the Don Cossacks did not benefit from an administration comparable to those of the Crimean or Kazan Khanates. Hence, they depended on access to food and military resources and were subject to the ever-present risk of poor harvests in neighbouring regions.[45]

This dependence left a door open for Moscow's strategies, particularly its attempts to control the Cossacks through systems of support and supply financing. For that same reason, Moscow weakened trade routes in Don territory, a source of revenue for the Cossacks. As early as the 1620s, Moscow endeavoured to set up a central political organization and a Cossack pseudo-state that would transcend temporary alliances between clans and offer institutional stability. Such stability was supposed to be in the hands of Cossack elites with close ties to Moscow, but it was not achieved until the last quarter of the seventeenth century. Initially, at least, Moscow granted subsidies to the Cossacks as a whole, but later on restricted them to loyal commanders who were responsible for distributing them among the Cossack population. It was a winning strategy, combining integration and control over local elites with forms of economic and military dependence. It was reminiscent of the strategy adopted by the Manchu towards Mongol populations, but it differed in the relative military autonomy Moscow allowed to the Cossacks for a long time. From this standpoint, it was closer to the strategy used by the Mughals in India with professional warriors, but avoided its main limitation, i.e., combining military and financial autonomy. Moscow preferred to fund the armed groups itself; in that way, the groups had no tax resources of their own, and unlike their counterparts in India during the same period, they had no means of taking root in the territory. One last element gave Moscow control over the Cossacks: the construction of the fortifications in the south curbed raids into Muscovite territory by Tatars from Crimea as well as sorties by the Cossacks themselves. As a result, the Cossacks could not finance themselves by taking prisoners in Ottoman territory or raise the stakes with Moscow by threatening to pillage the Ottoman regions and Crimea.

The strategy adopted with other populations of the steppe was similar but even tougher than those adopted vis-à-vis the Cossacks. As we have seen, Nogays, Kalmyks and other 'nomads' were not only military aggressed, they were also deprived of their main monetary and in-kind resources. Slave and other trades fell under the control of Russians or forbidden; at the same, Moscow progressively took the control of horse feeding and reproduction in the steppe by establishing an unprecedented system of mass conscription and colonization.

Military service and social order

As early as the fifteenth century, the princes of Moscow demanded exclusive control over the military services provided by cavalrymen. When Ivan III defeated

Novgorod, he exiled its elites and introduced compulsory service for the Moscow elites. The legal definition of the elites was in fact specified at the time of Ivan III and Vasily III (between 1459 and 1533): alongside hereditary estates (*votchina*), the law made land grants in return for military service known as *pomest'e*. This type of estate, very similar to the Mongol and Muslim institution in Central Asia called the *iqta*, could be inherited only if the descendent also served the prince. If not, ownership of the land reverted to state upon the officer's death. The *pomest'e* could not be sold or mortgaged, and could be exchanged only for another *pomest'e*. With this system, the princes of Moscow sought to achieve two objectives: control the elites and dispose of a relatively stable cavalry.

In terms of manpower, very few landowners in the mid-sixteenth century possessed a *votchina* (about 2,000), whereas about 5 per cent of the population (i.e., 25,000 cavalrymen) owned a *pomest'e*. On average, they possessed five or six peasants, which meant their social status was rather precarious. These institutions were one of the pillars of Muscovy's expansion; social and political frontiers were interconnected. To encourage military enlistment and strengthen the army, the Muscovite princes increased *pomest'e* grants in frontier regions, particularly in the south. The problem was that, unlike the other regions of Russia, in this case the status was given to people of a different social origin: the personnel at urban garrisons (*gorodovaia sluzhba*) and those stationed in the countryside (*polkovaia sluzhba*).[46] This distinction was initially intended to differentiate cavalrymen from peasants, but the conditions facing cavalrymen were often harsh and it was not unusual for them to shift from one status to another. During the 1660s and 1670s, the shortage of peasants drove many cavalrymen to take part in agricultural activities and they therefore asked to be assigned to the countryside, alongside the peasants.[47] This movement also led to the merging of estates. The notes of recruiting officers at the time indicated that the mergers aimed to reduce the services provided by the military and improve the cavalrymen's standard of living. Such social fluidity was opposed by some of Moscow's top leaders as well as landowners in other regions. In 1678, the authorities decided to restrict access to hereditary military service and to the nobility, especially as the increasing use of firearms and new tactics had expanded the role of the infantry and consequently of peasants within the army.

This trend took another turn with the legal creation of the *odnodvortsy*: these individuals were unmarried owners of small estates who were identified as landowners by their tax and military system in decrees adopted between 1710 and 1724. At the time, the *odnodvortsy* included 600,000 Muscovites and their dependents, most of whom had settled along the Belgorod Line and in the region of Sevsk. The *odnodvortsy* were similar to state peasants: like the latter, they paid taxes (in money and in kind), but they also had military obligations and enjoyed property rights over the land,[48] which meant land ownership was no longer a distinguishing feature of the 'nobility' as opposed to the peasantry. Indeed, along the southern frontier, peasant-settlers also benefited from a *pomest'e*. The problem in the newly conquered regions was the lack of peasants; Moscow made wide use of the colonization of the steppe to reinforce its territorial as well as military power. The first waves took place in the sixteenth century after seizing Kazan in 1552, and again during the 1580s and 1590s following the withdrawal of the Tatars of Crimea and the Nogays, and the agricultural crisis in central Russia. The emigrants were fugitive peasants, deserters and service elites who had no *pomest'e* in the other territories of Muscovy. They helped erect fortresses and colonize the neighbouring areas. As a result, the Muscovite authorities allowed the peasants that performed their military service in these regions to pass their small estates on to their descendants. At the same moment, members of the lower service class were sometimes salaried and sometimes they received a parcel (*nadel*) of land that was collective property of, for example, all musketeers serving in Belgorod province.[49] These policies, clearly at odds with the official ones in Moscow, had become especially urgent due to the advent of firearms, which required stable numbers of trained soldiers recruited from the peasantry. However, during the second half of the seventeenth century, financial difficulties of the state led to its inability to pay salaries and thus enhanced the distribution of land in exchange for the service. By the 1690s unconventional usages meant that service landholding in the south was no longer an attribute predicated upon membership in an elite family or hereditary military service.[50]

Of course, these policies did not fail to create problems between state elites and estate owners in the core of Russia. Throughout the sixteenth and seventeenth centuries, several rules were adopted that had the effect of limiting peasant mobility. Until the first half of the seventeenth century, the restriction was assumed to be temporary; by the 1630s, landlords even came to enjoy the right to allow their peasants to move, as can be seen expressed in many documents (the *otpusknaia gramota*). Such documents were signed by landowners, for example, to let their peasants marry on another estate, move to towns, etc. In exchange for mobility, peasants had to pay a fee. The process was by no means simple, as is evidenced by the numerous legal disputes and petitions drawn up by landlords' families against other claimants to their properties, whether landlords, merchants, *boyari*, or others. The alliance between the state and the provincial elites was supposed to offer a solution, with new rules on runaways being adopted in exchange for landowners' acceptance of a cadastre. However, this alliance proved to be ineffective, because different state administrations were unable to cooperate in achieving a cadastre, returning runaways, or punishing owners whose claims were illegitimate. To that must be added the lack of cooperation among landowners, who continued to retain peasants on the move – so-called runaways. Petitions multiplied between the 1620s and the 1640s, and the central state responded by lengthening the time to recover fugitives from 5 to 9 to 15 years (decrees of 1637, 1641, 1645, 1648).

This is where the famous *Ulozhenie* intervention of 1649 comes in; according to many interpretations – Russian, Soviet, and Western alike – it marked the final adoption of the servile regime in Russia and thereby the central role of the state in the process. The available sources reveal clear attempts by the state to enforce rules,[51] but as the records of litigation among landowners and between urban merchants and landowners plainly show,[52] the legal definition of those who had the right to own and transfer populated estates was not clear. The great landlords became notorious for luring peasants away from smaller estates.[53] This game became even more complicated when urban elites (with fiscal motives) and peripheral authorities (interested in increasing the local population) pushed to keep the runaways in place. Negotiations concerning this occurred on the legal, administrative, and political level.[54]

Annexation of new territories and the colonization of the steppe further weakened these already barely enforced rules. In 1635 a decree authorized commandants of local garrisons and southern governors to guarantee residence to fugitive peasants and not to return them to their legitimate owners. The following year, a new ordinance freed all those whose mobility had been restricted after 1613. Petitions by estate owners increased so much that in 1636, the central authorities decreed the obligation to return fugitive peasants to their legitimate owners. The *Ulozhenie* of 1649 sought to reinforce these rules. However, in the southern areas even more than in the heartland, the rules were barely enforced.[55] In the eyes of some tsarist elites, geopolitical considerations overwhelmed the political and social defence of estate owners in the central areas of Russia. For a few fugitives who were returned to their 'legitimate owners', millions of other peasants were left in their new places. Colonization could not have worked without a more or less accepted emigration and, thus, a limitation of the power of estate owners of central Russia on their peasants.[56] Thus, by 1656, despite the Ulozhenie of 1649, a new decree stated that three years of service rendered a migrant and also a fugitive, immune to return so as not to empty the defences in the South. In short, Moscow's policies were a mix of bureaucratic lack of organization and conscious attempt to 'leave fugitive peasants where they are' in order to occupy the steppe.[57]

As a consequence, between 1678 and 1897, peasants' settlements in the central forest heartland fell from 69.9 to 41.22 per cent of the total cultivated land, while those in the steppe areas increased from 28.78 to 41.22 per cent. During this same period, settlement in Siberia rose from 1.32 to 7.54 per cent. In the southern and eastern settlement areas, one-third of the population increase was due to natural growth and two-thirds to immigration. By the 1680s the peasant population in the Ukrainian territories was about half a million people; it doubled by 1720.[58] By 1678, 3.7 million peasants had emigrated and settled in Siberia, the north-western areas, the Urals, the south-eastern steppe, and the Volga.[59] As a whole, the population of Russia increased from 7 million in 1600 to about 9 million in 1678, 14 million in 1719, 17 million in 1762, and 21 million in 1782.[60]

To sum up, in order to stabilize Muscovite and later Russian territory, the social status of the population had to be defined by the state. However, this operation did not correspond to the traditional description provided by historiography, i.e., the sharp distinction between landlords and peasants and the bonded status of the latter were pillars of Russian expansion. For one thing, the landowners – especially of the smallest estates – were opposed to territorial expansion, which they correctly associated with a shortage of peasant manpower and social instability. Moreover, the Russian peasants were not serfs (*serfs de la glèbe*), but bonded labourers who could partially negotiate the terms of their bondage and above all their departure. In the end, the distinction between peasants and landowners remained vague in the colonized regions.

These elements can help us to understand the innovations of Peter the Great. In 1700, he expanded recruitment when Russia found itself engaged in a militarily conflict with Sweden: 335,000 men were concerned (out of a population of fifteen million) between 1700 and 1713. The army stabilized this figure at between 160,000 and 200,000 people. Peter accomplished this by conscripting one man for every 20 bonded labourers (thus peasants and lower-class city dwellers). For this purpose, he established a direct link between demographic calculation, tax pressure and recruitment. In particular, he changed the fiscal system from taxation by household to per capita taxation, which was not introduced in Europe until after the Napoleonic Wars a century later. With the per capita tax, Russian state revenue rose from 3 million roubles in 1701 to 8.5 million in 1725. The money was used not only to maintain the army but also to buy Western weapons, produce their own armaments in the Ural and finally to set up the first cadet training schools in the world. His success stemmed from two realities that Westerners all too often fail to perceive: Russian serfdom was far more flexible and the Mongols far less primitive than we tend to assert. Peter was able to take advantage of this heritage and blend it into social and administrative policies to suit his ambitions.

The power of the steppe

Muscovy, the last to arrive in the steppe, managed to gain control over territories that were by no means empty but in fact occupied by solid powers such as the Ottoman Empire, the Mongol Khanates and the Safavids. These territories were difficult to conquer and holding onto them proved even harder. Muscovy succeeded above all through diplomacy: it set neighbouring powers against each other; it sometimes sought financing from one power and sometimes from another, while convincing both it was not a threat and could be a useful tool to weaken their competitors. Moscow played with the monopoly on violence: the Muscovite princes sought first and foremost to subordinate the military and landowning elites. From a military standpoint, they accomplished this first by calling upon European mercenaries, then on the Cossacks and other steppe warriors and finally the peasants, aided by the 'military revolution'. Military solutions and the colonization of the steppe at the expense of local population were internally linked. The former could not work without the latter. From a social standpoint, Moscow owed its success to distinctions in social status laid down by laws that were increasingly strict in some cases, much more flexible in others and still more fluid in practice. A typical example was the difference between hereditary landowners and service elites, a distinction that evolved not only over time but even in everyday practice and in different regions in Russia.

The same coexistence of in principle fixed but actually flexible social status was found among the peasants. On the one hand, the peasantry was officially subject to heavier constraints on their mobility to meet the demands of intermediary echelons, small landowners and, in part, conscription needs. At the same time, these constraints were largely reduced when it came to territorial expansion: peasants were encouraged to emigrate and colonize the new regions, over the objections of landowners in emigration territories. Once they arrived, their legal status as peasants could even be called into question, as the borderline separating them from the intermediary ranks of society was quite flexible. Finally, such social experimentation, which began in the frontier, spread to the rest of Russia.

Through these policies, the Russian elites controlled the estate owners and won the loyalty of the peasants. They offered a form of political and social domination that was compatible with territorial expansion, which the landlords opposed. The expansion relied on the massive use of peasant-soldiers, a solution developed by Russia for want of an efficient road network and a sufficiently centralized bureaucracy. The presence of peasant-soldiers allowed Moscow to maintain a regular army without the need for large-scale transport of food. The subordination – if not the massive killing of 'nomads' – was a by-product of this aggressive expansion. As a result, merchants played a smaller role in supplying the army in Russia than in China. That does not mean that Moscow was hostile to markets. On the contrary, the whole point of territorial expansion was to take control of Eurasian trade networks; it was designed not just to demand tribute but to support Russian merchants at the expense of the other market communities that had dominated those regions for centuries. In any case, Russian trade expansion was more far-reaching than Western observers have acknowledged.

Our aim here is not to oppose an ideal Russian model to Western dynamics nor to endorse or refute historical modes of development but simply to understand them. The cities of these empires do not fit the European conception of the city, made up of middle class inhabitants and guilds and defined in opposition to the peasants, *villici* and rural lords. Russian cities were administrative centres and at the same time extensions of the countryside and especially the steppe, forming full-fledged economic worlds. The latter were not the kingdom of nomads, but rather complex military, fiscal and administrative entities that passed on to imperial constructions their notion and experience of the frontier as a movable space and locus of social and political experimentation.

In fact, there is no clear connection between war and economic growth. Imperial powers of varying dimensions quite often engaged in conflicts. Important resources were sometimes destroyed, but it was not systematic. The outcome depended, among other things, on interaction between the environment, the administration and social hierarchies. The short-, medium- and long-term success of Eurasian empires stemmed from the way they combined forms of recruitment, army and social order, military supplies and overall economic organization. Compared with the West, these solutions can now be seen as less 'primitive' and simplistic than is usually claimed. Trade and capital have played an important part in Russian development and it is therefore hardly credible to compare a despotic, coercive Asia to a capitalist Europe. Capital and coercion overlapped in Asia just as they did in Europe. Coercion relied on capital and capital in turn made wide use of coercion. The real question is how these two elements interacted in social organization, military strategies and state construction. Russia was distinctly less coercive than is usually asserted, and China made supplying the army an integral part of its market dynamics.

The notion of Asian despotism is thus of little relevance in analysing Russia. (Incidentally, others have shown that it does not help us to understand China and Central Asia either, or even the ancient empires.) On the contrary, we find capitalism overlapping with coercion, along with social distinctions that were strictly specified by law (depending on the time and place, even within Muscovy and later the Russian Empire) but quite flexible in practice. The idea of Asian (or Oriental) despotism was invoked in three different contexts: Montesquieu when absolutism was undergoing reform; Marx and the laws of development after 1850, when the capitalist world was changing; Wittfogel during the Cold War. These three reflections have something in common: they are all concerned with the transformation of capitalism and the relationship between the West and Asia. The first point is still with us but it has changed: we too can see the transformations of capitalism, but unlike during the three earlier periods mentioned, no alternative is being proposed today. The second point has also changed: Asia is now viewed not only as the reign of barbarians, but as a dangerous competitor – and a capitalist one at that, though in its own way. The new variants of despotism emphasize the lack of democracy in China and Russia. That is true, but it does not make their capitalism any less efficient.

As a result, our conventional image linking the rise of capitalism to wage labour, private property and trade is called into question. If Russia and Europe can both be characterized as a blend of capital and coercion, then how did specific mix and forms of them influence political and economic dynamics?

We have already discussed the impact of recruitment on labour and labour markets and the superposition between peasants, colonists and soldiers in the steppe. We need now to widen this perspective and include serfdom, slavery and peasant labour into our picture. Is it true that coerced labour opposed market development?

After Oriental despotism, notions of freedom and (social and economic) dependence require to be discussed. Again, we will make use of Russian and Inner Asian history as a heuristic to critically analyse conventional answers to these questions.

4

Slavery and Trade in Central Asia and Russia

Introduction[1]

To what extent can we qualify different forms of bondage, to which different words and rules have been applied, among them 'slavery'?

This question has been raised for various forms of bondage in Africa, India, China, the Ottoman Empire, Latin America, Southeast Asia, etc. On the one hand, several scholars have stressed the existence of slavery in these various places at different times. On the other hand, many other specialists on these areas have replied that local forms of bondage (and the related words to express them) cannot be translated as slavery insofar as these particular forms of bondage involved reciprocal obligations, voluntary submission, temporary bondage and still other kindred phenomena that would seem to exclude them from being considered slavery in a strict sense.[2]

One position minimizes the historical weight of transatlantic and Western colonial slavery in the Americas by lessening the perceived ubiquity of its oppressiveness, while the latter position stresses the historical specificity of forms of bondage and dependence and of the uniqueness of 'Western slavery'. The stakes in these debates are high, possibly including reparations from old European colonial countries and the United States to countries from which slaves originated. Contemporary debates over the nature of twenty-first-century informal forced labour (i.e., Eastern European sex trade, African child soldiers, etc.) grapple with historical definitions of slavery.[3]

Two main sources are usually mentioned in studies of ancient, medieval and modern slavery: debt (widely conceived as a form of individual and/or social obligation) and capture by war parties or belligerent armies. Roughly speaking, the first is internal to a given society while the second is generated by transgressing territorial boundaries.[4] This taxonomy requires some important qualifications; for example, war captives may be offered for ransom, but they may also enter the category of slaves by being sold; sale of captives within the internal market of the victorious war party was quite widespread. However, this shift requires the agreement of the leaders of the clan or of the state. That is to say that the boundary between a war captive and a slave is flexible and depends on the relative power of military commanders, political leaders, slave brokers and slave owners in negotiating among themselves the disposition of war captives. In this respect, slaves and captives in ancient Rome or in modern Africa are quite different phenomena.

In turn, debt and 'obligated' slaves cover a much wider and debated category extending from debt bondage, through voluntary or involuntary submission, and finally to pawnship. Enslavement by consent occurred frequently in Africa, India, China and Southeast Asia. It was usually indigenous and its prohibition was a feature of Islam and Western Christianity, but not of the Greek Orthodox Church, Hinduism, Confucianism or Buddhism.[5]

In this respect, Russia and Eurasia provide a stimulating historical environment to discuss the appropriateness of the terminology adumbrated above and whether envisioning the phenomena encompassed by such wording is warranted historically. On these topics, available historiographies provide answers that we can sketch as follows: Russia constituted a peculiar historical case in which slavery was practised on Russians themselves. Russia's backwardness in comparison with the West is confirmed by the persistence of despotism and bondage. In turn, Oriental despotism went along with the long-term persistence of the nomadic powers in Central Asia; ultimately, these features contributed to keeping Central Asia and Russia out of the world dynamics, namely the rise of capitalism in the West, and to the marginalization of these areas in the world economy.

Over the last several years, some aspects of these views have been revisited. Particular emphasis has been put on the nomadic powers of Central Asia as a long-term cultural, commercial and political force; to a certain extent, Eurasian history now has become a fresh topic, no longer necessarily associated with despotism, nomadic powers and backwardness. In this, war captives and domestic bondage were far from being a symptom and a source of backwardness and instability. Such a judgement is based upon the presumption of the superiority of free labour over bonded labour and of territorial states over pirates and nomads.[6]

A similar judgement orients the main interpretations of Russian forms of bondage resulting from capture in war. The existence of slavery in Russia is little known outside the circle of pre-Petrine Russia specialists, despite slavery's importance not only for Russian but also for global history, e.g., the link between slavery and serfdom; the relationship between the lengthy Russian history of bondage (most prominently slavery and serfdom) to the Gulag; and last but not least, bondage as testimony to the Mongol influence on Russia or, vice versa, as a response to European world expansion. Answers to these questions require careful analysis of slavery in pre-modern Russia. Such investigation must focus on war captives, domestic slaves and bonded people in their historical definitions and overlapping. So, who were they?

A current historiography follows the main, if not sole reference work in a Western language on Russian slavery, Richard Hellie's book *Slavery in Russia, 1450–1725*.[7] Hellie considers that the *kholopy* were slaves. He initially translated *kholopstvo* as bondage, but later preferred the term 'slavery'. Herbert Leventer objected to the latter translation, emphasizing that the status of Russian *kholopy* was not transferred to their children, that their servitude was temporary and that they could accumulate and transfer property. He therefore thought that *kholop* corresponded instead to the English word 'servant'. Hellie retorted that, in Russian, *kholop* was a synonym for *rab* (slave), and that even if the conditions of the *kholopy* were different from those of slaves in antiquity and the Americas, they were perfectly compatible with those of other forms of slavery.[8]

This actually is a quite common problem met by everyone who has worked on forms of bondage and slavery.

We consider that any general definition of slavery will miss the point, that is, how different societies in different times identified legal status and labour conditions and assigned hierarchical duties, obligations and, eventually, rights to the people in question. We prefer to adopt this last approach, which, in turn, does not avoid comparisons but, quite the contrary, seeks to identify multiple criteria for comparing labour conditions and legal status in different historical contexts.

Our investigation pathway is as follows: we will start with Russian words expressing forms of legal bondage and then try to understand their social and institutional role by comparing legal texts and social practices. We will see that the Russian language generated one single word (*kholopstvo*) to express bondage; at the same time, within this rubric, different forms and gradations of dependence existed, from debt bondage and self-sale into bondage to indenture and chattel slavery. This taxonomy reflected the fact that *kholopstvo* was much less a precise category or invariant legal status (as the term 'slavery' connotes in Western language) than a spectrum of bondage-related phenomena, each of which was addressed specifically by statutory definitions and regulations and/or by contracts.

This situation is not unique to Russia: in African *pawnship*, for example, the major difference from Western slavery and other forms of African bondage and slavery was that ownership and transfer concerned the contract and not people.[9] The same argument can be made for Russian *kholopstvo*. To parallel recent debates about slavery, the critical issue is not whether any system of bondage was 'harsh' or 'mild', but rather which conditions were exceptional and which were typical in it.[10] In Russia, hereditary slaves comprised barely 10 per cent of the *kholopy* (who in turn comprised 10 per cent of the population), and they were mostly recorded for Novgorod in the aftermath of the *Oprichina* (1565–1572, when the Tsar Ivan IV split the state in two and ravaged much of it) and during the Time of Troubles (from 1598, when the establishment of the Romanov dynasty in 1613 ended the 700-year-old Riudrikid dynasty). All other contracts, as we will see, were limited in time or could last until the death of the master. This difference certainly mattered, although more detailed empirical analyses would be required to determine the percentage of renewed contracts that ended up erasing this difference. At the same time, two major features differentiated these relationships from hereditary *kholopstvo*: a contract remained part of the legal status and, therefore, the condition of *kholopstvo* did not automatically transfer to children (even if this issue was not de facto impossible).

The second part of this chapter focuses on war captives. Unlike *kholopy*, war captives often entered permanent slavery. They constitute a historically highly important element of normative and unusual political activity and even turmoil. Over centuries, if not millennia, war captives, pirates and nomadic powers were the rules and not the exceptions in geo-political and economic equilibriums.[11] From the twelfth to the eighteenth century, captives and slaves were part of the common world of Mongols, Berbers, Ottomans, Chinese and European powers. All of them took part in raids and the trade in captives and made use of slaves. This also implies that the Eurasian history of slavery cannot confirm the clear-cut opposition between slave and captive, on the one hand, and nomadic and territorial powers, on the other hand. Theorists of state building[12] as well as economic historians[13] persistently contrast predatory units to centralized states. The Mongols are placed in the first category, Europe the second one. The history of war captives and slaves will lead us to adopt a different approach, close to that of those who have recently revisited the history of the steppes and, more generally, the contrast between national states, on the one hand, and nomadic and predatory powers, on the other.[14]

Sources for studying these problems are numerous, but they are scattered. Regarding *kholopy*, the Russian archives provide whole series of contracts, civil statuses and other litigations. Partially exploited by Iakovlev, Paneiakh and Hellie, these sources provide a quite complete picture of the phenomenon. The *kabal'nye knigi* (i.e., the *kholopy* registration books) are particularly valuable and so are the records of the *kholopy prikaz* settled in 1571.[15] Contracts are also available in the Saltikov-Shedrin library (see the following notes).

The sources for studying war captives raise distinct problems, since so much of the paperwork has been lost and what has survived is in Middle-Russian script. The *kholopy* registers introduced in the sixteenth century and diplomatic sources provide some information.[16] However, despite official rules, war captives were not systematically recorded, and therefore their real number must be substantially greater than what extant records tell us.

This lacuna does not apply to the other important powers in the area under study, namely the Byzantine Empire, Venice, Genoa and, later on, the Ottoman Empire, for these polities left an important archival legacy on war captives and the Eurasian slave trade. Ottomanists have already provided important studies on the market for slaves between Crimea, Russia, Central Asia, and the Ottoman Empire, in particular in the seventeenth through nineteenth centuries[17]; historians of medieval and early modern Venice and Genoa have also provided some remarkable studies. Sources in Genoa and Venice include a few in Latin, but more in pre-modern Italian. Much of our knowledge about the trade of Caffa is derived from the commercial deeds and contracts drawn up by the Genoese notary Lamberto di Sambuceto between 1128 and 1290.[18] A precise date for the foundation of the Genoese colony at Caffa on the Crimean coast cannot be given. The first historical fact relating to Caffa in the Genoese chronicles is the dispatch of three vessels by the consul of the port, Paolino Doria, to the aid of Tripoli in 1289.[19]

Kholopy: Slaves, serfs, or indentured servants?

Translating *kholop* as 'slave' is partly justified by the fact that when Peter the Great abolished this status in 1725, documents then associated the *kholop* with a slave (*rab*). This association of ideas dates from the early eighteenth century, however, and occurred in the special context of the reforms of Peter the Great. At the time, insofar as slavery in the strict sense was prohibited, *rab* designated either a former slave, one mentioned in the Bible, or the symbolic relationship that the landlords maintained with the Tsar.[20] It is not without interest that, over previous centuries, *kholop* meant any 'subject of' the tsar or any superior Russian political authority; this word was particularly in use for Muslims and Tatars.[21] In turn, the meaning of *rab* changed over time. Iakovlev thinks it was of Turkish origin and was used to designate Mameluke slaves from Africa, who were as such distinct from slaves from Central Asia and Eastern Europe. At the same time, in the southern part of the future Rus', the word *rab* designated Cumans and Pechenegs. It is nevertheless meaningful that, in Russian legal and common language since the twelfth century, *raba* means the *kholop*'s wife.[22] However, any free person who married a *kholop* was subject to the legal constraints applying to the latter ('po rabe kholop, po kholopu rabe').[23] Even more important, the relationship between a *kholop* and his wife is associated with that between the *kholop* and his master, the *rab* and his master, a son and his father. In all these cases, a mutual although hierarchical relation (of dependence) is established. Children, wives and *kholopy* had limited but existing rights in relation to their 'masters' (this category being inclusive of husbands and fathers).[24]

Let us try to grasp the meaning and content of the word *kholop*.[25] According to Iakovlev, the word *kholop* derived from a Polish word that, since the eleventh century, was associated in common Eastern Slavic and later in Russian with war captives.[26] This is extremely important to us, insofar as it testifies to the common origin of war captives and other bonded people.

The word *kholop* then entered the *Russkaia Pravda*, a collection of legal acts that began to be compiled in 1016 and was put together in its near final version in the mid-twelfth century.[27] Three main origins of slavery were listed: accepting work associated with a slave; marrying a slave; selling oneself into slavery. In the version of the twelfth century, the general category of *kholopy* was already highly differentiated and ranged from full *kholopstvo* (*obelnyi kholop*)[28] to indentured servant (*zakup*).[29] All of these categories had legal personality and rights.[30]

Indeed, the word *kholop* appeared in quite disparate sixteenth and seventeenth century sources: law collections, judicial cases, private transactions, contracts, memoranda, estate accounts, registrations with notaries, etc. These documents never speak of *kholopstvo* in general, but qualify the word with adjectives: *starinnoe* (hereditary), *polnoe* (full), *dokladnoe* (registered), *dolgovoe* (obligated, indebted), *zhiloe* (limited to a period of time), *dobrovol'noe* (voluntary) and *kabal'noe* (limited service contract). The latter was by far the most widespread term, found in 80–92 per cent of the known contracts of *kholopstvo*, depending on the period.[31] This multiplicity of qualifiers is significant, for it indicates a set of distinct kinds of contracts rather than a single formal personal status. Elite *kholopy* (mostly entered in the category of *dokladnoe kholopstvo*) served in the central government/palace administration and in the provincial administration until the mid-sixteenth century, in the cavalry probably until the third decade of the seventeenth century and as estate managers until the time of Peter the Great.[32] The institution seems to have arisen around the end of the fifteenth century, and the last extant registered slavery document is dated before the end of the sixteenth century. Some of the major factors in this decline were the evolution of the central government from a royal household to an administration run by lay bureaucrats. Next was the radical decline of the large patrimonial estate (*votchiny*), which had needed stewards to manage them, in favour of an increase in smaller service estates (*pomest'ia*) that were increasingly managed by members of the middle service class.

Let us take now the most widespread of these contracts, the *kabal'noe kholopstvo*, which appears in legislation, disputes, contracts between private individuals, wills and estate inventories.[33] All these documents mention the length of service and the possibility of transforming a six-month or one-year contract into a contract of unlimited service.[34] However, the latter practice was prohibited in the early seventeenth century.[35] Before that, the code of 1550 already emphasized that the *kabal'nye* were not *dolgovye* (indebted). In subsequent years (1586 and 1597), new provisions confirmed that the *kabal'nye* could remain obligated only for the duration of the creditor's life, and that the latter could not transfer the obligations to anyone, in the form of either a sale or an inheritance. These same rules forbade the *kholop* to repay his debt.[36] This latter provision could be interpreted as the desire to maintain the *kholop* in a state close to slavery, but it is equally legitimate to interpret it as a provision aimed to exclude that form of dependence, and the link with the previous provisions would seem to confirm the latter interpretation. This conclusion is bolstered by all the contracts that have been found, which indicate the length of commitment, usually limited to one year.[37] The evolution in the rules concerning the *kabal'nye kholopy* between 1586 and 1597 was inspired by the previous evolution of rules on military captives, notable the law of 21 August 1556, which prescribed that a military captive was to be enslaved no longer than the period of his captor's life and could not pass as a slave to his children.[38] From this standpoint, the change in the nature of limited service contract *kholopstvo* was instituted to safeguard the interest of the middle service class, whose members were at a disadvantage in competing with other members of the upper service class for *kholopy*.[39]

It remains to examine the most extreme forms of *kholopstvo*. The 'full' (*pol'noe*) variety was already developed in the *Russkaia Pravda* since the twelfth century and had three main sources. The *kholop* himself or herself might ask to be included in this category, as a form of repayment of a debt to the authorities.

Second, if a female *kholop* married a free man, without the authorization of the person entitled to the wife's service, her husband became a *pol'nyi* (full) *kholop*. The third source was domestic service contracts established for an unlimited length of time, but such contracts have been found only between 1430 and 1554, with none appearing after that date. The most widely accepted hypothesis is that this form of dependence tended to be transformed into other forms of *kholopstvo* of a temporary nature.

The hereditary variety (*starinnoe kholopstvo*) seems to come closest to slavery in the strict sense. It expresses the condition of those whose parents were *kholopy*. It was possible to transfer such *kholopy* in wills or as a dowry or gift. In the contracts examined by Hellie, there were 5,575 *kholopy* between 1430 and 1598, 483 of whom were hereditary. The *kabal'nye knigi* (*kholopy* registration books) at the end of the seventeenth century mention 418 hereditary *kholopy* out of a total of 2,168 registered at the time. The available sources do not allow us to say whether this higher percentage testifies to the poor economic situation of the time, or to a long-term trend, because this type of commitment was prohibited by the decrees of 1586 and 1593.

To be sure, Iakovlev and more recently Paneiakh have found disputes and contracts concerning *starinnye kholopy* in the middle of the seventeenth century, decades after the official abolition of this type of contract.[40] In other words, despite the official prohibition, several lords continued to impose forms of contractual servitude of a hereditary type. The authorities devoted much attention to what amounted to illegal slavery and attempted to penalize transgressors. By banning this kind of servitude, the government sought to limit the power of landlords over peasants and thereby strengthen state authority over the owners of large estates. Furthermore, the *kholopy* were exempt from taxation, which reduced the revenue of the state. This was a measure intended to strengthen small landowners and to encourage their alliance with the state. Among other things, the specialization of warfare in the early seventeenth century reduced the importance of cavalry while increasing the importance of infantry wielding firearms. As a result, bureaucratic and military service continued to be meritocratic; but those possessing or developing merit were from outside the traditional service class.[41] The evolution of kinds of *kholopy* and those of people entitled to own *kholopy* enter these broader dynamics. In particular, measures to get rid of hereditary servitude had important consequences. Rather than exclude part of the population from all legal rights, as in the case of slavery, the solution consisted in assigning highly differentiated rights to the various strata of the population and dividing them into legally distinct groups. The peasants saw their rights severely restricted, while city dwellers were prohibited from subjecting themselves, even voluntarily, to any form of *krepost'* or *kholopstvo*. Numerous provisions defined those entitled to sign *kholopstvo* contracts as creditors or debtors. Thus, in 1641, the following were excluded from the category of creditors entitled to demand labour service: all *tiaglye liudi* (people subject to *tiaglo*, i.e., the unit of taxation), including peasants and artisans as well as other taxpayers, priests, artillerymen and monastery servants.[42] Conversely, starting in 1590, city dwellers subject to taxation (*posad*) were prohibited from offering these forms of labour service. In 1628, this prohibition was extended to include musketeers, soldiers and all the intermediate ranks of the civil service and the military. The interpretation of these norms posed problems, because the categories were rather general. In the case of professions such as barbers, seamstresses, trappers and small craftsmen, the question arose whether they could legitimately enter into *kholopstvo* contracts. The many petitions sent to the *kholop* chancellery concerning such individuals demonstrate their involvement in these contracts, their desire to be able to continue being taken on as *kholopy* and their use of the law to challenge the claims of their counterparts.[43]

From this point of view, the 119 articles of chapter 20 of the *Ulozhenie* of 1649, devoted to *kholopy*, reproduced in large part the provisions of earlier legislation. For those who failed to meet their legal obligations (debts, penalties, fines, theft, etc.), the text indicated the amount of work required to repay their debt or, in general, to fulfil their obligation. Once the work was completed, the creditor brought the debtor back before an official, who released the debtor from all obligations. Section 20 of the *Ulozhenie* also mentions other conditions for release from *kholopstvo*. Various articles speak of both debts and *krepost'*, with the latter viewed as justifying the debt.

The core provisions of chapter 20 of the *Ulozhenie* depart from the rules found in many slaveholding systems (including the ancient Rome and the Western colonial codes), although they are not very different from slavery in Islamic and Catholic areas. *Kholopy* were free to marry, and such an act was inviolable. The wife of a *kholop* was obliged to remain in residence until her husband's debt was repaid, but, upon the death of the husband, his wife's dowry passed to her family, and not to the landowner-creditor.[44] The *kholop* could be called as a witness in a trial, which means that legal personality was acknowledged. Diverging most from systems of slavery elsewhere, a master of *kholopy* had no obligation to feed or provide care for elderly *kholopy*, whereas this obligation formed part of a master's commitment throughout the length of the contract itself.[45]

The available contracts show that about 20 per cent of the *kholopy* were children between 5 and 14 years of age whose parents placed them under one-year service contracts that were often renewable. Some contracts were for rather long periods. Such contracts were signed by the most disadvantaged among the city population, and their numbers rose at the turn of the seventeenth century, a time of serious economic crisis. In a way, it meant placing children in service to ensure their survival. From this point of view, the *kholopstvo* contract for children sprang from the same motives as several contracts of this type that were widespread during the same period in France and England (servants in husbandry), albeit with different legal terms and institutional conditions.[46] The other *kholopstvo* contracts referred to adults working as servants. Loans were sometimes the formal reason for these contracts, but the terms of the loans often suggest that these were really servants' wages.

Taking these facts into account, we can conclude that, especially following the decline of its hereditary forms, most of the aspects of *kholopstvo* resemble other types of indebtedness and limitation on mobility, such as forms of contractual servitude widely found in the same period among Hindu populations in India and in parts of China. Temporary servitude fell within the scope of contracts that were considered 'free' and voluntary from a legal standpoint. Freedom of commitment did not exclude the renewal of contracts for up to several decades, or even throughout the lifetime of the 'indebted' person.[47] However, the Russian situation differed from the one prevalent in the Islamic world, where sharia law forbad all forms of bondage for debt, crimes and indigence, even if they occurred in practice under customary or sultans' law.[48]

In virtually all the known Russian contracts, and increasingly so over time, the status of *kholopy* could not be transferred to descendants; this is essentially what distinguished this system from slavery in antiquity and the Americas. In other words, by their very existence, forms of voluntary bondage testify to the variety of labour commitments and to continuity rather than opposition between these forms, ranging from statutory and hereditary slavery to 'free' labour. Fugitives from the ranks of apprentices, domestics and the indentured were caught by the state's police forces and were subject to criminal proceedings. Such 'penal sanctions' also applied to the Russian *kholopy*.

It is possible to distinguish two main tendencies in the disputes over *kholopy*, either involving several 'claimants to title' or between these people and *kholopy*. In the first case, the question arose when someone claimed to have established a *kholopstvo* contract in good faith and the other party had previously signed one with another master. Such an individual was legally a 'fugitive'. In the early sixteenth century, the *Russkaia Pravda* (article 118) stated that the first claimant to rights could recover the fugitive, but had to compensate a buyer who had acted in good faith. However, the *Sudebnik* of 1550 adopted the principle of *caveat emptor*: the buyer of a title over a *kholop* could not be compensated, especially if he had been negligent.[49] Finally, the *Ulozhenie* of 1649 returned to the previous principle. In every case, written documents were required to prove the validity of a plaintiff's claims.

There were also disputes between those who claimed rights over people and those in a situation of obligation, who might object to the original obligation or to the terms of its cancellation. These conflicts were so numerous that a *kholopii prikaz* (chancellery) was set up in 1571 to resolve issues of this kind.[50] Among the most frequent disputes concerned types of *kholopstvo*. The prohibition against hereditary *kholopstvo* towards the end of the seventeenth century did not end this practice. Many cases were brought before the court at this time, by *kholopy* themselves, often by the children of *kholopy* or by new masters who were claiming their rights.[51] These disputes confirm that it was not impossible for the *kholopy* to win a case, although the chances were slim compared with those of 'claimants to title'. At the same time, this use of rights was possible because it intersected with the interests of other lords, other claimants over *kholopy* or of the state itself, for the reasons mentioned above. This also explains why the few suits *kholopy* won concerned the kind of *kholopstvo* and their obligations and rights towards one lord rather than another one. On the contrary, brutality against *kholopy* was punishable by law, but was extremely rarely enforced. The solution to this problem was rather found in the strong, disloyal competition among estate owners; the *kholop* could easily find another master, flight was easy and recovery extremely hard and costly. This implies that masters were obliged to treat their *kholop* with relative decency or they would run away.[52]

Overall, when Peter the Great abolished the *kholopstvo* status in 1725, it applied to 10 per cent of the population.[53] Of the 2,500 contracts and documents that have been recovered, 92 per cent are from the Novgorod region and 80 per cent of the contracts were signed between 1581 and 1603. According to Hellie's calculations, 23 per cent of the cases involved single men and 60 per cent couples without children. The rest were couples with a minor child (1.6 per cent), widowers (four per cent), widows (3.7 per cent), married women (2.5 per cent) or unmarried women (4.2 per cent), while the status of the others was unknown. In the majority of cases, the *kholopy* were between 10 and 34 years of age, but about ten per cent were between the ages of 10 and 14 and another 10 per cent between the ages of 5 and 9. Finally, men made up at least two-thirds, and often virtually all, of the *kholopy* throughout the period under study, from the sixteenth to the late seventeenth centuries.[54] Nearly all the *kholopy* were domestic servants, and they were rarely assigned to farm work.

The link between *kholopy* and debt bondage is clear when one relates the number of new contracts concerning *kholopy* – mostly *kabal'nye* – and the dynamics of harvest between the 1580s and 1610. In the province of Novgorod, the number of *Kholopy* rose by a factor of anywhere from eight to ten after bad harvests.[55]

However, the *kholopy* were seldom intended for farm work, at least in Muscovy and European Russia. One reason that slaves and *kholopy* were infrequently found in Russian agriculture could be that masses of serfs performed such functions. *Kholopy* and serfs, therefore, appear to have been complementary, and this may have constituted one of the dominant features of Russian history.[56] *Kholopy* initially were domestic, elite and/or urban bonded people in a still unstable, although expanding state; later, their dismissal was linked to the solidification of state power with its fiscal and military needs and the rise of clear legal differentiations between hereditary and service estate owners peasants, artisans, urban groups, etc. The merging of *kholopy* with peasants was linked to state fiscal and military needs; since the early eighteenth century, *kholopy*, *dvornye* and *delovye liudy* could enlist in the army; *kholopy* were initially exempted from soul tax; their transfer into existing legal-social groups (*sostoianiia*) corrected this situation. In other words, the long history of *kholopstvo* in Russia reflects that of the progressive formation of state power, the evolution in the relationship between various social groups and labour. In 1720, Peter replaced the household tax with the soul tax; this reform made it unacceptable that *kholopy* (10 per cent of the population) were not submitted to the tax. Their conversion into 'peasants' or lower urban groups solved this problem. In the military realm as well, since the fourteenth century at least, *kholopy* (and fugitive *kholopy*) serving in the army were freed of their 'debt' and became free people. This situation changed during the second half of the seventeenth century, when the authors of the *Ulozhenie* of 1649 quickly realized that freedmen were not likely to make good cavalrymen, and thus allowed members of the middle service class who had been *kholopy* to return to their condition if they found military service not to their liking.[57] In 1700, Peter the Great, faced with the Northern War, ordered that manumitted limited service *kholopy* be enlisted in the infantry; the order was repealed in 1703. The reason was that during the second half of the seventeenth century, the nature of warfare had changed, and the old middle service class cavalry had been largely phased out. This was a crucial step towards the abolition of *kholopstvo*. To a certain extent, the transformation of *Kholopstov* in connection with domestic and internal affairs cannot be isolated from the evolution of Russia on the international chessboard. War captives and the slave trade are part of this wider dynamics. In the following pages, we will study warfare and the slave trade in Eurasia in detail.

War captives at a crossroads of empires

Central Asian slaves for the Mediterranean, from the thirteenth through the fifteenth centuries

The importance of captives and slaves on the expanding Russian territory reflected changing power constellations in Central Asia, the southern Balkans, the Crimea and the Mediterranean. The history of war captives in Russia and Asia is linked to that of the main trade routes and changing geopolitical situations over the centuries. The first phase, during the thirteenth and fourteenth centuries, was mostly connected to the Silk Road; the second, from the fourteenth into the sixteenth century, followed a Russian-Iranian-Indian path; and the third, from the sixteenth into the eighteenth century, was linked to the expansion of Russia and its integration of Mongol khanates. Each of these waves had commercial and geopolitical dimensions; our aim is to add the ransom-captive and slave markets to the picture and thereby shed new light on the entire process.

The origin of the words *esclaves* and *sclavus* in use in medieval and early modern Italy expressed less the linguistic and legal heritage of ancient Rome than it did a link with the market for bound people from the Slavic areas.[58] The slave trade had an economic prop in traffic from Central Asia to the Black Sea[59] and in the growing presence of Venetians and Genoese in this area.[60] In both Venice and Genoa, traders sold Circassian and Abkhazian slaves previously bought mostly in Caspian and Black Sea ports. We have evidence from as early as 1246 that the Mongols sold Greeks, Bulgarians, Ruthenians and Rumanians to merchants from Genoa, Pisa and Venice, who in turn sold them to the Saracens. The Italians had purchased these slaves in the northern Black Sea ports of Maurocastro at the mouth of the Dniester and Caffa in the Crimea; in the latter, the Genoese received permission from the Mongol khan in 1266 to establish a colony. In Caffa, Genoese merchants bought Circassians, Tatars, Russians, Iranians, Poles, etc. The other centre of the slave trade in the Black Sea during the fourteenth century was the Crimean port of Tana, which the Venetians had colonized in 1333. In spite of the unstable favour of the Mongol ruler of Tana and resulting breaks in the trading activities, Tana still remained a place of high strategic value, ensuring better access to the Oriental markets and the Far East than the Genoese had in Caffa. The potentially high profits to be expected from trips to the eastern Black Sea area can be seen in the increased revenue of *incanti* for the galleys bound for Romania in the first half of the fourteenth century and after the 1370s. The main trading goods were furs, wine, grain and slaves, the latter becoming increasingly important in the late fourteenth century when Venice needed slaves for its colony on Crete. As a consequence of the growing Ottoman menace, the Venetian trade shifted to the western Black Sea (Maurocastro and the Danube estuary), Egypt and the Middle East in the course of the first half of the fifteenth century. At Kilia, Tatar subjects were sold by their compatriots to Genoese, Venetians and Greeks from Constantinople.[61] Genoa, Venice and Catalonia were also in competition for the trade in slaves. In 1263, the Byzantine Empire re-opened the trade between Egypt and the Black Sea, and Genoa became the first supplier of slaves for both the armies and the harems of the Mameluke sultans. Male slaves were also sent to the alum mines of Genoa at Focea and, of course, to Genoa and Spain. Women were particularly welcome for domestic services, while men were valued for ship work or sold to Spain. In early 1400, almost 10 per cent of Genoa's population was unfree – that is, between 4,000 and 5,000 people.[62] In Caffa, the revenue from the *gabella capitum* allows us to calculate the following numbers of slaves: in 1374 at least 3,285 slaves, in 1385/86 about 1,500, in 1387/88 about 1,600 and in 1381/82 at least 3,800 slaves. During the fifteenth century, the *gabella* was farmed out. For 1411 one can assume 2,900 sold slaves; from the 1420s until 1477 there were 2,000 per year at most. The fall of Constantinople provoked a massive decline (to about 400 or 600 slaves per year). Thus, during a single century, the numbers fell by around 80 per cent, and this decline was already apparent before 1453; both the *gabella* incomes of February and June follow this trend.[63]

Resembling later transatlantic slavery, here too it was war captives and people already enslaved in internal areas who were then sold to Genoa. But, according to Genoese sources, 'voluntary' enslavement was equally widespread – that is, people who were still legally 'free' in Caffa and were seized there by Genoese. However, neither Genoese nor Venetian traders organized expeditions with this specific aim in Central Asia.[64] This was probably due to the small scale and high transaction costs of the operations. It was simply not worth extending to Central Asia the credit and commercial arrangements in place on the Black Sea, and this was all the more true for slaves, a minor market compared with that in luxury items. The caravan trade, much too wide-ranging for European powers, was solidly based on the interaction between non-pastoral nomadic activities and caravan merchants. Increasingly stable communities in Central Asia offered a reliable environment. Islamization of the area further drove this process but did not immediately marginalize Venice and Genoa; at first they even benefited from the decline of the Byzantine Empire, in terms of not only commercial trade but also the captives' market.[65] At the same time, the rivalry between Venice and Genoa prevented either one of them from controlling the Black Sea trade. In 1462, after the fall of Constantinople, Genoese Caffa placed itself under the protection of Poland. From 1466 to 1474, intervention by the Genoese became particularly marked. Ultimately, Muhammad the Conqueror captured Caffa in 1475 and controlled the trade of goods and slaves from Central Asia. In 1459 the Venetian Senate lamented the scarcity of slaves, most of the Slavic and Tatar slaves now being sent to the Near and Middle East, in particular to Egypt and Turkey.[66] Genoa therefore turned to other sources, that is, to Islamic Spain and North Africa, where it acquired slaves to sell in Seville and in the Canary Islands. It was at this point that Genoa tried to enter the market for slaves in the New World but was quickly overtaken by Spanish, Portuguese and finally British vessels.[67]

At first glance, this outcome would seem to confirm the traditional historiographical view of a progressive shift from the Mediterranean to the Atlantic.[68] According to this view, the decline of Venice and the Italian republic was linked to the rising power of Spain and the Western European powers (Portugal, the Netherlands, Britain and France) in connection with the discovery of the Americas. This view, while not totally incorrect, is nonetheless a prejudiced one insofar as it ignores what was meanwhile transpiring in Central Eurasia, Russia and the Ottoman Empire.

The Indian network, from the fourteenth to the seventeenth centuries

Indeed, the traffic between Central Asia and Venice and Genoa intersected with the resurgence of the caravan trade; this was linked to Mongol and Ming political stabilization, which was achieved from the fourteenth to the sixteenth centuries.[69] In the early sixteenth century, the Uzbeks, Kazakhs and Kirghiz dominated the steppes. Muscovite expansion and increasing division among Mongol groups and heirs to the Golden Horde strongly contributed to reshaping the caravan trade in Central Asia from the fourteenth century on,[70] while the traffic in slaves increased. Caravan trade among China, Persia, Central Asia, the

Ottoman Empire and Russia, on the one hand, and among Russia, Central Asia and India or the Ottoman Empire, on the other, accorded with the systematic traffic in slaves. The Indian-Central Asian caravan trade was, in large measure, a latter-day continuation of the enterprise that, centuries earlier, had led Indian Buddhists to move out along the same routes.[71] Indian slaves had been exported from Central Asia since ancient times. Indian chroniclers mention slaves in the tens and even hundreds of thousands,[72] while Central Asian sources suggest that slaves were put to work in masonry, construction engineering, agricultural production, and other forms of skilled and unskilled labour. Even if slaves were drawn from a number of regions – including the nomadic steppes, Iran, Afghanistan, the Caucasus and Russia at the turn of the sixteenth and seventeenth centuries – judicial sources show that Indians accounted for at least 58 per cent of all slaves.[73]

In the sixteenth century, Indian slaves, both Hindus and Muslims, were sold on the markets of Tashkent and Samarkand, along with other slaves from Lithuania, Russia and the Caucasus.[74] Between the twelfth and seventeenth centuries, there are indications of bonded people being part of the caravan trade from Central Asia to India and China[75] and vice versa, i.e., from India to Central Asia. This trade went along with the general trade in luxury items and horses along the same axes.[76] This traffic had begun in ancient times but evolved dramatically during the medieval period, particularly in conjunction with the expansion of Islam in India in the early eleventh century and later when the Indian merchant diasporas emerged in the sixteenth century.[77] The Indian merchant diasporas, and in particular the Indian community in Astrakhan, strongly supported this traffic; Persian merchants also contributed to it.[78] Samarkand was perhaps the quintessential caravan city – near to where the east-west route intersected the north-south highway between India and Russia, embedded in a fertile garden and what would be the future political capital of Tamerlane (and the regional capital of earlier dynasties).[79] Indian slaves reached Central Asia in different ways; some of these slaves were secured in exchange for Central Asian goods, horses in particular; some were war captives; while many others were captured during raids on trading caravans.[80] In 1014, the sultan of Gazna brought 200,000 Indian slaves into his town. In Turan in the early fourteenth century, sultans owned between 50,000 and 180,000 slaves each. Indian slaves worked in agriculture and were employed in other domestic activities in Bukhara in the late fourteenth and the early fifteenth centuries.[81] Skilled slaves were particularly valuable, which is why rival political powers commonly enslaved and relocated artisans in the wake of successful invasions.

Indian slaves were also sold in Bukhara and Astrakhan. At the same time, the Safavid Iranians were also sold as slaves, in particular after wars between the Uzbeks and Safavids. Enslavement of Iranians lasted until the mid-nineteenth century, when Russian and British sources spoke of some 10,000 Iranian slaves in Khiva and over 100,000 slaves in the Khivan, Bukharan and Turkmen territories.[82] In the eighteenth century, at the markets of Bukhara, Khiva and Kashgar, most slaves came from Africa or from the mountains and desert fringes of Iran and Afghanistan.[83] Many owners manumitted their slaves, mostly when they were over 50 years old, whereupon they spent the rest of their lives in extremely poor conditions. There are also a number of cases of young slaves manumitted at the death of their master, which was in conformity with Islamic law.[84]

No less important, however, were the strong Islamic scholarly scientific and cultural links that overlapped the trade routes, connecting Bukhara and Istanbul, the Ottoman capital and extending across the Muslim Qazaq steppes all the way to Chawchak (i.e., Chuguchak, Tacheng) and beyond. India's Muslim and even Hindu merchants knew Farsi Persian, the main trading language, and some knew Turkic dialects, useful in Muscovy/Russia. Indian merchants developed some of the same techniques made famous in Renaissance Italy – palazzo-like trading houses (called *havelis*), kin networks and credit – but they did *not* enjoy a corresponding Italian-style political organization, that is, strong city-states to support them.[85]

However, in the eighteenth century, Indian slaves were comparatively few on the markets of Bukhara, Samarkand, Khiva and Kashgar.[86] This was the case because, as usual, the traffic in slaves reflected the commercial trade and geopolitical equilibrium; the strong links between Turkestan and South Asia appear to have suffered with the tsarist advance into the region. Tensions and rivalries between and within these political entities strongly contributed to the advance of Russia in the north and that of the European powers in the south.[87] At the same time, Indian exports of slaves decreased insofar as the Mughal Empire reduced – without completely eliminating – the practice of enslavement in India. This process was concomitant with a progressive fragmentation of the Muslim world, which consisted of Central Asia and the Ottoman, Mughal and Safavid Empires. By the seventeenth century, India had begun to manufacture enough textiles to clothe nearly the whole of Central Asia as well as Iran, and thus there was no longer any need to exchange Central Asian horses and other goods for Indian slaves.[88] According to some scholars, the most important development in the eighteenth century was the emergence, under Durrani rule, of Afghanistan as a powerful polity with particularly close links to northern India.⁸⁹ To this one should add the progressive withdrawal of the Ottoman Empire from India and its general decentralization, which resulted in less traffic in slaves. In the seventeenth and eighteenth centuries, when Indian slaves almost disappeared in Central Asia, Indian goods entered this area; the Punjab in particular witnessed an unprecedented economic and demographic growth in the seventeenth century, but this commerce later came to a halt with the rapid decay of the Safavid Empire and the Uzbek khanates, the Punjab's most important customers.⁹⁰ India's communications with Central Asia were not only maintained, but even enhanced. Contrary to widely held beliefs, active bilateral trade between India and Central Asia continued between 1550 and 1750. In other words, recent historiographical trends do *not* see the decline of Indian slaves and certain Indian networks in Central Asia as indicating a general decline of India, but as the result of new destinations for its textiles and the emergence of new centres in Central Asia that were mostly dominated by Russians.

Khanates, nomads and Russia, from the sixteenth to the nineteenth centuries

The establishment of new trade boundaries between India and Central Asia paralleled the reconfiguration of the balance between Central Asia and Russia. This process is important to us for it links the historical dynamics of the Inner Asian slave trade to the evolution of slavery in the Mediterranean, on the one hand, and to the rising of serfdom in Russia, on the other hand. Without the long-standing tradition of the trade in slaves and war captives, we cannot understand the peculiar link in Russia between territorial expansion, military concerns, fiscal problems and serfdom. Ultimately, the geo-political evolution of Russia and Inner Asia will provide insights into the link between war, trade and forced labour. Now, the dissolution of the Golden Horde produced not only fully nomadic steppe societies such as the Nogays (a confederation of Turkic and Mongol tribes), but also city-states such as the Crimean and Kazan khanates. Turkic Kazakhs, Bashkirs and Tatars competed with Mongol Kalmyks. Thus, Central Asian political formations cannot be lumped together simply on the basis of an allegedly common 'nomadic' nature. Russian expansion there continued for over 300 years, from the fifteenth through the eighteenth centuries. In the late fifteenth century, the alliance between the Crimea and Muscovy continued to be based on their mutual interests against their respective foes, the Great Horde and Poland. With disbandment of the Horde in 1506, Crimea, Moscow, the Nogays, and Lithuania remained the major players in the region. Moscow actually began its real expansion eastward by conquering the steppe state of Kazan in the mid-sixteenth century. This marked an end to Muscovy's active participation in steppe politics for over 70 years; during this period, Muscovy turned westward and expanded across Siberia while fighting against Polish and Lithuanian states. In pursuing this strategy, Moscow was first allied with Crimea against Poland; then it weakened its relations with Crimea while strengthening ties with the Ottoman sultan. At the same time, the nomadic Nogays, unable to resist the predations of the Kazakhs, abandoned their pastures east of the Yaik River and moved west, crossing the Volga into the pastures of the Astrakhan khan. The new khan of Kazan ravaged the provinces of Nizhnii Novgorod and Vladimir and moved towards Moscow. However, a confrontation was avoided insofar as Moscow and the Nogays had similar interests in the area. For Moscow, the Nogays were a critical force capable of checking the Crimean raids and aiding Moscow in the conquest of Kazan.[91]

In this same period – as a result of their action against the Genoese of the Crimea in 1475 – the Ottomans made their presence more strongly felt among the Crimean Tatars and on the Pontic Steppe in general. By 1478 the Ottoman power established the right to appoint and dismiss the khans. It was thus with a single blow that Moldavian and Polish-Lithuanian access to Black Sea markets was brought to an end. By the beginning of the sixteenth century, the Black Sea had turned into an Ottoman lake.

Between 1555 and 1578, a number of events affected the Ottoman presence on the Black Sea. Muscovy took Astrakhan in 1556. Trade ties between Muscovy and Britain commenced about the same time, and soon the English Muscovy Company was sending its traders into Persia in quest of spices and silk. British woollens, hardware and firearms in turn whetted the appetite of the shahs. However, in Istanbul, despite initial concerns over Moscow's conquest of Kazan and Astrakhan, containing Muscovite ambitions did not become a priority insofar as Istanbul was engaged with the Habsburg power in the west and Persia in the east. By the early 1560s, the sultan had adopted a more aggressive attitude and laid claim to Astrakhan; but war was avoided for the sake of the shared geopolitical and commercial interests of Moscow and Istanbul. The Ottomans established their suzerainty over the Crimean khanate between 1575 and 1578. The long war of 1579–1590 resulted in the establishment of Ottoman direct rule over much of the Caucasus. This was all the more important for Moscow in that it suffered two humiliating defeats by Poland-Lithuania and Sweden in the 1570s and early 1580s. Since then, the Nogays experienced increasing divisions and were ultimately debilitated by the arrival of the Kalmyks in the 1630s. This did not prevent them from launching raids into Russia. Moscow thus undertook a new initiative: it began construction of fortification lines in the south; this went along with colonization of the region and explains the refusal of central and local authorities to return fugitive peasants from central Russian areas to their legitimate masters – as we shall see.

As in previous centuries, the captive-ransoming and slave trade followed the same paths as other commercial trade. As in previous centuries and in the 'north-south' axes, the horse trade was important for the local Muscovite economy and its military, but it also acquired increasing commercial and political significance. In the sixteenth and seventeenth centuries the horse trade was strictly controlled by the Russian authorities and was transacted in several Russian towns along the Volga. Nogays and Kalmyks sold horses to Russians and to the Crimea khanate. From 1551 to 1564 the Nogays bought for sale an average of 7,400 horses a year.[92] The Russian market held enormous lure for the nomads; in the sixteenth century, the Nogays sought to obtain from Moscow a wide variety of products (furs, woollens, armour, etc.), while in the seventeenth century the Kalmyks increasingly sold their horses to buy many of these items on the Russian markets.

The horse trade was important for the local Muscovite economy and its military, but it was the trade with the Muslim powers in Central Asia and with the rising Ottoman Empire that linked Muscovy to world markets.[93] Russians sold horses that they acquired from steppe powers to the Crimeans and Ottomans. Merchants from the Central Asian khanates – Crimea, Persia and the Ottoman Empire – brought merchandise to Moscow while Russian merchants travelled to the Crimea; the Ottoman cities of Istanbul, Bursa, Azov and Kaffa were the most important trade centres along a well-established trade route.

Most important, in the seventeenth century exports of silk from Iran confirmed this new role of Russia. At that time raw silk produced in Iran was funnelled into local Persian industry and was exported to India, the Ottoman Empire and Europe. Historians have mostly studied exports from Iran to Aleppo and Venice, and their decline in the seventeenth and early eighteenth centuries due to the development of the British East India Company and its traffic between China, India and Europe has thus been cited as confirmation of the 'rise of the West', namely Britain and its industry.[94] But this conclusion does not take into account the considerable increase in the export of raw silk from Iran to Russia through Astrakhan, which varied from 20,000 to 100,000 kilograms per year at the turn of the eighteenth century.[95]

In other words, Moscow entered routes already in place, running east to west, north to southeast (India) and to the south (Ottoman Empire). At the same time, these routes and this traffic associated slaves with other goods in accordance with long-term established practices and routes. This was a situation quite similar to that in the Mediterranean area. As Mikhail Khodarkovsky has put it, if the steppe was akin to the sea and the Russian towns to ports, the nomads were the seamen. Many of the seamen were pirates living off the 'ports' or looting the passing ship convoys.[96] This indeed was the principal goal of the Russian government – to turn the pirates into merchants; and it was in this regard that the Russian authorities acted exactly as Ottoman and European powers had done in the Mediterranean.[97] Pirates were alternately encouraged and stopped, co-opted and fought against in the competitive rise of territorial states. Nomadic economies and powers were still inseparable from those of the neighbouring sedentary societies. And so it is on these grounds that Perdue correctly stresses the necessity of overcoming later historiographic constructions of both the Russians and Chinese and of seeing the rise of stable territorial powers (China and Russia) as helping to secure the area and put a halt to long-term nomadic raids and stem powers that were detrimental to development and growth. While accepting this argument, one may still wonder whether (as per Perdue's argument) political and military instability in Eurasia during the sixteenth and seventeenth centuries – and not European expansion – reduced long-distance trade while benefitting the market for captives.[98] Moscow's expansion in the south and changes in regional geopolitics certainly brought the trade with Crimea and the Ottoman Empire to a halt, at least for commercial items, while the traffic in captives and slaves increased because of this instability. At the same time, Muscovy competed with the Grand Duchy of Lithuania and Tver' and with the successor khanates.[99] Kazan' fell in 1552, but this did not mark the beginning of Russian conquest of the steppe; Muscovite rulers sought first to expand westward at the expense of the Polish-Lithuanian state. It was during this effort that they occasionally allied with one or another khanate to exploit the latter's internal divisions. In 1501, during the campaign in Lithuania, Crimean Tatars seized 50,000 Lithuanian captives.

During the second half of the sixteenth century, Russia once again moved eastward, into Siberia and certain Cossack areas, namely the territory of the Iaik Cossacks.[100] The resulting prisoners of war and captives held for ransom fed a consistent market for slaves. It is symptomatic that the Russian word for captive, *iasyr* or *esyr'*, was a direct transliteration of the Turkish and Arab equivalent as used in Central Asia and the Ottoman Empire.[101]

In the fourteenth century, some 2,000 Slavic slaves a year were sold by Crimean Tatars to Ottomans, with that figure rising in the fifteenth century. The Tatars either bought them at Central Asian markets or captured them themselves.[102] Slave-raiding forays into Muscovy reached crisis proportions after 1475, when the Ottomans took over the Black Sea slave trade from the Genoese and the Crimeans began slave raiding as a major industry, especially between 1514 and 1654. In 1529 half of the slaves in the Ottoman Crimea were identified as coming from Ukraine and Muscovy. Between 150,000 and 200,000 Russians were captured in the first half of the seventeenth century.[103]

Peace treaties led to the release of slaves. In 1618, for example, the Nogays signed a treaty with Moscow and released 15,000 Russian captives.[104] In 1661 the Kalmyks did the same with Russian captives they had previously acquired from the Tatars; in 1678, these same Kalmyks signed a treaty with Moscow and again returned Russian prisoners.[105] There were specific criteria for redeeming Russian captives. Thus, the Kalmyk Mongols agreed in 1661 to free Russians whom they had acquired through Tatars and in 1678 to return Russians whom they themselves had taken captive.[106] The Russians were redeeming slaves from Turkistan as late as the mid-nineteenth century.[107]

The *Ulozhenie* of 1649 devoted a whole section (number eight) to the issue of ransoming Russian captives.[108] A ransom tax was introduced to this purpose in 1551 and remained in place until 1679. The ransom was stipulated in accordance with the captive's status. For example, the ransom for a high-ranking Russian boyar, B. V. Sheremetev, was estimated at 60,000 silver thaler. At the other extreme of the ransom scale, peasants were ransomed at about fifteen roubles per person.[109] Those who were not ransomed became slaves and were assigned various duties. In the Crimea, some were employed in agriculture or used as interpreters and guides to lead war parties into Russian territory. Those sold on the slave markets of the Ottoman Empire or Central Asian khanates were employed as craftsmen, labourers and domestics.[110] Fugitives returning to Russia often gained the protection of local authorities, thereby provoking vehement protests from Nogays leaders who laid claim to these fugitives as their property.[111]

Conversely, above all during the seventeenth century, Russians seized war prisoners and captives for ransom from both Muslim and Catholic areas. According to the *Sudebnik* of 1550, captives were intended to serve the elite as administrative assistants or servants. Their maximum term of service was supposed to be until the death of their master. They could also be redeemed by an agreement between the Russian state and their country of origin. If they had converted to Orthodox Christianity, they might be emancipated, although this was not mandatory. Such a decree might be issued by the state. This occurred in 1558 when the government ordered the manumission of any war slave who converted to Orthodoxy so that he might enter the tsar's service.

If war captives were not redeemed or returned to their country of origin, they then entered the category of full or limited *kholopstvo*. Since the early seventeenth century, the state had tried to compile a register for military captives so that the central authorities could eventually return them to their home countries in case of a diplomatic agreement. However, several sources note the problems the Moscow authorities encountered in ensuring compliance with these norms, and servitude for war captives persisted. After the conclusion of the Smolensk War, in October 1634, the government ordered the release of all Poles and Lithuanians who had been seized. However, the effect of this provision was quite limited, and in 1637/38 another decree was promulgated on foreign military captives, insisting that they had the right to choose whether to return home or stay in Muscovy.

After the Thirteen Years War (1654–1667), Lithuanian and Polish captives distributed to members of the upper and middle service classes were not registered by the latter, who tended, in practice, to treat them as genuine slaves.[112] In 1655, Poles, Lithuanians and miscellaneous others, both adults and children, were openly sold in the streets of Moscow.[113] As a result of this war, many people were sold in Russia, at times becoming *kholopy*.[114] The Nogays, who had joined the Muscovite forces, purchased German and Polish prisoners in Moscow.[115] Frequently, Muslims were captured and occasionally sold in violation of Islamic law; the Ottoman and Islamic authorities therefore sent injunctions to Moscow in order to redeem them without compensation.[116]

In 1690, the Russian government thus returned to its position of 1556, decreeing that military captives were to be manumitted by the Slavery Chancellery upon the death of their owners. As in previous times, this process went along with a renewal of trade routes. From the late sixteenth century on, delegations of traders had regularly travelled from Central Asia to Muscovy and – though less often – in the opposite direction. Bukharan interest in trade with Western Siberia also dates from the late sixteenth century. By the late seventeenth century, Muscovy was trading with China itself, often through the mediation of Bukharan traders who were familiar with all the major routes between Muscovy and China. Some of these routes followed traditional itineraries, leading down along the Volga to Central Asia and then on to Xinjiang and China.[117]

Fuelled by this traffic, Siberian fairs emerged strongly during the seventeenth and eighteenth centuries; at Irbit, Russian traders, native Tartars and Bashkir merchants exchanged horses and cattle from the southern Urals for Chinese goods (tea, cloth, silk). Persians, Bukharans and Greeks also attended the fair, where servants and perhaps slaves were also for sale.[118] By the late eighteenth century, Orenburg surpassed Astrakhan and became the largest market on the steppe, bartering horses and sheep while trading luxury items from the Far East. With the help of peddlers from Bukhara, Russians revived the caravan commerce.[119] This was the case not only for the northern Eurasian caravan routes but also for the Indo-Iranian routes, which continued operating during the eighteenth century. The establishment of the Orenburg line did much to advance Russia's Asian economic frontier and increase Russo-Central Asian trade. At the same time, the Orenburg line was a fortified frontier and a welcoming gateway for newly created trade opportunities. Diplomatic archives show that the Russian administration also made efforts to motivate Asian merchants to shift their trade from the Iran-Caspian-Astrakhan line to overland routes through Central Asia to Orenburg.[120] Asian merchants progressively began to favour Orenburg, Omsk and Ufa; this in turn caused a shift in the relative importance of different areas in Central Asia. In particular, in the middle of the eighteenth century, one-third of the total Persian silk production was directed to Moscow and not only the market towns of Germany and the Low Countries.[121] Russians also expressed increasing interest in the Kokand khanate (Uzbekistan) because of the role played by Kokandi merchants in the trade between Orenburg to Tien Shan, Yarkand and other Xinjiang cities. The khanate became all the more important when cotton crops were developed in the Fergana Valley. Tashkent's role increased and with it the role of 'colonial' Russian production of textile-substitute imports from Iran and India. At the same time, Russians used their influence in steppe politics to implement a rather successful strategy of divide and rule, in particular among the Kazakhs, which in the short term enhanced the market in captives. In the early eighteenth century, though with less and less frequency, Russians could still be seized as captives or slaves. In 1717, the Kalmyks, this time temporarily allied with the Kuban Nogays, brought back 12,000 captives seized in the middle Volga provinces. In 1742, the Karakalpaks captured 1,000 Russian women and children in Siberia, and between 3,000 and 4,000 Russians are estimated to have been captives in the Karakalpaks' hands.[122] This occurred at a moment in history when the Russian authorities were adopting an ambivalent attitude towards the Kazakhs, wishing as they did to dominate the area.[123]

However, by the end of the eighteenth century the only slaves and ransom captives in the Russian Empire were Tatars or Circassians. The highest-volume traffic in slave chattel and captives was with the Ottoman Empire. The Russian Empire interacted with Islamic regions where chattel slavery was common and regarded as the only legitimate form of coerced labour under Islamic law. Muslim Tatars of the Crimea raided widely for Russian subjects as well as other eastern Slavs, Poles and Lithuanians, and they exported most of their captives to the Ottomans.[124] In 1529, half of all the slaves in the Ottoman Crimea were identified as coming from Ukraine and Muscovy; the other half were the Circassians.[125] From the 1570s on, about 20,000 slaves were sold annually in the port of Caffa on the Black Sea.[126] Until the early seventeenth century, Russians and above all Cossacks also sold captives to the Tatars or directly to the Ottomans.[127] The Ottoman rules on slave trade distinguished between slaves who were brought from the Tatar and Circassian areas and those from Ottoman territories such as Azov and Taman. The tax on the latter was half of that on the former group.[128]

The Russian Empire also gradually incorporated areas in which local populations had long practised various forms of servitude and slave trading.[129] Many inhabitants of the Caucasus – especially Christian Georgians and Armenians, together with heterodox Muslim Circassians – were sent as slaves to the Ottoman Empire, whether overland or across the Black Sea. For the first three-quarters of the nineteenth century, the Ottomans imported between 16,000 and 18,000 such slaves every year.[130] Some male slaves entered the servile administrative elite of the Ottoman Empire, while many women ended up in the harems of the rich and powerful. Circassian families at times sold their own children to intermediaries, who transported them to Ottoman territory. Under British pressure, the flow of slaves from the Caucasus was suspended in 1854, but it grew again after the end of the Crimean War. Moreover, the brutal Russian conquest of Circassia led to an influx of between half a million and a million refugees into the Ottoman domains between 1854 and 1865, of whom perhaps a tenth were of servile status.[131] These massive arrivals increased the number of agricultural slaves, which had been relatively small until then (except in Egypt and Oriental Anatolia).[132]

In short, real slaves were present in Russia. As in other historical situations, they were typically taken in frontier raids where boundaries were uncertain, or during military operations in the strictest sense. From a geopolitical standpoint, these forms of slavery were linked to conflicts within the Islamic world and between Russia and Central Asian powers, as well as to the conflicts that tore Europe apart in the seventeenth century.[133] At the same time, this phenomenon did not mean that this large geographical area was backward, for flourishing trade and vital markets developed despite raids and military expeditions. The market for slaves and the markets for products were complementary, underscoring the fact that nomadic powers and territorial states were much more integrated with one another than usually stated in the historiography. One cannot simply associate captives and slaves with political instability or, for that matter, with stable powers, insofar as bondage could enhance or burden either configuration.

Slavery in Central Eurasia: Its estimation and overall interpretation

Over the long run, the history of bondage in Russia and Eurasia provides useful insights into a number of historical questions: the link between bondage and war captives and between slavery and other forms of bondage; the dimension of bondage in Central Asian history; and the long-term links between Central Asia, Russia the Turk-Ottoman powers, India and the Mediterranean area.

On a more abstract level, these topics lead to a discussion of several interlinked perspectives.

The historical relations between nomadic powers, pirates and national territorial states, that is, the monopoly of violence and the emergency of legal rights; and the relations between bondage, coerced labour and economic development.

Our main answers to these questions may be summarized as follows: not all Russian *kholopy* can be identified as chattel slaves insofar as all but a small minority had no hereditary status; they benefited from limited legal rights; and they could inherit and marry. *Kholopstvo* expressed a form of bondage, quite common in other contexts in Asia and Africa and linked to two major phenomena: tensions and competition among the elites for the control of labour and mutual and hierarchical forms of dependence within the society. *Kholopy* had far fewer rights than their masters, but they still had legal rights. The master had some obligations as defined in the contracts of *kholopstvo*. If we term these relations 'slavery', we miss the specificity of Russia in comparison with trans-Atlantic or classical Roman slavery, and we compromise our understanding of the dynamics of Russian society. Any multiplication of different forms of bondage and relations of dependence reflects the way social links are established. *Kholopstvo*, like forms of bondage in other Asian and African societies, often was a form of inclusion, not of exclusion in society (as chattel slavery is). This explains why, as in these other societies, this form of bondage applied to people of the same ethnicity and religion as their masters. From this standpoint, Russia does not constitute an exception in the worldwide history of slavery and bondage. Chattel slavery was mostly imposed on non-Russians. According to Hellie, in 1725, when Peter the Great abolished *kholopstvo*, *kholopy* constituted around ten per cent of the Russian population. However, their importance changed over time and from area to area. For example, the Moscow military census of 1638 listed 7,672 households containing 10,787 adult males, of whom approximately 1,735, or 16.1 per cent were *kholopy*. About 15.1 per cent of the households reported having *kholopy*.[134] In a broader census taken in 1678, in 93 central provinces between 75,839 and 79,855 adult males were listed as *zadvornye* and *delovye liudi* (domestic servants) out of a total rural population (excluding those on properties that belonged to the royal court) of between 1,988,622 and 2,041,277 males, for proportions of between 3.7 and 4.0 per cent.[135]

The evaluation of war captives and slaves in Inner Asia is more complicated than that of *kholopy*. Clearly, no definitive census of this trade is possible, since any research must depend upon suspect observations. Some of the observations are based upon custom reports, which represent the closest evidence we have to the working records from which the best statistics are derived. However, unlike the accounts of merchants themselves, custom records only reflect that portion of a trade that is visible to government officials, and we are dealing here with regions where governments had only limited control over private-sector activities. Moreover, we only learn about that portion of trade that was legal. Even worse, external trade was only a residual of local trades. Much of the slave trade was conducted by land, and in this case evidence is scanty. We may therefore only give some estimation, cautiously using sources that have already been exploited. On the basis of what we have seen in the previous pages, Genoa's imports of slaves from Caffa are estimated at around 250,000 between the 1370s and the 1470s; Venice is estimated to have imported another 100,000 slaves from Tana and the Balkans. Some of them were sold in Italy, but most in Egypt. However, current research suggests we must be cautious about these figures; Caffa customs data did not make any distinction between slaves and other passengers and the first detailed analyses of the archives of daily registers and ships confirm the suspicion that the number of slaves per boat and those declared at the customs office were far fewer than usually stated (100s rather than 1,000s per year).[136]

Quantitative information on our second network and trade route between India, Persia, and Inner Asia is even scantier than for Genoa and Venice. As a whole, we can estimate that there were about 200,000 Indian slaves in Bukhara, to which we may add other 200,000 Iranian slaves.

Ottoman and Russian archives provide good data on third network, connecting Inner (maj) Asia, Russia and Crimea. Russians seized by Tatars between the sixteenth and the first half of the seventeenth century are estimated at about 200,000. Many of them were sold to the Ottomans, but an undetermined portion was kept in Inner Asia and Crimea. In particular, between the fourteenth and the sixteenth centuries Crimean Tatars sold at least 2000 slaves a year, or a total of 400,000, to the Ottomans.

In the following centuries, a compilation of estimates indicates that Crimean Tatars seized about 1,750,000 Ukrainians, Poles and Russians from 1468 to 1695.[137] Crimean export statistics indicate that around 10,000 slaves a year, including Circassians, went to the Ottomans, suggesting a total of around 2,500,000 from 1450 to 1700.[138]

From 1800 to 1909, the Ottomans imported some 200,000 slaves from the Caucasus, mainly Circassians, with another 100,000 or so arriving with their Circassian masters in the 1850s and 1860s.[139] On average, between 1800 and 1875, the Ottomans imported 18,000 slaves per year from Caucasus, and Crimea, for an overall figure of 1,350,000 slaves.

The available and still incomplete data provide the following numbers for the exports of slaves from Inner (maj) Asia and Russia: 4,000,000 to the Ottoman Empire; 400,000 through Venice's and Genoa's ports on the Black Sea; 700,000 Persians and Indians traded in Central Asia. We lack data on internal trade, caravan trade and the number of people who died during transportation. If we want start from a lower hypothesis, we may affirm that the Inner (maj) Asian slave trade that escaped customs statistics might reach half of this latter trade. We therefore reach about 6,000,000–6,500,000 people traded as slaves in Central Asia between the eleventh and the nineteenth century. This figure surely underestimates reality; however, even our minimal evaluation permits some conclusions. First, the slave trade in Central Asia and Russia was the most important in pre-modern era and it is not far below the later slave trade in other areas: 11 million people traded along the trans-Sahara, the Red Sea and the Indian Ocean routes between the seventh and the twentieth century and 11 million slaves on the transatlantic route from the fifteenth to the nineteenth century.[140]

From this standpoint, the history of slavery in Russia and Central Asia confirms what previous studies on Mediterranean slavery have already stated, that is, the importance of pre-colonial slavery, in particular outside the transatlantic route, and, therefore, the importance of the role these previous routes had in terms of the organization of labour, legal rules and trans-national powers. The slave trade in Russia and Central Asia was connected to the stabilization of territorial powers, the evolution of warfare and the monopoly on violence. Indeed, the history of war captives and *kholopy* in Russia is linked to that of the incredible expansion of Muscovy and Russia and to the evolution of inner social relationships. Between the thirteenth and the sixteenth centuries, captives and slaves were commonly exchanged between the khanates, Safavid Persia, the Byzantine Empire, India, Genoa and Venice. The slave trade accompanied general trade. Previous historiography estimated a decline of the caravan trade in Central Asia in connection with the development of the sea trade in the Mediterranean,[141] then in connection with European powers' penetration into the Indian Ocean.[142] A number of studies have recently re-evaluated the efficiency of inland trade and confirmed that Central Eurasian trade did not decline after the seventeenth century but only shifted its objects, tools, leading groups, centres and axes. The Mongols' power had guaranteed trade for centuries; their decline did not mean that of Central Asia, insofar as the Russians progressively took their place, while in the south, over all those centuries, the Safavids, the Mughals and the Ottoman Empires also ensured trades and economic growth.[143] The horse trade previously mentioned was central: between 60,000 and 100,000 horses were imported each year from Inner Asia to Kabul and from then to India.[144] In the eighteenth century, this trade reached 400,000–800,000 horses per year.[145]

Textiles were the other major item traded in Inner Asia. In the mid-seventeenth century, India sent 25,000–30,000 camel loads of cotton to Iran. This trade did not disappear with the arrival of the British, which means that, as the imports of Indian textile in Britain enormously increased in the eighteenth century, Indian production also increased to meet British and Central Asian demand. The silk trade between India, Iran and Russia was also important; as mentioned before, Russia and Britain each took half of the raw silk from Iran at the turn of the eighteenth century. Now, these figures are scattered and incomplete; most new evidence comes from archaeology and is hard to quantify. More generally, statistics from the Western trading companies and non-Western merchants in Inner Asia leave out data from Russia and the Ottoman Empire. Even if the Ottoman Empire's economic decline in the face of the expansion of the West did not clearly materialize before the eighteenth century, in the seventeenth century real wages in Istanbul and other Ottoman towns were already lagging behind those of major Western European areas.[146] If we recall that the Inner Asian trade did not collapse with the 'rise of the West', the point is not to enter the debate on the great divergence and the relative rates of growth between Western

Europe and Asia. Even if, for example, the importance of the textile and horse trade between India and Inner Asia is relevant to the debate about the impact of British expansion on India, and, eventually, on the Ottoman Empire, these topics lie beyond the scope of this book. Instead, we have stressed the persisting vitality of the Inner Asian trade in its connection with geopolitical dynamics and the slave trade in order to understand the main features of the expansion of the Muscovy and the rise of the Russian Empire. Starting from this, we are ready to face the main questions directly related to our investigation: the relationship between the slave trade and general trade in Inner Asia and the rise of serfdom in Russia and, the temporality and rhythm of the ensuing Russian growth as compared to that of the West. For sure, the fall of Constantinople and Byzantium had major consequences for Western Europe. The core of its world economy subsequently shifted from the Mediterranean to the Atlantic. However, it also closed the eastern slave trade and led to the search for alternative supplies of slaves. Thereafter, Western Europe and the Islamic powers increasingly turned to two new sources of slaves – captives in Christian–Muslim conflicts[147] and sub-Saharan Africa.[148]

Yet this well-known history fails to take into consideration the contemporary dynamics of Russia and Eurasia which paralleled the expansion of the West. The traditional view that slavery, common in the classical Greece and Rome, disappeared in medieval times has now been discredited. Research has demonstrated that debt bondage, serfdom and slavery existed in medieval Western Europe and they played a major role in the resurgence of slavery under colonialism. Our investigation has added a new piece to this puzzle: this long-standing history of slavery did not exclusively involve the Mediterranean, Africa and the Atlantic, but Inner Asia and Oriental Europe were essential ingredients of it, in terms of both supply of slaves and global dynamics. Indeed, Russian expansion in the steppes went along with the increasing importance of war captives (in institutional and economic terms, as we have shown) and, then, with the end of *kholopy* and the generalization of new forms of bondage, namely serfdom, in the Russian Empire. The question is whether slavery and serfdom were complementary or substitutes; in the first case, they responded to different although related pressures and dynamics, while in the second one, they developed one after the other, as slavery and the indentured system did in the Atlantic and the Indian Ocean. In order to answer this question, we need to carefully study the institutions of serfdom and their chronologies.

5

Neither Feudalism nor Capitalism: Agrarian Markets under Coercion

The institutions of Russian serfdom

Liberal, radical and Marxist historiography and such different authors as Kula, Wallerstein and North agree on this: in early modern times, Eastern Europe responded to the commercial, agrarian and, then, industrial expansion of the West by binding the peasantries to the land and its lords.[1] According to this view, the enserfment of the peasantry in the East contrasts with the rise of 'free' wage labour in the West. These dynamics are supposed to have accompanied an increasing international division of labour in which the periphery (Asia, Africa) and quasi-periphery (southern and eastern Europe) were subordinated to the core (northern and western Europe).

The fact that very different authors agree on these arguments confirms the persistent strength of two assumptions common to liberal and Marxist historiographies: first, an ethnocentric approach (Europe and Britain are supposed to be the core in modern and contemporary history) and, second, a clear-cut and ahistorical opposition between free and unfree labour. It is only on the basis of these assumptions that the overall economic dynamics of the early modern world can be depicted in terms of a 'periphery', dependence and the opposition between freedom and unfreedom, markets and institutions. It is interesting that even new approaches in world history such as Pomeranz's 'great divergence', while contesting China's backwardness and European ethnocentrism, still consider Russia the paradigm of unfree labour and lack of markets and as such opposed to both the Lower Yangtzee and Britain.[2] The questions this chapter considers are: Were Russian peasants obliged to provide corvées? Were corvées a major obstacle to, if not the antithesis of, market relations?

Already in 1921, Marc Bloch warned against the use of the word 'serf' and the expression 'serf of the glebe'. He showed in particular that the notion was absent in the Middle Ages and, on the contrary, enjoyed success after *l'Esprit des lois* by Montesquieu in 1748. From this point of view, the 'serf of the glebe' was used to identify a largely stylized feudal system and to contrast it to an equally stylized liberal economic system.[3]

Since then, medieval studies have widely adopted this conclusion for France and Britain.[4] More recently, a similar reassessment has been made for the German 'second serfdom' (notably in criticizing Brenner's argument).[5]

Discussions of Russian serfdom have adopted a much more cautious attitude; they have mostly focused on its origin (the state[6] and/or the landowners[7]) and its profitability,[8] rather than on the interplay between its legal rules and economic activity. The most remarkable contributions are those of Confino, Hoch, Wirtschafter, Melton and Moon, who have effectively revisited the simplistic definition and functioning of Russian serfdom.[9] Serfdom's dynamics and rules have been questioned; it has been suggested that serfdom was never officially introduced[10] and that it was much more a set of practices than a formal system.[11] Starting from this, some have argued that serfdom could have been profitable, if not all around Russia, at least in many areas.[12] As I have already developed the analysis of the origin and evolution of serfdom rules,[13] I will briefly summarize them before moving to the study of labour on the Russian estates. Indeed, throughout the sixteenth and seventeenth centuries, several rules were adopted that had the effect of limiting peasant mobility; however, these rules actually aimed to establish a cadastre in order to improve tax income and military conscription, but also to settle disputes over estates to which there were various claimants, including different categories of estate owners, the crown, the Church and monasteries. Until the first half of the seventeenth century, it was assumed that the restriction was temporary; the process was by no means simple, however, as is evidenced by the numerous legal disputes and petitions drawn up by landowner families against other claimants to their properties, whether other estate owners, merchants, *boyari* or others.[14] The alliance between the state and the provincial and lesser estate owners was supposed to offer a solution, new rules on runaways being adopted in exchange for landowners' acceptance of a cadastre. However, this agreement proved to be ineffective, because different state administrations were unable to cooperate in achieving a cadastre, returning runaways, and punishing owners whose claims were illegitimate. To that must be added the lack of cooperation among landowners, who continued to retain peasants who were on the move – 'runaways'. Petitions multiplied between the 1620s and the 1640s, and the central state responded by lengthening the time to recover fugitives from 5 to 9 and then to 15 years (1637, 1641, 1645, 1648).

The great landlords became notorious for luring peasants away from smaller estates.[15] This game became even more complicated when urban elites (for fiscal needs) and peripheral authorities (interested in increasing the local population) pushed to keep the 'runaways' in place. Negotiations on this occurred on the legal, administrative and political levels.[16]

As we have shown, annexation of new territories and the colonization of the steppe further weakened these already barely enforced rules. In the eyes of some tsarist elites, geopolitical considerations overwhelmed the political and social defence of estate owners in the central areas of Russia. As a consequence, between 1678 and 1897, peasants' settlements in the central forest heartland fell from 69.9 to 41.22 per cent of the total, while those in the steppes areas increased from 28.78 to 41.22 per cent. During this same period, settlement in Siberia rose from 1.32 to 7.54 per cent. In the southern and eastern settlement areas, one-third of the population increase was due to natural growth and two-thirds to immigration. By the 1680s, the peasant population in the Ukrainian territories was about half a million people; it doubled by 1720.[17] By 1678, 3.7 million peasants had emigrated and settled in Siberia, the northwestern areas, the Urals, the southeastern steppe and the Volga.[18] As a whole, the population of Russia increased from 7 million in 1600 to about 9 million in 1678, 14 million in 1719, 17 million in 1762 and 21 million in 1782.[19]

From the mid-sixteenth century until the last quarter of the eighteenth century, Muscovite, Russian and Imperial Russian rules of land ownership did not refer to serfs but mostly aimed to define who was entitled to own and then dispose of populated estates and, as a consequence of that entitlement, who could retain runaways. This solution had far-reaching consequences: it showed that the main goal of the state was not to bind the peasantry, but to link the very possibility the right estate owners had to possess and transmit them to these owners' acceptance of the state rules regarding the cadastre and thus property. In turn, this put the entitled nobility under the legal control of the state. Third, defining the estate owner rather than the serf meant that the former was informally allowed to exert her or his authority over the latter – which means to exert seigniorial justice and possibly require forms of coerced labour. The state simply delegated the local demesne legal authority to the estate owner. But ultimately, earlier sets of rules meant that while the peasant could not refuse corvées, he could contest the estate owner's ownership. Attempts by estate owners to refuse access to land and status to such other groups as service elites and the bourgeoisie were constantly mitigated by the ambivalent approach of the state elite, which wished to allow yet at the same time restrict the access to estate ownership and higher official ranks, in order to win support for reform and ensure social stability.[20]

Starting from this, we need to examine whether, despite the institutional long-term evolution of serfdom and the lack of official rules 'binding' the peasantry, bondage was not informally practised on the estates.

Labour on Russian estates

In Russia, landlords could ask peasants either for quitrent or for labour services (corvées). Western, Russian, and Soviet historiography all traditionally argue that quitrent encourages trade and economic growth, whereas labour service restricts both.[21] This argument has been widely echoed by historians of serfdom in Western[22] and Eastern Europe.[23] Of course, many others maintain that trade and economic growth can also take place under a system of corvées labour or even slavery in the strict sense.[24] Any satisfactory answer to this question requires an assessment of labour productivity and the overall demesne efficiency: some consider that corvées require high supervision costs while reducing labour productivity and peasants' interest in increasing both productivity and market production. Some others have objected that labour supervision is not necessarily stricter under corvées than under quitrent. In particular, Hoch has shown that serf owners were able to exploit serf labour with minimum supervisory costs by harnessing the patriarchal authority structure of the peasant household.[25]

The question underlying this debate is important: were historical forms of forced labour compatible with the market, innovation and capitalism? We may note that an increased dissemination of quitrent is recorded during the first half of the eighteenth century, followed by the greater success of labour services during the second half of this century. Finally, in the first half of the nineteenth century, the quitrent came back into prominence, although to a lesser degree than during the previous century. Within this overall framework, significant regional differences can be seen: forced labour was more widespread in the 'black earth' (the central, most fertile regions of European Russia), whereas the quitrent system was more widely practised near industrial areas.[26] Based on this observation, several historians concluded that forced labour restricted trade and economic development.[27]

This approach requires serious revision; empirical analysis shows that the revival of labour services went along with an increasing integration of the demesne in proto-industrial activity as well as in local and national markets for agriculture and manufactures. Overall trends provide evidence of an important link, since the eighteenth century, between rural estates and markets. Of course, regional variations were important and even beyond this, institutional constraints, social hierarchies and market dynamics varied from one area to another and even from one estate to another. Most microeconomic studies focus on large estates[28] – even if some Soviet scholars like Koval'chenko exploited several estates' archives. In part, this creates a bias insofar as large estates were more inclined to adopt 'modern' techniques and also, because of advantages of scale, won higher yields and rates of commercialization than smaller units. Yet this bias does not invalidate but rather confirms our argument: despite the better performances of big estates, overall data show quite good outcomes for the Russian economy as compared with most Western economies,[29] and this despite the well-known tendencies of statistics to underestimate products, yields and revenues.

Proto-industry, trade and growth under serfdom

Proto-industrialization has long been considered an obstacle to 'modernization' and 'industrialization'. This view is firmly rooted in the hypothesis that large manufactures and the 'British' way are the only path to industrialization. This view has more recently been strongly modified: the continental European, Asian and Latin American paths mostly anchored to small units were the rule.[30] Recent analyses have also shown that, in contradiction to the first theories, guilds declined even without proto-industrialization (this was the case in most parts of England, Flanders and the Netherlands).[31] Conversely, in many other parts of Europe (Bohemia, Northern Italy), community, seigniorial institutions[32] and guilds remained strong despite the diffusion of proto-industry.[33] To what extent does Russian history confirm or invalidate these issues?

In eighteenth-century Russia, agricultural prices continued to climb, rising by a factor of two and a half, which no doubt made service labour more profitable than quitrent.[34] At the same time, this solution was possible only if the estates were efficiently supervised, hence the aforementioned increased interest in supervisors on the part of landowners. The supervisor was supposed to adopt good working methods, carry out an inventory of goods, land and harvests, and keep the landowner informed about the running of the estate.

In this context, there is no evidence of an increasing autarchy of the demesne coupled with increasing wheat exports from 'backward' Russia to the benefit of 'advanced' Europe, as Wallerstein and Kula have argued. Exports undoubtedly rose, and, as Mironov has shown, Russian markets were more and more integrated into the international and European markets. At the same time, the growth of exports did not take place at the expense of local and national markets; indeed, by 1760 the demand for grain in the heartland created a rise in grain prices.[35] Russian local markets were therefore increasingly integrated into a national market during the second half of the eighteenth century.[36] The nobility's role in the expansion of rural trade is reflected in the fact that much of the rural expansion took place on the pomeshchiki's (estate owners) estates. If in 1760 nobles' estates were the sites of 413 out of 1,143 rural fairs (36 per cent), in 1800 they had 1,615 out of 3,180 (51 per cent). This data clearly shows that not only landlords but also their peasants firmly entered the rural agrarian markets. Peasants' activity in rural markets surpassed that of merchants and small urban traders.[37] Therefore, contrary to traditional arguments, trade in estate production increased with *barshchina* (corvées), which was compatible not only with exportation and long distances, but also with the rise of local and national markets.[38]

It was all the more important that local markets were widespread not only for agriculture produce, but also for proto-industrial products. Since the mid-eighteenth century, peasants had been buying important shares of proto-industrial products while benefiting from increasing incomes. For example, the larger accessible labour market of peasants already familiar with linen weaving gave Moscow and Ivanovo firms a greater competitive viability than Saint Petersburg.[39] To control this market, landowners were taking back control of the sale of products from their estates and entering into urban trade circuits with a certain degree of firmness.[40] Proto-industry became ruralized.[41] The urban population dropped from 12 per cent to 8 per cent of the total population between 1742 and 1801.[42] Thus, agricultural and industrial rural areas were sometimes differentiated and sometimes overlapped.

Thus, while 5 per cent of all private factories belonged to nobles in the 1720s, the percentage rose to 20 in 1773. In 1725, 78 per cent of industrial activity was located in cities; that percentage dropped to 60 in 1775–1778 and 58 in 1803.[43] On the whole, during the second half of the eighteenth century, landlords massively entered the proto-industrial sector; the 'ruralization' of proto-industry was not a symptom of demesne autarchy, but, quite the contrary, testified to the demesne's increasing commercialization. Both peasants and landlords entered the market in cereals as well as going in for proto-industrial activities and trade and transportation activities. Numerous 'serf-entrepreneurs' registered, on behalf of the landowner or sometimes quite independently, to start up businesses or even proto-industrial and industrial activities.[44] Serf-entrepreneurs often employed workers in their proto-industrial activity. They came from the same villages or from neighbouring districts.[45] During and after the mid-eighteenth century, peasants bought an important share of proto-industrial products while benefiting from increasing incomes.

All this increased the need for labour and exacerbated competition for goods and proto-industrial and labour markets. Competition therefore rose not only between landowners and merchants, but also among estate owners even more than in the first half of the eighteenth century, landlords were in competition with each other to keep the best master-peasants, who trained other artisans. Litigations on runaways and estate records confirm this picture. As a consequence, many estate owners sought to keep their peasant-workers on the estate instead of sending them to town. As in the case of the sale of products, it would be reductive to see the landowners' orientation towards factories merely as a desire for estate autarchy and market closing, and hence as a regression of the Russian economy. In reality, what the landowners wanted was to take over the proto-industrial and manufacturing sector, once dominated by peasants and merchants. This accounts for their request, which Catherine granted, to prohibit any form of serfdom in factories owned by non-nobles.[46] Estate archives show that landlords had every interest to develop a sort of 'protectionist' politics beneficial to the estate's peasants and craftsmen.[47] For example, Count Sheremetev did not hesitate to publish an *instruktsiia* giving priority to local peasant-traders over urban merchants in the commercialization of the Pavlovo estate's products.[48] Peasant-artisans also demanded from Count Sheremetev the exclusive right to sell their products in Nizhegorod.[49] Sheremetev's estate-law court regulated conflicts between peasants and merchants, and the decisions were often favourable to the former.[50] In other words, peasants and landlords made arrangements to shape markets and competition rules to their own advantage and to exclude urban merchants and producers.

Labour relations were therefore extremely complex. In Nizhnyi-Novgorod province (250 miles east of Moscow), on the Demidov estate in particular, there was a mix of both compelled and hired labour. The latter was used for some processing of products and as supervisory personnel in the mills and brickworks; compelled labour was used to mill rye and wheat and for cottage industry, including spinning yarn and making linen cloth.[51] Relations of 'dependence' among peasants, merchants and manufacturers have to be included in this context. One of the key factors was the control of raw materials. As long as every stage in the production process took place within the peasant household, the producer remained more or less an independent craftsman. The fact that flax cultivation was so widespread in the non-black-soil provinces helped make linen production especially resistant to change. But in sectors like cotton and silk weaving, where the cottage weavers depended on outside sources for their materials, wage relations grew more rapidly. For the supply of raw materials for metalworking, the development of production in the Ural region modified the networks and the hierarchies. This was true in particular after the 1760s, when the Demidov estate in the Ural region 'exported' raw materials for metallurgy to the proto-industrial districts of Tula, Nizhni Novgorod and Moscow.[52]

Peasants could buy materials themselves, but sometimes landlords provided raw materials and made advances to their peasant-master. In such cases, too, after the end of the eighteenth century, landlords developed a clear strategy to enter and control networks that had been previously dominated by traders and merchants. It is interesting that landlords adopted the same strategies as merchants in order to control the output system (i.e., advancing money and/or raw materials).[53] Again, this confirms that legal limitations to mobility alone did not suffice; otherwise estate owners would have not developed this system of advances to keep peasants-workers bound to them.

To sum up, the rebirth of *barshchina* (corvées) during the second half of the eighteenth century was accompanied neither by increased exploitation of peasants solely with a view to export trade nor by a crisis in manufacturing business and markets in general, as predicted by Witold Kula's model. The demesne economy and the Russian economy as a whole were more efficient, flexible and market-oriented than he stated. Agriculture and proto-industrial markets developed intensively, and so did national income and per capita income. Agriculture and proto-industry expanded, and the competition between landowners and merchants was institutional before it became economic. The former wanted to enter into trade and industry at the expense of the latter and succeeded, thanks to the support of institutional measures such as the exclusion of 'serfs' from factories managed by merchants. Thus, labour services raised commercial produce, and proto-industrial activity became strongly integrated into the demesne activity.

At the same time, these multiple activities increased competition for labour time between estate owners and peasants, landlords and merchants, and even within the peasant family. Institutions (state law, demesne law and peasant commune law) provided a set of rules to solve this problem. These arrangements were not without conflicts, but, as a whole, rural institutions worked well enough to ensure coordination. The decreasing impact of bad harvests on the standard of living and the increasing integration of the peasantry and the landlords into market networks testify to this increasing coordination among the involved actors. Evidence suggests that the output of both agricultural produce and proto-industrial products increased throughout the eighteenth and nineteenth century; in turn, this sustained the demand for manufactured goods, which was mostly satisfied by local proto-industrial activity that utilized labour-intensive technology.[54]

Briefly, the growth in productivity and in the standard of living and the commercialization of agriculture in Russia can hardly be explained by the potentialities (i.e., the possibility of extorting more and more surplus by force) of a system of serfdom, which did not exist as such, at least in its 'pure' form, but rather by the flexibility of a world made up of inducements and constraints, central law and local customs. Thus, the coexistence of service labour and quitrent enabled the peasant economy and that of the landowners to cope with the fluctuations of the economy by limiting their impact on the level of activity, standard of living and investments.

Price fluctuations were more pronounced during the first half of the nineteenth century than during the second half of the eighteenth century, and this led again, as during the first half of the previous century, to mixing corvées and quitrent.[55] At the same time, estates were concentrated; the number of small estates declined while large properties became the rule, to such an extent that in 1857 estates with less than 21 peasants accounted for barely 3.2 per cent of all estates; those with between 21 and 100 peasants made up 15.9 per cent; and the great majority of estates had between 100 and 500 peasants (37.2 per cent), between 500 and 1,000 peasants (14.9 per cent) or even more than 1,000 peasants (28.7 per cent).[56] This trend was linked to the increasing indebtedness of the estate owners and the limited capital markets available to them; the growing institutional pressure of a tsarist state favouring peasants' emancipation and merchants' development also contributed to the concentration of estates.

Quitrent declined on state estates and on some private estates as well, while rising in the heartland (although this rise was generally moderate). Regional specialization also increased, with central and other industrial and proto-industrial areas tending to specialize while agricultural areas lost non-agrarian activities. In particular, in the steppe and central black earth areas, while factories shut down and proto-industrial activity was reduced,[57] the surface area of cultivated land expanded in the territory as a whole and inside the main estates. This process corresponded to an increase in agricultural production and, most important, a growth in marketed production and market integration. Grain prices in Russia showed a clear tendency towards homogenization and correlation on the national level.[58]

In the central industrial regions, the main difference from the previous century was that landowners no longer restricted peasant movements between city and country. This was for reasons of choice and constraint – in part, more volatile prices led some landlords to diversify their economic strategies; in part, industrial and tsarist elites pushed for increasing liberalization of the labour market. The main issue was that the use of *obrok* and the movements of peasants in the city and in neighbouring estates had intensified.[59] During the 1840s, in the north-western and western agricultural and industrial regions of European Russia, passports and tickets granted to peasants concerned between 25 and 32 per cent of the male population. By 1850, in Vladimir province, 92.44 per cent of the state peasants were involved at least part-time in one or another non-agricultural occupation; in Moscow province, the proportion was 89 per cent; in Kostroma province, 86.5 per cent; in Novgorod province, 80.5 per cent; in Pskov province, 80 per cent; in Iaroslavl province, 75.8 per cent; and in Nizhnii Novgorod, 65.7 per cent.[60] In these areas, the way back to proto-industry from countryside to town was not synonymous with a decline of the putting-out system (i.e., subcontracting while supplying raw materials). In 1828, 6,300 weavers worked in factories in the greater Ivanovo region (which included large swaths of both Vladimir and Kostroma provinces), while 18,224 (74 per cent) worked outside of factories. In 1849, the number of factory weavers had doubled to 14,854; the number of non-factory weavers had tripled, however, to 56,980 (79 per cent).[61] With a flexible network of knowledgeable peasant weavers, cotton-printing firms had little incentive to expend capital on centralized weaving establishments; in general, only high-end grades of cloth were factory-produced. In Vladimir province in the early 1850s, 18,000 factory looms merely supplemented the 80,000 peasant looms filling factory orders.[62]

Peasant-masters increasingly employed wage earners, often for short periods during which, however, they were under the strong legal and social control of the masters. Conflicts between peasant-masters and their working people increased; petitions were sent to local landlords, who were supposed to intervene in defence of the peasant-workers, which they often did.[63] Conflicts concerned wages and the possibility of moving. In 1802, P. B. Sheremetev received a petition from some local peasants asking him to intercede for them with their masters so that they might go and take in the harvest. Sheremetev thus issued an *ukaz* regulating the renting of land (limiting it to peasants in proto-industry) and proto-industrial activity as well.[64] As the putting-out system grew through the early 1800s, many independent domestic weavers found themselves increasingly tied to particular factories or particular putting-out middlemen because they had accepted loans or advances to buy yarn or more advanced looms. A law of 1835 stipulated that the employment of all workers be based upon the conclusion of a personal contract between employer and employee that specified the responsibilities of both sides. Since most workers were peasants whose period of residence in the city was determined by their passports, the period of the contract's validity was usually limited by the term of the passport. Workers were not supposed to leave their places of work until expiration of their contracts. This regulation, however, was difficult to enforce. Many entrepreneurs and managers complained that workers left their enterprises for the countryside or better employment opportunities before their contracts had expired.[65] Yet all this was a symptom of economic and social dynamics, not of stagnation. The Russian agrarian market developed further during the first half of the nineteenth century, and the convergence of prices testifies to the formation of a real national market. At the same time, regional specialization progressed: central and eastern agricultural areas increased productivity and marketable production, while proto-industrial areas created a denser network of urban towns and intensified product specialization. Russian growth took place on the basis of the coexistence of these different organizations and on the basis of a long-term trend in which proto-industry and manufacture units moved from the town to the countryside and vice versa.

Towards a reassessment of second serfdom in Eastern Europe

These outcomes confirm similar recent issues in Eastern European agriculture under serfdom.[66] For example, in Brandenburg-Prussia, by the turn of the eighteenth to the nineteenth century commutation payment increasingly eclipsed labour services. As in Russia, the government encouraged changes in the legal status of peasants.[67] However, before that, increasing labour service in the seventeenth and late eighteenth centuries was not synonymous with a retreat from the market, as previously stated in the historiography, but, to the contrary, commercialization of both peasant and demesne production (agriculture and proto-industrial products) quickly increased.[68] In contradiction to traditional historical literature on these matters (which conveyed the impression that East-Elbian agriculture was a simple affair of cereal monoculture based on coerced labour), new detailed analyses based upon estates' archives reveal a complex picture of a large and expansive workforce and high commodity sales. This was true not only of Brandenburg, but also of other regions of east central Europe, including Poland. Here peasant labour services provided only 40–50 per cent of the demesne labour force required during the summer months, and thus had to be supplemented by hired labour.[69] In all these areas, both peasants and seigniors employed hired labour.[70] There were also migrant day labourers who worked only during the harvest. In eastern Prussia, many of the day labourers lived in small towns, subsisting on wages earned during the peak season. Tracy Dennison and Sheilagh Ogilvie have recently stressed the strong similarities between Russia and Bohemia regarding 'serfdom' and social relations. Peasant and seigniorial institutions interacted in both systems and strongly contributed to the social and economic dynamics.[71]

Taken together, the experiences of Russia, Prussia, Lithuania and some parts of Poland lead to the conclusion that 'second serfdom' was not so much a form of slavery as it was a set of legal constraints on labour mobility and a form of institutional extortion. These rules were dictated much less by a scarcity of population than by increasing demand for agriculture produce and proto-industrial products. Labour services were not opposed to market development; quite the contrary, the two enhanced each other. Proto-industry developed, and the specialization of some areas went along with the seasonality of proto-industrial activity for many peasants. Estate relations sometimes opposed proto-industry but in some other cases were favourable to it, which did not necessarily enhance or retard the proletarization of peasants and craftsmen (as asserted in Franklin Mendel's model in which proto-industrialization slowed the growth of towns, and confirmed by Jan de Vries).[72] Agrarian development, proto-industry, demographic insights and institutional and legal hierarchies varied from one estate to another within the same country in accordance with the specific relations among the landlord, the peasant community and the involved markets. Still, despite this extreme variety, it is difficult to maintain that bondage and legal constraints on labour mobility were opposed to market and proto-industrial development and that developing markets in the West were at the origin of increasing bondage in the East. Indeed, existing studies provide the following picture: most microeconomic studies concern large estates with better-preserved archives. Certainly, on these estates the conditions of serfs were better, productivity higher, and integration in the market more developed than in smaller units. Also, all these indicators were more marked in industrial and proto-industrial areas than in agricultural regions. Yet, when one takes into account all the statistics available since the first half of the nineteenth century, even if the average values seem lower than on the big estates, the overall picture is not as dark as earlier commentators argued. First, because we know now that overall statistics underestimate peasant and landlord production: based upon interviews with producers or with indirect evidence, figures suffered from the producers' incentive to hide part of their production and income for fiscal reasons.[73] Statisticians were also concerned with the 'poverty of the peasantry' and exaggerated losses and crises.[74] Now, even if we do not correct the data, the final picture shows increasing productivity, well-being, and commercialization from the eighteenth century on. Between 1718 and 1788, the Russian aggregate national income increased fivefold, raising per capita income 85 per cent. After 1788 the annexation of rich southern provinces still increased this growth.[75]

These new estimations require us to revise the conventional views; the most pessimistic recent analyses show that, even if Russia's main economic indicators were persistently below those of main Western European countries, the gap was not that important and it did not widen until collectivization. Before that date, it was constant, or even reducing in terms of yields and commercialization in periods such as the second half of the nineteenth century.[76] Other, more optimistic recent interpretations even conclude that, by 1788, the average Russian was as rich as his English equivalent and only 15 per cent poorer than the average Frenchman, who at that time enjoyed the peak of his fortunes in the eighteenth century. During the period of the Revolutionary and Napoleonic wars, moreover, the Russian maintained his position, surpassing the Frenchman and rising with the Briton to the very top of the international league table.[77] This means that, unlike the conventional images of historiography, Russian economic growth was far from negligible.

This trend finds a confirmation in the rate of growth of the population. Recent analyses had sought to take into account the overall underestimation of birth rates in eighteenth- and nineteenth-century censuses, as well as the annexation of new territories and the resettlement (legal and illegal) of the peasantry. Once these biases had been corrected, the natural rate of population growth is considerable: on peasant estates, it was at about 0.70 per cent between 1678 and 1719, 0.62 per cent between 1719 and 1744, 0.97 between 1744 and 1762, and 0.96 per cent during the next 20 years. It fell to 0.60 between 1782 and 1795, rose again to 0.86 between 1795 and 1811 but collapsed during the Napoleonic wars to – 0.42 per cent. During the first half of the nineteenth century, the natural rate of growth of Russia's peasant population increased again to 0.94 in 1815–1833, 0.59 between 1833 and 1850, and 0.54 per cent between 1850 and 1857.[78] Of course, these general figures hide extreme variations among localities and great social inequalities. Soviet historians and then Western historians have highlighted the importance of regional differentiation and the impossibility of reaching overall conclusion for the whole of Russia.[79]

Certainly, the high birth rate corresponded to an equally high rate of death, in particular among children. This trend has usually been considered as an evidence of the 'backwardness' of Russia and its poverty. However, in recent years, this view has been seriously challenged: high child mortality actually had less to do with famine than with to diseases linked to lack of hygiene (in regard to water in particular), epidemics and wars.[80]

How can these new estimations on income, productivity and demographic rates be explained?

Answers have put the accent either on legal constraints (forced labour) or, just the opposite, on flexibility. In the first variant, growth has been linked to the profitability of serfdom; this is a revisionist approach that attributes the peasants a status close to that of slavery. According to this view, bondage and slavery are much more profitable than some liberal authors asserted and are perfectly compatible with economic growth, markets and capitalism. For sure, this variable played a role in Russia: the increasing power of landlords and forms of institutional extortion were able to extract more surplus from the peasantry.

At the same time, previous chapters also provide evidence of the second interpretation: economic growth was linked to flexible and increasingly relaxing legal constraints. In Russia, there were no official rules mentioning corvées before they were limited in the 1770s. Existing rules imposing limitations to peasants' movements were produced and implemented at the intersection of state, seigniorial and village institutions. These rules were not just the expression of the strength of the nobility over the peasantry, for they required the interaction between the rules of the nation, estates and villages. The real functioning of serfdom was founded upon these multiple institutions, actors and rules. There were no classes in the Marxist sense, but rather porous estates. Russian peasants were not *serfs de la glebe* but strongly dependent people with extremely limited legal rights. These rights, however, increased over time. They were not chattel slaves like American slaves. Since the early nineteenth century, private peasants increasingly moved to other legal and social categories and as a consequence their rights increased before the general abolition of serfdom in 1861. This is why labour services and strong legal constraints on labour mobility were not opposed to market development. Landlords and the demesne economy were not devoted to unproductive tasks and supporting monopolistic and parasitic attitudes, but instead sought to exploit imperfect competition to increase their profits. The peasant economy under 'serfdom' corresponded neither to the Chayanovian model of a peasant willing to satisfy his family's needs and entering the market only when obliged nor to Kula's model of peasants pushed to produce by the landlord, who took the entire product and sold it on the market. Peasants were already integrated into market activity, and proto-industry was not necessarily 'residual' (that is, an activity engaged in only after time and opportunities in agriculture had been fully exploited). Peasants' and landlords' integration into the market does not confirm the link between labour service and poor market development. 'Anti-economic' cultural values are used to oppose imaginary peasantries to proletarians, landlords to capitalists. In reality, Russian landlords and peasants were interested in profits and they were integrated into markets to various degrees. That they did not transform in accordance with some Western model does not mean that they were backward, but only that historical transformations of markets and societies may take different forms. Russian 'serfdom' was, in reality, a set of relatively flexible rules and norms that operated on a foundation of interacting landowners, managers, peasant elites (elders) and the rural community as a whole.

If privileges were not opposed to the market, then we can no longer study the history of pre-industrial worlds starting with ideal types such as the Junker, the *pomeshchik* (landowner), the *latifondista* or the *rentier*. Historians have claimed these actors were the opposite of English entrepreneurs and American farmers. Recent studies have shown, however, that the first group did not always use compulsory labour and was not made up solely of absentee landowners. In East Elbian Germany and Poland, Junkers and peasants took part in market development and innovation and their favourable attitude did not develop only after Napoleon and the French armies had passed through those territories. Since the eighteenth century, peasants and elites estate owners all across Europe, from France to Russia, had integrated markets and new economic dynamics. Of course, there were important differences, but, as in Russia, they did not correspond to such large areas such as France, East Elbian areas, etc. Discrepancies between regions or even villages and resemblances between distant areas were much more widespread than the similarities within a given area.

Yet, in political terms, European peasants lived under very different conditions. French peasants were formally free after the Revolution, although most of them participated in the labour market as seasonal workers and had far fewer rights than their masters and employers. Worse still, in the early twentieth century, most of them did not have the right to vote. Russian peasants were not serfs in the strict sense, yet the legal restrictions under which they lived were far more severe than those of their French counterparts.

This leads us to pose two main questions: first, to what extent did institutions affect the economic activity?

Second, from a political standpoint, the long-term strength of the European nobility and peasantry and their integration in market activity raises the questions of when and how the 'old regime' ended in Europe: in the eighteenth century? In connection with the rise of markets? After the French revolution? With the First World War?

To answer these questions, we have to study the continuities and changes in Russia after the official abolition of serfdom. Then we will compare this trend to that of Europe's main countries.

6

Beyond Economic Backwardness: Labour and Growth in Eurasia in the Long Nineteenth Century

Conventional views of pre-revolutionary Russia run as follows: reforms were inadequate and partial; the commune was strong; industrialization from above was unable to stimulate a wider process. Peasants' well-being decreased as political tensions rose, due mostly to the gaps between economic and social dynamics, on the one hand, and political conservatism on the other. In economic terms, the 'Russian case' after 1861 is mentioned in the historiography of Russia to discuss the limits of Tsarist reforms and the roots of the revolution in a clearly teleological approach common to 'liberal' and 'Marxist' scholars. In comparative studies, this same experience has been emphasized to suggest the role of institutions and/or mentalities in blocking development. The peasant commune is said to have stopped industrialization and urbanization, reduced the marketing of agricultural products and helped to keep Russia 'backward'. An initial approach stressed the social reasons for this and thus the 'mentalities' of Russian peasants and elites hostile to the market. An opposing interpretation has argued that institutional constraints artificially limited the market orientation of Russian peasants.[1]

In political historical analysis, the Russian case has been discussed to suggest a connection between a strong peasantry and the state, a weak landed aristocracy (in relation to the state) and revolution. According to this view, peasant backwardness and poverty stemmed from the political support given to peasant institutions and the ambivalent role of land aristocracies.

In order to discuss this argument, we may start with empirical data recently gathered on the well-being and the economic dynamics of the Russian peasantry. The global trend of Russia between 1861 and 1914 hardly corresponds to the conventional images that Gershenkron and many others have painted. Revised population trends show, on the whole, lower mortality and birth rates and better living conditions in the eighteenth and nineteenth centuries than previously thought.[2] Thus, pauperization of the peasantry and frequent famines did not in fact take place,[3] and both agriculture and living standards experienced stable growth during the period extending from 1861 to 1914.[4]

Indeed, this revised trend is easy to understand when we put it into the broader and long-term perspective that we developed in the previous chapters. Russian growth during the second half of the nineteenth century was important insofar as it had already been consistent during previous decades and as legal constraints on and bondage of the peasantry had already lessened before the official abolition of serfdom in 1861. As a consequence, during the second half of the nineteenth century and up through 1914, the rate of growth and commercialization of Russian agriculture was accelerated.[5] Between 1880 and 1900, the grain trade spread capitalism to even the remotest corners of the Empire[6] and Russia's wheat market was fully integrated into global markets.[7] Between 1861 and 1914, agriculture's contribution to the national income grew at a rapid pace, comparable to that of contemporary Western European economies. As Gregory evaluated it, Russia experienced rates of growth similar to those of Germany, France, America, Japan, Norway, Canada and the United Kingdom – 1.35 per cent average annual productivity growth in agriculture in the periods 1883–1887 and 1909–1913, which was three-quarters of the industrial productivity growth rate and nearly equal to the economy-wide 1.5 per cent.[8]

Net grain production rose to 3.1 per cent annually between 1885 and 1913; Russia produced more grain than any other country in 1861, and in 1913 it was second only to the United States.[9] The average annual rate of growth of gross cereal and potato production in European Russia for 1870–1913 was 2.5 per cent – 1.6 per cent for the first 30 years and 4.4 per cent from the turn of the century. This is in the range of estimates by Paul Gregory, who found the rate of growth covering the entire territory of Russia, including frontier regions during 1883–1887 and 1909–1913 to be 2.8 per cent, with some differences within the intervals of that period.[10] The value of the labour input increased between 1861 and 1913 by 42.6 per cent, or an average annual rate of 1.7 per cent.

Thus, unlike common view, capital intensification played its part in Russian growth, though labour played a dominant role. At the same time, the share of agriculture in the national income fell over the entire period (1881–1914) from 57 per cent to 51 per cent; but most of this decline occurred before Stolypin's privatization of common lands.[11] As opposed to the conventional view, the rates of growth of labour productivity in agriculture do not appear to have diverged significantly from the economy-wide average. In other words, if we look at the performance of agriculture and the main demographic index, recent estimations show that Russia was not falling behind most advanced countries, but rather keeping pace with them.

Growth relied on the evolution of basic Russian institutions – for example the peasant commune. It is no accident that during the past 20 years, when the history of enclosures in Britain and agriculture in Europe has been revisited,[12] the image of the Russian commune has been contested as well.[13] Recent estimations made for Russia confirm the lack of any correlation between land redistribution and productivity.[14] From this perspective, periodical redistributions were much less determinants of productivity than endogenous choices of investment decisions; communes often took soil investment decisions and the quality of the land into account when assigning new land rights. Repartitions allowed communities to respond to sudden unexpected changes in their size brought about by epidemics or out-migrations, recast the shape of the open fields and bring order into strip fields by reducing their number.[15]

Peasants' possessions more than doubled between the 1870s and the First World War, and acquisitions were made not only by the commune but also increasingly by individual households. Between 1863 and 1872, Russian peasants bought lands to add to their communal allotments. Over three-quarters of all peasant acquisitions on the open market were made by individuals. This trend accelerated with the foundation of the Peasant State Bank, which aimed at encouraging loans to peasants willing to buy lands. Peasant land properties doubled between 1877 and 1905. In 80 per cent of the cases, transactions were made by the peasant commune or by peasant associations. During the following years, between 1906 and 1914, the state sold 1.5 million *desiatina* to peasants (1 *desiatina* = 1.1 hectares); landlords lost one-fifth of their land, i.e., 10.2 million out of 49.7 *desiatina*. Two-thirds of the purchases were made by peasant societies and communes and one-third by individual families. Cossack and peasant ownership increased by 9.5 million *desiatina*, now reaching 170.4 million.[16] The acquisition of land thus offers further confirmation of the argument of increasing well-being of the peasantry between 1861 and 1914.

Added to this revised view of Russian agriculture is that of industrialization. In contrast to traditional judgements, between 1881 and 1913 the share of industry in national income rose from 25 to 32 per cent. Industrial labour productivity was 28 per cent higher than that of agriculture.[17] However, even if the rate of urbanization has been revised upwards,[18] peasant migrants still accounted for 93 per cent of all factory workers in Moscow in 1902,[19] most of whom worked in textiles. The industry remained geographically concentrated in the central provinces of Moscow and Vladimir as well as in and around the imperial capital. This means that despite an increasing rate of urbanization and of regional specialization, the peasant-worker was still the leading figure in the Russian economy. According to the 1897 census, 23.3 per cent of the active population was employed in non-agricultural sectors, half of which were in proto-industrial and craft activities and the rest in industry and services. Proto-industry and in particular rural cottage industry were still serious competitors for urban industry, not only in terms of production, but also on the labour market.[20] This seems to confirms Olga Crisp's and more recently Borodkin's and Leonard's argument that a lack of industrial labour was owing not to internal passports or legal constraints on mobility, but to the strength of agriculture, its profitability and the interest that people had in staying in rural areas and alternating these stays with seasonal urban employment.[21]

Mobility, on the one hand, and acquisition of land, on the other hand, weakened the unity of households and the overall economic and social equilibrium linked to it. Because of the social status of the head of the family in peasant communities, young male peasants tended to leave the paternal household early.[22] Young children and women working and living in towns several months per year were usually reticent to give the head of the household all their income and were also sensitive to urban fashion that called for increasing individual expenditures.[23] Local courts also registered increasing conflicts over these issues between 1870 and the First World War.[24] Thus, the number of households rose from 8,450,782 in 1877 to 12,019,255 in 1905. In fifteen provinces of European Russia, the rate of formation of new households was between 30 per cent and 60 per cent in the period 1861–1882. This rate was 2–4 times higher than the rate of population growth in these same areas. As a consequence, despite the increasing purchases of land and emigration to Siberia, land cultivated per family decreased from 13.2 to 10.2 *desiatina* between 1877 and 1905. In other words, social and economic developments were progressively depriving people of the social umbrella of the extended family and commune. The First World War would put a halt to previous economic dynamics and would exasperate social tensions within the village as well as between peasants and landlords.

To sum up, during the nineteenth century and up to the First World War, Russia experienced greater economic growth than is conventionally argued. It was rooted in the country's previous development and in the ability of Russian economic institutions to meet increasing demand. Although labour intensive, Russian growth also made use of increasing quantities of capital. Yet although this solution helped to compete with the rate of growth of leading Western countries, it did not catch up to them and, most importantly, it failed to resolve the tensions between economic development and social and political inequalities.

If this is so, then, the Russian specificity consisted in adopting extreme variations of Western solutions. Estate owners entered the proto-industrial and the cereal markets at the expense of urban merchants and producers and of occasional new 'bourgeois' estate owners. This outcome was politically relevant and specific in that it expressed an extreme defence of old agrarian aristocracies in a context of progressive transformation of the peasantry. In terms of economic growth, this solution was far from being catastrophic and confirms that markets and capitalism do not necessarily stand upon democracy and free labour. If this is true, then analogies and comparisons between Russia and Europe require a new basis.

Growth and labour in Europe and Asia

Over at least the last two decades, economic history has moved away from the interpretation developed in the early nineteenth century by the so-called 'classical' economists (Smith, Ricardo) and Marx, according to which the agrarian revolution and later the industrial revolution were accompanied by the substitution of labour by capital and the concentration of production units. In fact, this process mostly occurred in the twentieth century. Before that, in most Eurasiatic spaces, proto-industry, agriculture and even industry experienced a rather labour-intensive path. Agriculture first: conventional histories of economic growth stress a relative decline of agriculture during the industrialization process; at the same time, agriculture is supposed to provide goods to feed an increasing urban population. This outcome requires increasing productivity and yields, which, in turn, are obtained through a shift in the organization of economic units and in the relative weight of factors (decreasing labour and land and increasing capital). These views have been increasingly challenged, starting with the role of capital in agriculture; recent empirical analyses have shown that livestock densities in many parts of England were stable throughout the modern period up through the mid-nineteenth century[25]; however, in the same period, livestock was more important than commonly believed in Asia and eastern Europe.[26] That is to say that, in Britain, rising livestock numbers cannot explain the rise in yields that occurred before 1800.[27] On the rest of the continent as well, the long-term trend of rising wheat prices (roughly between 1680 and 1815) led to reducing the surface devoted to livestock and livestock feeding, while increasing that for wheat.

The role of machines and new sources of power is also under revision; after steam became the dominant form of power employed in manufacturing, the major sources of energy available to farmers continued to be men, animals, wind and water.[28] Mechanization in farming proceeded slowly because agricultural operations are more separated in time and space than industrial processes. Mechanization was therefore a relatively unimportant component of changes in agriculture technology up through the mid-nineteenth century[29] when the appearance of commercial fertilizers and the elaboration of mechanical harvesting equipment began significantly to affect methods of production.[30] Until the machine age, that is, after 1850, much of the rise in the productivity and the growth of output depended on intensive use of known technology than on novel methods. The so-called 'new husbandry' was indeed not so new[31] and it required more labour, not less.[32] Only in agriculture systems characterized (as in the United States) by high opportunity cost for labour did economic pressure to mechanize become similar to that experienced by some sectors of industry. On the contrary, not only in Russia and France, but also in Prussia, since the seventeenth and up through the second half of the nineteenth century, labour was not only the major input in agriculture, either direct or embodied in land improvements, but its weight even increased during this period.[33] Recent analyses converge towards the same conclusion: labour and labour intensity are identified as the main source of agriculture growth before 1850, with human and physical capital playing a secondary role.[34] Labour-intensive techniques linked to the diffusion of knowledge and attractive market (with increasing agriculture price) were at hand between the seventeenth and the last quarter of the nineteenth century, when this trend reversed (decreasing agriculture prices and increasing wages).[35]

However, increasing labour demand in agriculture had to compete with similar processes in proto-industry and manufacture. Original theories of proto-industrialization associated proto-industry to demographic growth and proletarization, on the one hand, and to a decline of urban guilds and feudal institutions, on the other.[36] Further analyses have put all these assertions under question and nowadays it is widely accepted that on a comparative scale no one single uniform link between proto-industrialization and each of the mentioned variables can be detected. Proto-industry developed in Western, Central and Eastern Europe since the end of the seventeenth century, in response to market demand and demographic pressure.[37] It played a central role all over Europe at least until the mid-nineteenth century, after which some areas declined and manufactures and industries replaced the putting-out system.[38] However, this issue was far from being general, and in many European areas and districts, proto-industry continued to play a leading role during the second half of the nineteenth century and even in the twentieth century.[39]

This timing was even more relevant in Asia; authors such as Lee and Sugihara have maintained that the 'industrious revolution' De Vries had identified in Europe[40] was at hand also in some Asiatic areas.[41] As in Russia, in Japan and China too, the success of proto-industry, in particular of rural proto-industry, was at the root of a labour-intensive path of growth.[42]

In all these areas, as in most Russian regions, agriculture did not turn into a simple supplier of produce and labour-force for industry; quite the contrary, estates and peasants took part in the development of local and national markets, for both wheat and proto-industrial products. In Russia, as in Japan and in Central Europe, peasants' commercialization was not always nor necessarily 'forced' (by the landlords and/or the state); economic and legal dependence of many peasants was not in contradiction with the attraction the market exerted on many others.[43] In Japan, as in many areas in Russia and Western Europe, increases in agricultural output and income led to a growth in demand for manufactured goods that was met by an expanding rural industry utilizing labour-intensive technology. The resulting growth in rural non-agricultural activity in turn generated increased incomes for rural households and hence increased demand for agriculture output.[44]

Similar results are now available on India; contrary to the traditional view, stressing the decline of the cottage industry under the British rule and the growing international markets, fresh research shows that 'traditional' labour-intensive techniques were well developed; thanks to their flexibility, these techniques allowed a labour-intensive pattern of growth linked to family units integrated in both agriculture and industrial markets.[45]

However, such a persistent and global strength of agriculture and proto-industry had an unanticipated effect: urbanization and the supply of labour for urban manufacture were mostly seasonal.

Not only in Russia, Japan and France,[46] but also in Britain, until the mid-nineteenth century double employment (mostly in rural and urban areas) was the rule rather than the exception. According to Lindert and Williamson, for the larger occupational groupings, such as 'agriculture', 'commerce' and 'manufacturing trades', the census and statistical error margins are probably within the range of minus 40 to plus 66 per cent!![47]

Seasonal needs in agriculture were the crucial variable here. Not only in Russia, China and Japan, but also in Britain, France, and Central Europe, seasonal and local shortages of manpower were overcome by interregional migration and, eventually, only later in the nineteenth century, by a transformation of hand harvesting techniques and tools.[48] In fact, labour requirements of harvesting were particularly important since labour input peaked sharply at the harvest.[49] Thus, landowners in Brandenburg satisfied part of their manorial labour by requiring the children of their peasant tenants to serve on the manor for a period of three years. However, at harvest time, the labour services provided by peasants and their children fell short and recourse to seasonal day labour was widespread. The part of rural dwellers who worked part time for corn growers depended on what they did outside the peak season.

These attitudes were extremely embarrassing for the rising manufacture and industry, which, as the other segments of the economy, mostly relied upon labour. Because of the still high price of capital, urban employers sought to face labour shortages with legal pressure on labour as well on competitors (interdiction to move before the end of terms, strong penalties for unfair competition, etc.). The first industrial revolution in Britain was far from being the realm of capital over labour. Feinstein's estimations show that in Britain, capital and labour grew at about the same rate from 1760 through 1830, so that there was effectively no change in the capital/labour ration in these seven decades. In the last three decades the ratio slowly rose, as capital per worker increased at a rate of about 0.5 per cent per annum.[50] As a whole, the rate of capital formation in Britain was relatively slow until the mid-nineteenth century and the capital/labour ration strongly increased only afterward.[51]

By 1850, relatively few workers were employed in factories: only a small proportion worked in technologically advanced industries such as cotton, iron and steel, and metalworking; and the full impact of steam power in transport and production was yet to be felt.[52] These issues break with the traditional view of the first industrial revolution and strongly reduce the gap between Britain and other countries, especially France. Historiography considered France as 'backward' in comparison with Britain, precisely because of its slow rate of concentration and capital intensification in industry.[53] Recent analyses have consistently modified this view: while British capital intensification and the increasing capital/labour rate in industry have been revised downwards, French dynamics have been corrected upwards. From this standpoint, the relatively slow pace of growth of capital in France, and the increasing rate of labour/capital in industry are no more considered as exceptional nor 'inefficient'.[54]

This means that not only in Russia but also in France and most of the European countries, economic and industrial growth of the eighteenth and nineteenth centuries remained at a small scale and was labour intensive. Growth was most mostly achieved through a movement along the same production function whose scope slightly moved upwards until the mid-nineteenth century.[55] There is evidence that a lot of productivity increase was not associated with specific innovations, but with workers operating more machines.[56] Christine Mac Leod has found out that the most declared goal of the innovation was either improving the quality of the product or saving on capital, not labour. And if inventors were not particularly intent on saving labour, those who judged their inventions were even less so. In other words, economic actors did not wish to substitute labour with capital and the final outcome for the whole economy was an increasing demand for labour.[57]

As a whole, during the second half of the eighteenth century, in the British industry, labour input grew at about 1.2–1.3 per cent, two-thirds of which was caused by a larger population, and the remaining coming from longer working hours.[58] Following E. P. Thompson,[59] legions of historians have endeavoured to show that working time actually increased with the industrial revolution. Indeed, this process started well before it, in the seventeenth and eighteenth centuries, with the 'industrious revolution' and the multiple farming and industrial activities.[60] Thus, the global history of the eighteenth and nineteenth centuries shows a similar evolution of working time in all the countries we mentioned, i.e., the workdays became longer as labour became more intensive.[61] The innovations and technical improvements recorded in agriculture, industry and trade did not take place at the expense of labour but actually fostered employment. This mechanism is confirmed in the study of manufactures in France and England, Japan and India. From the point of view of labour institutions and the relationship of labour to other production factors, it thus became a common 'wave of capitalism' (to borrow Braudel's expression but not his chronology) that lifted up Eurasian capitalism as a whole from the seventeenth to the early twentieth century.

In view of these facts, it is possible to conclude that, not only in the seventeenth but also in the eighteenth and much of the nineteenth centuries, the continuing importance of cottage industries and frequent migration between the city and the country created a strong link between two types of constraint: presence at work and compliance with working hours, on the one hand, and competition among employers (including heads of households), manufacturers, landowners and trader-entrepreneurs for the control and appropriation of labour, on the other hand. This is where presence at work and discipline encountered institutions and labour law. Along with the rules governing workshops, agricultural estates and plantations in Europe and Asia, a set of provisions was devised to control mobility and presence at work, such as the worker's booklet, laws against poaching workers and begging, forms of bondage, etc. Constraint in the organizational sense became linked to institutional constraints; presence at work conveyed concerns about internal organization, competition and public order.

Conclusion: Russia in a Globalizing World

Backwardness, dependency, Orientalism, and Asiatic (or Oriental) despotism: all these notions have influenced European perceptions of Russia and Asia since the eighteenth century. According to the period and the authors, they reflected major transformations in European societies and policies. In the eighteenth century, notions of backwardness and despotism developed in the realm of the Enlightenment and wished to contrast 'new' political philosophy and politics of Western Europe to those of other areas. In the following century, together with Orientalism, they expressed the new ambitions and fears of liberal regimes, namely, democracy and socialism. During the same period, dependency, backwardness and freedom played a part in the long debates and implementation of colonialism, slavery, serfdom and their demise.

In the twentieth century, these categories were used to interpret Russia and Asia in reflections on communism, decolonization, the Cold War, post-colonial economic development and the transformations of the welfare state. Despite differences in context and time, approaches that refer to economic backwardness, Oriental despotism and dependence share a common faith in History (with a capital 'H') and its discernible meaning and laws. 'Otherness' enters into a broader historical determinism aimed at showing the necessity and superiority of capitalism over feudalism and communism, of freedom over un-freedom (as the West identifies it), of Europe over Asia, the nation-state over empire, of rational settlers over nomads and pirates, etc.

We have tackled these approaches mainly on empirical grounds and shown that they cannot explain the historical dynamics of Russia and Eurasia. Contrary to conventional views, Oriental despotism relied on capital while European markets made extensive use of coercion. Their encounter in the steppe should be expressed in terms of a convergence rather than the opposition between two worlds. In the steppe, European military techniques and organization did not prove superior to Mongol techniques until very late, let us say the eighteenth century. Before that date, Russian expansion relied not on weapons but on modern conscription and settler-soldiers, capable of providing both armed force and wheat. The same was true in the expansion of China and the Moghul Empire, where the presumed superiority of Western weapons and tactics was not achieved until the early nineteenth century. Military innovations in the steppe did not depend solely on their effectiveness but also on how they were linked to underlying social and economic practices. In the rural worlds that characterized the period we are studying, recruitment influenced agricultural activities and the relationships between landowners and peasants. Muscovite and later Russian expansion relied upon state control over landlords and their incorporation in the state apparatus as well as social and institutional dynamics in the steppe that were quite different from those in the heartland. In the steppe, peasants were granted rights to land with the obligation to provide limited labour services. In exchange, they colonized the area and provided wheat for themselves and the rest of the army. On the eastern border, Muscovy was more eager to adopt Western military strategies but it avoided using the market or pillage to feed troops. Military granaries and cereal stocks were developed in those areas.

China adopted a similar solution with peasant-soldier-colonists in the north-western steppe. In contrast to Russia, however, this solution proved weak because of persistent tensions between Manchus and Hans, on the one hand, and the importance of market solutions in the rest of China, on the other. The latter left the army and the city vulnerable to the speculation of merchants and, later in the eighteenth century, to monetary instability linked to the expansion of the West and the increasing circulation of metals from the Americas in Asia. Russia avoided both these difficulties.[1]

If Russian militarization proved ultimately to be more efficient than that in China, India or the Ottoman Empire, it also rivalled the solutions adopted in Western Europe. The modernization of European armies was a long, complex evolution and in no way a revolution. The transformation of supply techniques and logistics was also a slow process and Europe's main armies faced considerable supply problems at least until the First World War.[2] Systems of recruitment slowly evolved over time and modern conscription as we know it today – with a stable army in peace time – became established only with the Napoleonic wars, in other words more than a century after Peter the Great had introduced it in Russia. War turned out to be disruptive for Spain and Portugal, but not for Britain or Russia, for both similar and different reasons. Russia could count on its centralized state and power, the collection of non-monetary resources and the gradual integration of Mongol techniques of war and administration. Pax Russica was a late by-product of war and razzias. Power in Britain, on the other hand, was less centralized than in France and Russia and its landed aristocracies less dependent on the central power and a gradually disintegrating peasantry. Yet Britain, Spain and Russia built up their empires from the peripheries of Europe. Over the long term, Britain and Russia were more successful in keeping their territories than Spain. The reasons were different: Britain relied upon maritime power, trade, and the (mostly failed) attempt to impose its own rules over its territories. Russia relied upon land power, soldier-colonists and coexisting/simultaneous wars and tolerance towards conquered people. These different models of expansion used equally different fiscal models and forms of labour.

Indeed, four main sources are worth mentioning: trade; pillage and razzias; economic growth; taxes. From the seventeenth through the early eighteenth centuries, trade in the steppe, including slave trade, provided increasing resources. We have seen that Muscovy gradually took control of the main trade routes linking Inner Asia to the North, Eastern Europe, China, India, the Ottoman Empire and the Mediterranean. Silk, textile, furs, spices and slaves were the main traded items. Yet slave raids and trade were not so much economic resources in themselves as diplomatic weapons; Muscovy and later Russia used them to take control of the steppe. Once this process was completed, the pacification of the area and the decline of the slave trade became a single issue. In a broader perspective, the Eurasian slave trade paved the way for two major events: the development of slavery in the Mediterranean area and thus a model for the Atlantic slave trade, and the establishment of serfdom in Russia. Increasing production of consumption items under coercive, labour-intensive systems was common to both. However, the differences were also important: chattel slavery related to racial differences was used to produce luxuries (coffee, sugar) and ordinary items (cotton) items for Europe. In Russia and Eastern Europe, strong restrictions on mobility within complex relationships between landlords, peasants and their communities and the state produced wheat for both Europe and Russia. In the modern era, peasants and landowners were more involved in market life than is commonly believed, not only in capitalist England but also in France under the *ancien régime*, in Central Europe, Prussia, Eastern Europe and Russia.

Social hierarchies and rights were also different on the sea and in the steppe. Russian colonists experienced more freedom than inland peasants. The opposite was true for European colonists in the Indian Ocean and the Americas during the seventeenth, eighteenth and early nineteenth centuries, when the rights of indentured immigrants were extremely unequal and their conditions harsh. Yet over time those trends reversed, and post-slavery and post-serfdom societies developed along different paths. In North America at the turn of the nineteenth century, there were important differences between white settlers and 'free' white immigrants, on the one hand, and Chinese coolies and former slaves on the other. During the same years, the abolition of slavery in Africa gave European powers a pretext to occupy the continent and introduce new forms of forced labour. Post-emancipation Russia maintained significant inequalities between peasants and landlords. We find three different sources and forms of inequality here within a common global trend.

The rise of the fiscal state is another crucial variable. In this case as well, we now know that we cannot compare 'Europe' to 'Asia'; the fiscal regimes in some European countries were closer to those in certain Asian areas than the ones adopted by their European neighbours.[3] In this panorama, Russia did not correspond to the way it is usually depicted. Its military expenditures in the eighteenth century were slightly higher than those of France or Britain but lower than that of Prussia. Indirect taxes dominated the fiscal burden; salt tax, consumption tax, etc., provided 45 per cent of national income in the 1680s compared with 34 per cent from direct taxation. In 1701, the weight of direct taxation had fallen to 20 per cent. In 1718, Peter introduced the soul tax. It was a single tax, calculated to match the needs of the army, to be collected by landlords and municipalities on peasants and lower-class urban groups. In 1724, the soul tax provided 54 per cent of the revenue budget. However, despite huge price increases, particularly during the second half of the eighteenth century, the poll tax was not raised until 1794.

France followed a similar path, although at a different level: direct taxation declined from 44 per cent in 1726 to 35 per cent in 1788. In Britain, direct taxation declined from 47 per cent in the 1690s to 21 per cent a hundred years later. Though the British were relatively more successful than the French and the Russians in taxing the rich, a consistent step in this direction was achieved only under the impact of the Napoleonic wars.

During the second half of the eighteenth century, Catherine the Great found new sources of financing by confiscating the land and capital of the Church. In 1762, Russian monasteries owned two-thirds of Russian ploughed land; only 13 per cent of the nobility possessed more than a hundred peasants, whereas 70 per cent of landed ecclesiastical institutions did so. The Church's peasants constituted one-seventh of the rural population in 1762. The secularization of those lands brought the state 3.6 million roubles in 1784.

At the same time, resources were not redistributed to the presumed 'lazy' aristocracy, first because a great deal of money was used to free peasants and build infrastructure, and second because the Russian aristocracy was deeply involved in market processes and investments. As we have seen, Russian landlords invested and actively participated in markets, much like Junkers and Austrian landlords. In turn, this fact confirms that, contrary to conventional historiographies, landlords and landed aristocracies were not just rentiers, but played an active role all over Europe in the process of modernization.

On the political and fiscal side, Russian landlords were only at a first sight more protected than, say, their English or French equivalents. Even if this was partly true in terms of taxation, the fact is that the rights of Russian landlords were never fully guaranteed. The tsar could withdraw their rights, titles and properties; indeed, the policies adopted after the end of the eighteenth century consisted in emancipating more and more peasants by administrative and political decision.

In contrast, European landlords relied upon solid property rights and unequal fiscal regimes; this system remained in place until the First World War. In short, the success of nineteenth-century Europe also depended on unequal taxation and the continuing power of the landed aristocracy, together with rising industrial and urban elites. This confirms Arno Meyer's thesis: the old regime in Europe did not come to an end until the First World War.[4] How did these regimes affect economic growth?

As early as the seventeenth century, considerable agricultural growth and changes in mentality were taking place everywhere. In the eighteenth century, the Russian aggregate national income increased fivefold, raising per capita income by 85 per cent. In agriculture, the gap between Russia and Western Europe was constant, or even diminishing in terms of yields and commercialization.[5] In sum, differences in the rate of growth of both national income and agriculture, though relevant, were not the most significant between Russia and Europe. This was due first to the fact that the commune was not always and necessarily an obstacle to agrarian development – at least until mechanization, which came late, even in Western Europe. Commons slowly disappeared in France and even in England the process took more time than conventional historiography asserted.

The second reason why the differences between Russian and European agriculture were not of major importance was that forced labour was a complex notion and practice and was not necessarily unproductive. In Russia, peasants were not *serfs de la glebe* but peasants with restricted rights, subject to institutional extortion by landlords, while in Europe there were no 'independent' peasants or rural proletarians, but only servants with highly limited rights. They undoubtedly enjoyed greater freedom than Russian peasants and fewer restrictions on their mobility. In the end, the differences were not extreme but rather gradations of the same world. Coercion did not necessarily limit productivity; abolition of slavery and serfdom in the nineteenth century was the outcome of political not economic forces. In other words, given the techniques and scope of agriculture in the nineteenth century, differences in productivity and yields were only tangentially connected to coercion. The differences in terms of political and social rights were far more significant; over time, especially since the last quarter of the nineteenth century, political rights increased for most people in Europe but they continued to be unequal in Russia. This affected income distribution and political equilibrium. At the turn of the century, the real wages of working people in the United States, France, Britain and Germany increased after decades during which landlords and entrepreneurial capitalists had chiefly benefited from economic growth. In Russia, peasants had access to land and their living standards improved, whereas the new, relatively small proletariat was on the sidelines.

The collapse of those systems in the West was linked to a twofold process: increasing mechanization and decreasing prices of foodstuffs, colonial products and wheat; and stronger resistance from 'subaltern' groups. All these phenomena, though occasionally present in the late eighteenth century and early nineteenth centuries, took on decisive weight only in the last quarter of the nineteenth century. The second industrial revolution, the welfare state, the masses bursting onto the political scene and the decline of labour-intensive processes led to a disjunction between profitable production and coercion, at least in Europe and in many of its colonies. Free wage labour became more productive than coerced labour.

However, this shift was far from universal; the accommodation between large-scale, intensive production and new forms of bondage came back to the forefront with the First World War and its aftermath, as the revival of coercion in Africa and Nazi and Soviet Europe shows. Soviet Russia was not only the land of coercion; more specifically, it marked an attempt to achieve the second industrial revolution using the methods and organization of the first, i.e., with increasing labour intensification, longer labour time and little attention to the quality. The Soviet experience consisted in combining large-scale production and mechanization with labour intensification in terms of time and extremely unequal rights between working people and state masters. From this perspective, the main feature of Russia over the long run is not so much 'economic backwardness' as persistent, strong social inequalities inside an industrializing economy and society.

Nowadays, after the collapse of the Wall and the end of the Cold War, we are invited to refresh our own notions of freedom, democracy and economic growth.

Oriental despotism was a notion Montesquieu developed to contrast enlightened despotism with absolutism. It was further refined in the nineteenth century to contrast the liberal order with continuing old regimes. In the twentieth century, Oriental despotism became an intellectual and political weapon in the Cold War. All these approaches tended to link freedom to civil and political rights rather than to social rights. However, the revisited history of Russia and Eurasia we have presented here – as well as the new Asian capitalism of China and India today – shows that economic growth and markets are perfectly compatible with lack of democracy and unequal social rights. On a global, comparative scale, the new, difficult relationship, if not the divorce, between democracy, capitalism and social rights is a persistent problem not only in Russia, the post-colonial South and Asia, but also in the West. It is time for us to invent new bridges.

Notes

Introduction

1 Dominic Lieven, *Empire, The Russian Empire and Its Rivals from the Sixteenth Century to the Present* (London: Pimlico, 2003).
2 Immanuel Wallerstein, *The Modern World-System: Capitalist Agriculture and the Origins of the European World-Economy in the Sixteenth Century* (New York, London: Atheneum, 1974, 1976); Witold Kula, *An Economic Theory of the Feudal System* (London: New Left Books, 1976); Douglass North, *Structure and Change in Economic History* (New York: Norton, 1981).
3 Kenneth Pomeranz, *The Great Divergence* (Princeton: Princeton University Press, 2000).
4 John Keep, *Soldiers of the Tsar: Army and Society in Russia, 1462–1874* (Oxford: Clarendon Press, 1985).
5 Jane Burbank and Frederick Cooper, *Empires in World History: Power and the Politics of Difference* (Princeton: Princeton University Press, 2010).
6 Jerome Blum, *Lord and Peasant in Russian from the Ninth to the Nineteenth Century* (New York: Atheneum, 1964); Alexander Gershenkron, *Economic Backwardness in Historical Perspective* (Cambridge, Mass.: Harvard University Press, 1962); Richard Hellie, *Enserfment and Military Change in Muscovy* (Chicago: University of Chicago Press 1971); Peter Kolchin, *Unfree Labor: American Slavery and Russian Serfdom*, (Cambridge: Cambridge University Press, 1987); Michael Bush, ed., *Serfdom and Slavery: Studies in Legal Bondage* (Manchester: Manchester University Press, 1996); Daniel Field, *The End of Serfdom: Nobility and Bureaucracy in Russia, 1855–1861* (Cambridge, Mass. Harvard University Press,1976).
7 Steven Hoch, *Serfdom and Social Control in Russia. Petrovskoe, a Village in Tambov* (Chicago: University of Chicago Press, 1986).
8 Ivan D. Koval'chenko, *Russkoe krepostnoe krest'ianstvo v pervoi polovine XIX v.* (The Russian serf economy during the first half of the nineteenth century), (Moscow: Nauka,1967); Evsey Domar and M. Machina, 'On the Profitability of Russian Serfdom,' *The Journal of Economic History*, 44, 4 (1984): 919–955.
9 Michael Confino, *Domaines et seigneurs en Russie vers la fin du XVIIIe siècle: Étude de structures agraires et de mentalités économiques* (Paris: Mouton, 1963); *Systèmes agraires et progrès agricole en Russie aux XVIIIe–XIXe siècles: Étude d' économie et de sociologie rurales* (Paris: Mouton, 1969); David Moon, *The Abolition of Serfdom in*

Russia, 1762-1907 (London: Pearson, 2001); David Moon, *The Russian Peasantry, 1600-1930* (London: Longman, 1996). Elise Kimerling Wirtschafter, *Structures of Society: Imperial Russia's 'People of various ranks'* (Dekalb: Northern Illinois University Press, 1994); Elise Kimerling Wirtschafter, *Social Identity in Imperial Russia* (Dekalb: Northern Illinois University Press, 1997).

10 Roger Bartlett, 'Serfdom and State Power in Imperial Russia', *European History Quarterly*, 33, 1 (2003): 29–64; David Moon, 'Reassessing Russian Serfdom', *European History Quarterly*, 26, 1 (1996): 483–526.

11 Examples of this are found in Tracy Dennison, *The Institutional Framework of Russian Serfdom* (Cambridge: Cambridge University Press: 2011).

12 Ian Blanchard, *Russia's Age of Silver: Precious Metal Production and Economic Growth in the Eighteenth Century* (New York and London: Routledge, 1989).

13 Alessandro Stanziani, 'Revisiting Russian Serfdom: Bonded Peasants and Market Dynamics, 1600–1800', *International Labor and Working Class History*, 78, 1 (2010): 12–27; 'Serfs, Slaves, or Wage Earners? The Legal Status of Labour in Russia from a Comparative Perspective, from the 16th to the 19th century', *Journal of Global History*, 3, 2 (2008): 183–202.

14 Steven Hoch, *Serfdom and Social Control in Russia. Petrovskoe, a Village in Tambov* (Chicago: Chicago University Press 1986); Moon, *The Russian Peasantry, 1600–1930*.

15 Stephen Wheatcroft, 'Crisis and Condition of the Peasantry in Late Imperial Russia', In Esther Kingston-Mann, Timothy Mixter eds., *Peasant Economy, Culture and Politics of European Russia, 1800–1921* (Princeton: Princeton University Press, 1991): 101–127.

16 Elvira M. Wilbur, 'Was Russian Peasant Agriculture Really That Impoverished? New Evidence From a Case Study From the "Impoverished Center" at the End of the Nineteenth Century', *Journal of Economic History*, 43 (March 1983): 137–144; Esther Kingston-Mann, 'Marxism and Russian Rural Development: Problems of Evidence, Experience and Culture', *American Historical Review*, 84 (Oct. 1981): 731–752; James Y. Simms Jr., 'The Crop Failure of 1891: Soil Exhaustion, Technological Backwardness, and Russia's "Agrarian Crisis"', *Slavic Review*, 41 (Summer 1982: 236–250).

Chapter 1

1 Alessandro Stanziani, 'Free Labour-Forced Labour: An Uncertain Boundary? The Circulation of Economic Ideas between Russia and Europe from the 18th to the Mid-19th Century', *Kritika: Explorations in Russian and Eurasian History*, 9, 1 (2008): 1–27.

2 Alexander Gershenkron, *Economic Backwardness in Historical Perspective* (Cambridge, Mass.: Harvard University Press, 1962).

3 A useful discussion on the historiography of the industrial revolution in Peter Temin, 'Two Views of the British Industrial Revolution', *The Journal of Economic History*, 57, 1 (1997): 63–82.
4 Jerome Blum, *Lord and Peasant in Russia from the Ninth to the Nineteenth Century* (New York: Atheneum, 1964); Richard Hellie, *Enserfment and Military Change in Muscovy* (Chicago: University of Chicago Press, 1971); Peter Kolchin, *Unfree Labour: American Slavery and Russian Serfdom* (Cambridge, Mass.: Harvard University Press, 1987).
5 Alessandro Stanziani, *L'économie en révolution. Le cas russe, 1870–1930* (Paris: Albin Michel, 1998).
6 Stanziani, *L'économie en revolution. Le cas russe, 1860–1930*.
7 Nikolai Kablukov, *Posobie pri mestnykh statistichekikh obsledovaniiakh* (Remarks for local statistical surveys) (Moscow: Leman, 1910): 8–10.
8 Alessandro Stanziani, 'Les enquêtes orales en Russie, 1861–1914', *Annales HSS*, 1 (2000): 219–241.
9 Alexander Mendel, *Dilemmas of Progress in Tsarist Russia. Legal Marxism and Legal Populism* (Cambridge, Mass.: 1961); Paul Rosenstein-Rodan, 'Problems of Industrialization of Eastern and South eastern Europe', *Economic Journal*, June–September, 53 (1943): 202–211; Gunner Myrdal, *Economic Theory and Underdeveloped Regions* (London: Duckworth, 1956).
10 Douglass North and Robert Thomas, *The Rise of Western Civilization: A New Economic History* (Cambridge: Cambridge University Press, 1973).
11 Deidre McCloskey, 'The Open Fields of England: Rent, Risk, and the Rate of Interest, 1300–1815', in David Galenson ed., *Markets in History: Economic Studies of the Past* (Cambridge: Cambridge University Press, 1989): 5–51; Randall Nielsen, 'Storage and English Government Intervention in Early Modern Grain Markets', *The Journal of Economic History*, 57, 1 (1997): 1–33.
12 Tracy K., Dennison, 'Did Serfdom Matter? Russian Rural Society, 1750–1860', *Historical Research*, 79 (2003): 74–89.
13 Joseph Stiglitz, *Whither Socialism?* (Harvard: MIT Press, 1994).
14 Gregory Yavlinsky, *Laissez Faire versus Policy-Led Transformation, Lessons of the Economic Reforms in Russia* (Moscow: Center for Economic and Political Research, 1996); Shafiqul Islam, Michael Mandelbaum, eds., *Making Markets Economic Transformations in Eastern Europe and the Post-Soviet States* (New York: Council of Foreign Relations, 1993).
15 Gareth Austin, 'Reciprocal Comparison and African History: Tackling Conceptual Eurocentrism in the Study of Africa's Economic Past', *African Studies Review*, 50, 3 (2007): 1–28.
16 Alessandro Stanziani, 'Information, institutions et temporalités. Quelques remarques critiques sur l'usage de la nouvelle économie de l'information en histoire', *Revue de synthèse*, 1–2 (2000): 117–155.

17 Just a few references among a huge littérature: in economic anthropology: Arjun Appadurai, *The Social Life of Things. Commodities in Cultural Perspective* (Cambridge: Cambridge University Press, 1986); Philip Curtin, *Cross-Cultural Trade in World History* (Cambridge: Cambridge University Press, 1984); George Dalton, ed., *Research in Economic Anthropology* (Greenwich, Connecticut: JAI Press, 1983). In France: Bernand Lepetit 'Une logique du raisonnement historique', *Annale ESC*, 5 (1993): 1209–1219; special issue 'Histoire et sciences sociales', *Annales ESC*, 38, 6 (1983); and Jean-Claude Passeron, *Le raisonnement sociologique* (Paris: Nathan, 1991).
18 Par Arndt, *Economic Development. The History of an Idea* (Chicago: University of Chicago Press, 1987); Gerald Meier, James Rauch, *Leading Issues in Development Economics* (Oxford: Oxford University Press, 2000); Deepak Lal, *The Poverty of Development Economics* (Boston: MIT Press, 2000).
19 Clifford Geertz, *The Interpretation of Culture* (New York: Basic Book, 1973).
20 Christopher Lloyd, *The Structures of History* (Oxford: Blackwell, 1993); Paul Griffith, 'Ethnocentrism as Act of Kidnapping. The Procrustean Complex in the West', *American International Journal of Social Science*, 1, 2 (2012): 59–70; Roy Preiswerk and Dominique Perrot, *Ethnocentrism and History: Africa, Asia and Indian America in Western Textbooks* (New York: Nok. Print. 1978).
21 Edward Said, *Orientalism* (London: Penguin, 1977).
22 Larry Wolff, *Inventing Eastern Europe, The Map of Civilization on the Mind of Enlightenment* (Stanford: Stanford University Press, 1994).
23 Michael Confino, 'Reinventing the Enlightenment: Western Images of Eastern Realities in the eighteenth century', *Canadian Slavonic Papers*, 36, 3–4 (1994): 505–522.
24 Albert Lortholary, *Le mirage russe en France au XVIII siècle* (Paris: Éditions contemporaines, 1948): 14; Jan Struys, *Les voyages en Moscovie, en Tartarie, Perse, aux Indes et en plusieurs pays étrangers* (Amsterdam: Van Meers, 1681); Pierre de la Martinière, *Voyage des païs septentrionaux* (Paris: L. Vendame, 1671); John Perry, *État présent de la grande Russie* (La Haye: H. Dusanzet, 1717).
25 François-Marie Voltaire, *Histoire de l'Empire de Russie sous Pierre le Grand* (Paris: 1763), reproduced in *Oeuvres historiques* (Paris: Pléiade, 1957).
26 François-Marie Voltaire, 'Lettres à Catherine II en 1762, 1765, 1766', in *Correspondence* (Genève: Bastermann, 1953–1965).
27 Denis Diderot, 'Questions a Catherine II sur la situation économique de l'Empire de Russie', In Michel Maurice Tourneux ed., *Diderot et Catherine II* (Paris: Calmann Lévy, 1899), reproduced in 'Mémoires pour Catherine II', 11, 813–817.
28 Denis Diderot, 'Observations sur le Nakaz de Catherine II', in *Œuvres Politiques* (Paris: Garnier, 1963): 365.
29 Michel Duchet, *Anthropologie et histoire au siècle des Lumières* (Paris: Albin Michel, 1971): 134 sq.
30 Bonnot-Etienne Condillac, *Œuvres complètes* (Paris: PUF, 1947) vol. XX, (original published in 1798): 63–64.

31 Yves Benot, 'Condorcet journaliste et le combat anti-esclavagiste', in *Condorcet mathématicien, économiste, philosophe et homme politique* (Paris: Minerve, 1989): 376–384; Joseph Jurt, 'Condorcert: l'idée de progrès et l'opposition à l'esclavage', in *Condorcet mathématicien, économiste, philosophe et homme politique* (Paris: Minerve, 1989): 385–395.

32 On Raynal's influence on Radishchev: V.I., Moriakov *Iz istorii evoliutsii obshchstvenno-politiceheskikh vzgliadov prosvetitelei kontsa XVIII veka: Reinal' i Radishchev* (On the history of the evolution of the socio-political orientations of the Enlightenment in the eighteenth century) (Moscow: Nauka, 1981); Allison Blakely, 'American Influences on Russian Reformists in the Era of the French Revolution', *Russian Review*, 52, 4 (1993): 451–471.

33 On the impact of the American case on Russia at the time: Richard Hellie, *Slavery in Russia, 1450–1723* (Chicago: University of Chicago Press, 1982).

34 Marcus Green (ed.), *Rethinking Gramsci* (New York: Routledge 2011).

35 Dipesh Chakrabarty, *Provincializing Europe* (Princeton: Princeton University Press, 2000).

36 Frederick Cooper, *Colonialism in Question. Theory, Knowledge, History* (Berkeley: University of California Press, 2005).

37 A brilliant summary of criticisms of both subaltern studies and Wallerstein in Cooper, *Colonialism*, 2005.

38 Peter Burke, ed., *The New Cambridge Modern History* (Cambridge: Cambridge University Press, 1979), in particular the Introduction by Peter Burke; Fernand Braudel, *Civilisation matérielle, économie et capitalisme* (Paris: Colin, 3 vols. 1977–1979); Eric Hobsbawn, *On History* (New York, New Press, 1997).

39 Esther Kingston-Mann, 'Marxism and Russian Rural Development: Problems of Evidence, Experience and Culture', *American Historical Review*, 84 (Oct. 1981): 731–752. James Y. Jr., Simms, 'The Crisis in Russian Agriculture at the End of the Nineteenth Century: A Different View', *Slavic Review*, 36 (Sept. 1977): 377–398.

40 Steven Hoch, 'Famine, Disease and Mortality Patterns in the Parish of Boshervka, Russia, 1830–1932', *Population Studies*, 52, 3 (1998): 357–368. Steven Hoch, 'On Good Numbers and Bad: Malthus, Population Trend and Peasant Standard of Living in Late Imperial Russia', *Slavic Review*, 53, 1 (1994): 41–75. Steven Hoch, 'Serfs in Imperial Russia: Demographic Insights', *Journal of Interdisciplinary History*, 13, 2 (1982): 221–246.

41 Judith Pallot, *Land Reform in Russia 1906–1917: Peasant Responses to Stolypin's Project of Rural Transformation* (Oxford: Clarendon Press, 1999); Steven Nafziger 'Communal Institutions, Resource Allocation, and Russian Economic Development' (Unpublished Ph.D. dissertation, Yale University, 2006).

42 Paul Gregory, *Russian National Income, 1885–1913* (Cambridge: Cambridge University Press, 1982): 126–130; 168–194; 1999, 487–488.

Chapter 2

1. Karl Wittfogel, *Oriental Despotism. A Comparative Study of Total Power* (New Haven: Yale University Press, 1957).
2. To mention only a few references in a massive bibliography: François Barnier, *Un libertin dans l'Inde moghole (1656-1669)* (Paris: Chandeigne, 2008); Michèle Duchet, *Anthropologie et histoire au siècle des Lumières* (Paris: Albin Michel, 1971).
3. Claude de Grève, *Le Voyage en Russie* (Paris: Laffont, 1990).
4. Angus Maddison, *Contours of the World Economy, 1-2030 AD* (Oxford: Oxford University Press, 2007).
5. Charles Tilly, *Coercion, Capital and European States. AD 990-1991* (Cambridge-Oxford: Blackwell, 1990).
6. Marc Bloch, *Apologie pour l'histoire ou métier d'historien* (Paris: Colin, 1993, orig. 1949).
7. Nicola Di Cosmo, *Ancient China and Its Enemies. The Rise of Nomadic Power in East Asian History* (Cambridge: Cambridge University Press, 2002).
8. Arnaldo Momigliano, *Problèmes d'historiographie ancienne et moderne* (Paris: Gallimard, 1983).
9. David Morgan, *The Mongols*, (2e éd., Malden: Blackwell, 2007); Fernand Braudel, *La Méditerranée à l'époque de Philippe II* (Paris: Armand Colin, 1949); J. L. Anderson, 'Piracy and World History: An Economic Perspective on Maritime Predation', *Journal of World History*, 6 (1995): 175-199.
10. For a reassessment of the role of nomads: Scott Levi, *India and Central Asia. Commerce and Culture* (Oxford – Delhi: Oxford University Press, 2007). On pirates: Janice Thomson, *Mercenaries, Pirates and Sovereigns* (Princeton: Princeton University Press, 1994).
11. Nicola di Cosmo, 'State Formation and Periodization in Inner Asian History', *Journal of World History*, 10, 1 (1999): 1-40.
12. Reinhart Koselleck, *Le Futur passé. Contribution à la sémantique des temps historiques* (Paris: EHESS, 1990).
13. Eric Hobsbawn, 'The General Crisis of the European Economy in the 17th century', *Past and Present*, 6, 1 (1954): 33-53; Niels Steensgaard, *The Asian Trade Revolution of the 17th Century: The East India Company and the Decline of the Caravan Trade* (Chicago: University of Chicago Press, 1975).
14. Fernand Braudel, *Civilisation matérielle, économie et capitalisme* (Paris: Armand Colin, 3 vol., 1977-1979).
15. Barrington Moore, Jr., *The Social Origins of Dictatorship* and *Democracy* (Boston: Beacon Press, 1966).
16. Donald Ostrowki, *Muscovy and the Mongols: Cross-Cultural Influences on the Steppe Frontier, 1304-1589* (Cambridge: Cambridge University Press, 1998).

17 Jane Burbank, Frederick Cooper, *Empires in World History: Power and the Politics of Difference* (Princeton: Princeton University Press, 2010).
18 Muzzafar Alam, *The Languages of Political Islam. India 1200–1800* (Chicago: The University of Chicago Press, 2004).
19 Geoffrey Parker, *The Military Revolution and the Rise of the West, 1500–1800* (Cambridge: Cambridge University Press, 1988).
20 Jeremy Black, *European Warfare, 1600–1815* (New Haven: Yale University Press, 1994).
21 John Keep, *Soldiers of the Tsar: Army and Society in Russia, 1462–1874* (Oxford: Clarendon Press, 1985).
22 On these aspects: Carole Steven Balkins, *Soldiers of the Steppe: Army Reform and Social Change in Early Modern Russia* (Dekalb, Illinois: Northern Illinois University Press 1995); Alessandro Stanziani, 'The Legal Statute of Labour in the Seventeenth to the Nineteenth Century: Russia in a Comparative European Perspective', *International Review of Social History*, 54 (2009): 359–389.
23 Among those who maintain this position: Jerome Blum, *Lord and Peasants in Russia from the Ninth through the 19th Century* (New York: Atheneum, 1964).
24 For a comparison between Mughal India, the Safavid Empire and the Ottoman Empire: Stephen Dale, *The Muslim Empires of the Ottoman, Safavids, and Mughal* (Cambridge: Cambridge University Press, 2009); Rohan D'Souza, 'Crisis Before the Fall: Some Speculations on the Decline of the Ottomans, Safavids and Mughals', *Social Scientist*, 30 (September-October 2002): 3–30.
25 Duchet, *Anthropologie et histoire*.
26 Alessandro Stanziani, 'Free Labor-Forced Labor: an Uncertain Boundary? The Circulation of Economic Ideas between Russia and Europe from the 18th to the Mid-19th Century', *Kritika. Explorations in Russian and Eurasian History*, 9, 1 (2008): 1–27.
27 Frederick Cooper's summary in: *Colonialism in Question* (Berkeley: University of California Press, 2005).
28 Braudel, Hobsbawm and the *Cambridge Economic History* all emphasize the destruction of resources due to war. Braudel, *Civilisation matérielle, économie et capitalisme*; Eric Hobsbawm, *The Age of Empire* (New York: Vintage books, 1987).
29 Christopher Duffy, *Russia's Military Way to the West: Origins and Nature of Russian Military Power, 1700–1800* (London: Routledge, 1981).
30 David Holloway, *Stalin and the Bomb: The Soviet Union and the Atomic Energy, 1939–1956* (New Haven: Yale University Press, 1994).
31 Robert Allen, *The British Industrial Revolution in Global Perspective* (Cambridge: Cambridge University Press, 2009).
32 Kenneth Pomeranz, *The Great Divergence. China, Europe, and the Making of the Modern World Economy.* (Princeton: Princeton University Press, 2000).
33 Eric Hobsbawm, *The Age of Extremes: A History of the World, 1914–1991* (London: Vintage, 1996).

34 Jared Diamond, *Guns, Germs, and Steel: The Fates of Human Societies* (New York: Norton, 1999).
35 Mikhail Khodarkovsky, *Russia's Steppe Frontier. The Making of a Colonial Empire, 1500–1800* (Bloomington-Indianapolis: Indiana University Press, 2002).
36 Pierre Bonnassie, *From Slavery to Feudalism* (Cambridge: Cambridge University Press, 1991); Léopold Genicot, *Rural Communities in the Medieval West* (Baltimore: John Hopkins University, 1990); Georges Duby, *Les trois Ordres ou l'imaginaire du féodalisme* (Paris: Gallimard, 1978); John Munro, 'Crisis and Change in Late Medieval English Economy', *Journal of Economic History*, 58, 1 (1998): 215–219; Tom Scott ed., *The Peasantries of Europe. From the 14th to the 18th Centuries* (London: Longman, 1998).
37 Philip Hoffman, *Growth in a Traditional Society. The French Countryside, 1450–1815* (Princeton: Princeton University Press, 1996).
38 On relations between cities and the countryside in nineteenth century France: Gilles Postel-Vinay, 'The Disintegration of Traditional Labour Markets in France: from Agriculture and Industry to Agriculture or Industry', *in* George Grantham, Mary MacKinnon eds., *Labor Market Evolution: The Economic History of Market Integration, Wage Flexibility and the Employment Relation* (London-New York: Routledge, 1994): 64–84.
39 Sheilagh Ogilvie, Markus Cerman eds., *European Proto-industrialisation* (Cambridge: Cambridge University Press, 1996).
40 Arno Mayer, *The Persistence of the Old Regime: Europe from 1848 to the Great War* (New York: Pantheon, 1981).
41 Alexander Gershenkron, *Economic Backwardness in Historical Perspective* (Cambridge, Mass.: Harvard University Press, 1962). On Indian backwardness and its critique: Christopher Alan Bayly, *The Imperial Meridian* (London: Longman, Pearson Education, 1989).
42 Kirti N. Chaudhuri, *The Trading World of Asia and the English East India Company, 1660–1760* (Cambridge: Cambridge University Press, 1978); Denys Lombard, *Le Carrefour javanais* (Paris: EHESS, 3 vol., 1990; re-edited in 2004).
43 Khodarkovsky, *Russia's Steppe Frontier*.
44 Michael Pearsons, *The Indian Ocean* (London: Routledge, 2003).
45 Bin Wong, 'Entre monde et nation: les régions braudeliennes en Asie', *Annales HSC*, 56, 1 (2001): 5–41.
46 Stephen Dale, *Indian Merchants and Eurasian Trade, 1600–1750* (Cambridge: Cambridge University Press, 1994). Philippe Beaujard, 'The Indian Ocean in Eurasian and African World-Systems before the Sixteenth Century', *Journal of World History*, 16, 4 (2005): 411–465; Kirti N. Chaudhuri, *Asia Before Europe: Economy and Civilization in the Indian Ocean from the Rise of Islam to 1750* (Cambridge: Cambridge University Press, 1990).

47 Alam, *The Language of Political Islam*.
48 This point is also made by Bayly, *The Imperial Meridian*.
49 Natalia F. Demidova, Viktor S. Miasnikov eds., *Russko-kitaiskie otnosheniia v xvii veke: materialy i dokumenty* (Russian-Chinese relations in the 17th century: materials and documents) (2 vv Moscow: Nauka, 1969–1972); Natalia F. Demidova ed., *Materialy po istorii russko-mongol'skikh otnoshenii: russko-mongol'skie otnosheniia, 1654–1685 sbornik dokumentov* ('Materials for the history of Russian-Mongol relations: Russian-Mongol Relations, 1654–1685, collection of documents'), (Moscow: Izdatel'skaia Firma Vostochnaia Lietartura, 1995, 1996, 2000) with archive documents.
50 Oleg D. Chekhovich, *Samarkandie dokumenty, XV-XVI vv.*, (documents on Samarkand, 15th–16th centuries) (Moscow, 1974, in Persian with Russian translation); Rozia G. Mukminova, *Sotsial'naia differentiatiia naseleniia gorodov Uzbekistana v XV-XVIe vv*, (The social differentiation of the population of the cities in Uzbekistan in the 15th and 16th centuries) (Tashkent, 1985). The original documents in Persian are also translated by Scott Levi, *The Indian Diaspora in Central Asia, 1550–1900* (Leiden: Brill, 2002): Appendix one.
51 Sh. B. Chimitdorzhiev, *Vzaimootnosheniia Mongolii i Rossii v 17–18 vekakh* (Relations between Mongolia and Russian in the 17th and 18th centuries), (Moscow: Nauka, 1978); Igor Ia Zlatkin, Nikolai V. Ustiugov eds., *Materialy po Istorii russko-mongolskikh otnoshenii: russko-mongol'skie otnosheniia 1607–1636, sbornik dokumentov* (Materials for the history of Russian-Mongol relations: Russian-Mongol Relations 1607–1636, collection of documents) (Moscow: Izdatel'estvo vostochnoi literatury, 1959).
52 *Kazakhsko-russkie otnosheniia v 16–18 vekakh, Sbornik dokumentov i materialov* (Russian-Kazak relations in the 18th century. Collection of materials and documents), (Alma-Ata: Akademia nauk Kazakhskoi SSSR, 1961 and 1964): 88, 209, 33, 64, 76, 181, 184. *Mezhdunarodnye otnosheniia v Tsentral'noi Azii: 17-18vv. Dokumenty I materialy* (International relations in Central Asia, 17th-18th centuries. Documents and materials), (2 vol., Moscow: Nauka, 1989).
53 Katerina A. Antonova, Nikolai M. Gol'dberg, *Russko-Indyskie Otnosheniia v XVIII veke: sbornik dokumentov* (Russian-Indian relations in the 18th century: collection of documents), (Moscow: Nauka, 1965).

Chapter 3

1 David Moon, 'Peasant Migration and the Settlement of Russian Frontier, 1550–1897', *The Historical Journal*, 40, 4 (1997): 859–893.
2 Jerome Blum, *Lord and Peasants in Russia from the Ninth through the 19th Century* (New York: Atheneum, 1964).

3   Amitai Reuvan and Michal Biran eds., *Mongols, Turks, and Others: Eurasian Nomads and the Sedentary World* (Boston: Brill, 2005).
4   Brian Davies, *Warfare, State and Society on the Black Sea Steppe, 1500–1700* (London: Routledge, 2007).
5   The documents pertaining to these events were collected from archives by the Tsarist Academy of Sciences in the late 18th century. C. H. van Schoonveld (ed.), *Slavic Printings and Reprinting*, 251 (The Hague-Paris: Mouton, 1970): *Prodolzhenie drevnei rossiskoi vivliofiki*, 11 volumes. Original published by Imperator. Akademiia Nauk, Saint Petersburg, 1786–1801.
6   Williard Sunderland, *Taming the Wild Field: Colonization and Empire on the Russian Steppe* (Ithaca: Cornell University Press, 2004).
7   Michael Khodarkovsky, *Russia's Steppe Frontier: The Making of a Colonial Empire, 1500–1800* (Bloomington and Indianapolis: Indiana University Press, 2002).
8   Among the others: Khodarkovsky, *Russia's Steppe Frontier*; Sunderland, *Taming the Wild Field*; Andreas Kappeler, *The Russian Empire: A Multiethnic History* (London: Pearson, 2001); Francine Hirsch, *Empire of Nations. Ethnographic Knowledge and the Making of the Soviet Empire* (Ithaca: Cornell University Press, 2005).
9   Geoffrey Parker, *The Military Revolution and the Rise of the West, 1500–1800* (Cambridge: Cambridge University Press, 1988).
10 David B. Ralston, *Importing the European Army: The Introduction of European Military Techniques and Institutions into the Extra-European World, 1600–1914* (Chicago: University of Chicago Press, 1990).
11 Jeremy Black, *European Warfare, 1600–1815* (New Haven: Yale University Press, 1994).
12 Richard Hellie, *Enserfment and Military Change in Muscovy* (Chicago: University of Chicago Press, 1971); Carol Belkins Stevens, *Soldiers of the Steppe: Army Reforms and Social Change in early Modern Russia* (Dekalb: Northern Illinois University Press, 1995).
13 Hellie, *Enserfement*: 157, 185.
14 Prior to this date, bronze was expensive and Russians had to resort to iron-based leagues that produced poor quality canons and rifles.
15 Davies, *Warfare, State*: 73–76.
16 Aleksandr V. Chernov, *Vooruzhennye sily Russkogo gosudarstva v XV-XVI vv.* (The defence forces of the Muscovite estate in the 15th and 16th centuries), (Moscow: Ministerstvo Oborony, 1954).
17 Aleksandr' Z. Myshlaevskii, *Ofitserskii vopros v XVII veke* (The officer problem in the 17th century), (Saint-Petersburg: tipografiia Glavnoe upravlenie udelov 1899).
18 Belkins Stevens, *Soldiers of the Steppe*.
19 Nikolai I. Kostomarov, *Smutnoe vremia Moskovskogo gosudarstva v nachale XVII stoletiia, 1604–1613* (The Time of Troubles in the State of Muscovy at the early 17th century, 1604–1613), (Moscow: Charli, 1994).

20 *Akty, sobrannye v bibliothekakh i arkivakh Rossiskoi Imperii arkheograficheskii ekspeditsieiu imperatoskoi akademiia nauk* (Acts collected in the libraries and archives of the Russian Empire by the archaeographical expeditions of the Imperial Academy of Sciences), 4 vol., (Saint Petersburg, 1836, 1858, particularly volume 3).
21 Aleksei I. Iakovlev, *Zasechnaia cherta Moskovskogo gosudarstva v XVII veka* (The limits of Muscovy in the 17th century), (Moscow: tipografiia Lissner 1916).
22 Michael Khodarkovsky, *Russia's Steppe Frontier*.
23 David B. Ralston, *Importing the European Army*.
24 Davies, *Warfare, State*.
25 Cf. the special issue 'Noblesse, État et société en Russie. xvie-début du xixe siècle', *Cahiers du monde russe et soviétique*, XXXIV 1-2 (1993).
26 John Keep, *Soldiers of the Tsar. Army and Society in Russia, 1462-1874* (Oxford: Oxford University Press, 1985).
27 Belkins Stevens, *Soldiers of the Steppe*.
28 Viktor P. Zagorovskii, *Belgorodskaia cherta, (The Belgorod line of defence)* (Voronezh: Voronezhskii Gosudarstvennui Universitet, 1969).
29 Dianne I. Smith, 'Muscovite Logistics 1462-1598', *Slavonic and East European Review*, 71, 1 (January 1993): 35-65.
30 Richard Hellie, *Slavery in Russia* (Chicago: University of Chicago Press, 1982).
31 Davies, *Warfare, State*: 179.
32 John Le Donne, *Absolutism and Ruling Class: the Formation of the Russian Political Order, 1700-1825* (Oxford: Oxford University Press, 1991): 276-277, Table 15.1.
33 Evgenii V. Anisimov, 'Remarks on the Fiscal Policy of Russian Absolutism During the First Quarter of the Eighteenth Century', *Soviet Studies in History*, 28, 1 (1989): 10-32; EvgeniiV. Anisimov, *Podatnaia reforma Petra I: vvedenie podushnoi podati v Rossii 1719-1728 gg* (Tax reform under Pierre I: the introduction of per capita taxation in Russia, 1719-1728), (Moscow: Nauka, 1982); Paul Bushkovitch, 'Taxation, Tax Farming and Merchants in Sixteenth-Century Russia', *Slavic Review*, 37, 3 (1978): 381-398.
34 Belkins Stevens, *Soldiers of the Steppe*.
35 Tamara Kondrateva, *Gouverner et nourrir. Du pouvoir en Russie*, xvie-xxe siècles (Paris: Les Belles Lettres, 2002).
36 RGADA, fond 210 (Razriad), Belgorodskii stol, knigi 643, 772.
37 Belkins Stevens, *Soldiers of the Steppe*: 45.
38 RGADA, fond 210, Belgorodskii stol, knigi 118 and 152.
39 RGADA, fond 210,Belgorodskii stol, knigi 118 and 156.
40 Viktor M. Vazhinskii, 'Vvedenie podushnogo oblozheniia na iuge Rossii v 90-kh godov XVII veka' (The introduction of per capita taxation in the south of Russia during the 1690s of the 17th century), *Izvestiia Voronzhskogo gospedinstituta*, 127 (1973): 88-103.
41 Belkins Stevens, *Soldiers of the Steppe*.

42 Simon Dixon, *The Modernization of Russia, 1676–1825* (Cambridge: Cambridge University Press, 1999).
43 E. A. Razin, *Istoriia voennogo iskusstva, XVI-XVII vv* (Military history 16th-17th centuries), (Saint Petersburg: Poligon, 1994).
44 Hellie, *Enserfment*: 191, 227.
45 Mykhailo Hrushevsky, *History of Ukraine-Rus'*, vol. 7 and 8 (The Cossack Age to 1625 and from 1626 to 1650), (Edmonton: Canadian Institute of Ukrainian Studies, 2002).
46 Belkins Stevens, *Soldiers of the Steppe*: 67–68.
47 Vladimir P. Zagorovskii, *Belgorodskaia cherta* (The Belgorod line of defence), (Voronezh: Izdanie Voronezhskogo Universiteta 1969).
48 Thomas Esper, 'The odnodvortsy and the Russian Nobility', *Slavonic and East European Review*, 45 (1967): 124–135.
49 RGADA, fond 210 Belgorodskii stol, kniga 772.
50 Belkins Stevens, *Soldiers of the Steppe*: 146.
51 On peasant mobility, see RGADA, fond 294, opis'2. Emilia I. Indova, 'Rol' dvortsovoi derevni pervoi poloviny XVIII v. v formirovanii russkogo kupechestva' [The role of the village court during the first half of the eighteenth century in the formation of a Russian] *Istoricheskie Zapiski*, 68 (1961): 189–210.
52 RGADA, fond 615 (krepostnye knigi mestnyjh uchrezhdenii XVI–XVIII v), opis' 1; fond 294 (Manufaktor-Kontora), *opis-1-3*.
53 Edgar Melton, 'The Russian Peasantries, 1450–1860', In Tom Scott (ed.), *The Peasantries of Europe* (London: Longman, 1998), 227–268.
54 Arcadius Kahan, *The Plow, the Hammer, and the Knout: An Economic History of Eighteenth-century Russia* (Chicago: University of Chicago Press, 1985), 76–77.
55 RGIA, fond 379 opis'1; PSZ, sery 1, vol. 40 n 21779; vol. 32 n. 25150.
56 On this Link: Moon, 'Peasants Migration'; Khodarkovsky, *Russia's Steppe Frontier*; Sunderland, *Taming the Wild Field*.
57 Number of documents in that sense in RGADA, fond 16, opis' 1. For example delo 189.
58 Melton, 'The Russian Peasantries', 227–268.
59 Moon, 'Peasant Migration'; Williard Sunderland, 'Peasants on the Move: State Peasant Resettlement in Imperial Russia, 1805–1830', *Russian Review* 52, 4 (1993): 472–485.
60 David Moon, *The Russian Peasantry, 1600–1930: The World the Peasants Made* (London and New York: Addison Wesley Longman, 1999).

Chapter 4

1 This chapter is a revised version of Chapter 3 in my *Bondage. Labor and Rights in Eurasia, Seventeenth–Early Twentieth Century* (New York and Oxford: Berghahn Books, 2014). I amgrateful to Berghahn Books for having granted permission.

2 Among the scholars who have defended this argument: on India: Gyan Prakash, *Bonded Histories: Genealogies of Labor Servitude in Colonial India* (Cambridge: Cambridge University Press, 1990); on Africa: Paul Lovejoy, *The Ideology of Slavery in Africa* (Beverly Hills: Sage, 1981); Paul Lovejoy, Toyin Fayola, *Pawnship, Slavery and Colonialism in Africa* (Asmara: Africa World Press, 2003). On China: Anders Hansson, *Chinese Outcast. Discrimination and Emancipation in Late Imperial China* (Leiden: Brill, 1996); Harriet Zurndorfer, *Change and Continuity in Chinese Local History* (Leiden: Brill,1989); Chris M. Wilbur, *Slavery in China During the Former Han Dynasty* (Chicago: Field Museum of Natural History, 1943).

3 UNICEF, *The State of the World's Children* (Oxford: Oxford University Press, 1991); ILO, *International Labor Conference, Papers and Proceedings* (Geneva, 2001); IPEC, *Every Child Counts: New Global Estimates on Child Labor* (Geneva, BIT, 2002); Suzanne Miers, 'Contemporary Forms of Slavery', in Richard Roberts, Philip Zachuernuk, eds., *Canadian Journal of African Studies*. Special issue: On slavery and Islam in African History: a tribute to Martin Klein, 34, 3 (2000): 714–747.

4 Some references in a huge bibliography: Claude Meillassoux, *Anthropologie de l'esclavage* (Paris: PUF, 1986); Moses Finley, *Esclavage moderne et idéologie antique* (Paris: Editions de minuit, 1981); Suzanne Miers, Igor Kopytoff, eds., *Slavery in Africa: Historical and Anthropological Perspectives* (Madison: University of Wisconsin Press, 1977); Eric Williams, *Capitalism and Slavery* (Chapel Hill: University Of North Carolina Press), 1944; Michael Bush, ed., *Serfdom and Slavery* (Longman: New York and London, 1996); Stanley Engerman, ed., *Terms of Labor: Slavery, Freedom and Free Labor* (Stanford: Stanford University Press, 1999); Orlando Patterson, *Slavery and Social Death: a Comparative Study* (Cambridge: Cambridge University Press, 1982); Paul Lovejoy, *Transformations in Slavery: A History of Slavery in Africa* (Cambridge: Cambridge University Press, 1983). On the translation of Islamic institutions with slavery: Ehud Toledano, *Slavery and Abolition in the Ottoman Middle East* (Seattle and London: University of Washington Press, 1998).

5 Martin Klein, ed., *Breaking the Chains: Slavery, Bondage and Emancipation in Modern Africa and Asia* (Madison: University of Wisconsin Press, 1993).

6 On this: Jack Goldstone, 'The Rise of the West or Not? A Revision to Socio-economic History', *Sociological Theory*, 18, 2 (2000): 175–194.

7 Richard Hellie, *Slavery in Russia, 1450–1725* (Chicago: University of Chicago Press, 1982).

8 Richard Hellie, 'Recent Soviet Historiography on Medieval and Early Modern Russian Slavery', *Russian Review*, 35, 1 (1976): 1–36; Herbert Leventer, 'Comments on Richard Hellie', *Russian Review*, 36, 1 (1977): 64–67; Richard Hellie, 'Reply', *Russian Review*, 36, 1 (1977): 68–75.

9 Fayola, Lovejoy, *Pawnship, Slavery*.

10 Engerman, *Terms of Labor*, 'Introduction'.
11 Peter Perdue, *China Marches West: The Qing Conquest of Central Eurasia* (Harvard, Mass.: Belknap Press, 2005); Michael Khodarkovsky, *Russia's Steppe Frontier. The Making of a Colonial Empire, 1500-1800* (Bloomington and Indianapolis: Indiana University Press, 2002); Nicolas di Cosmo, 'Ancient Inner Asian Nomads: Their Economic Basis and Its Significance in Chinese History', *Journal of Asian Studies*, 53 (1993): 1092-1126, 'State Formation and Periodization in Inner Asian History', *Journal of World History*, 10 (1999): 1-40; David Christian, *A History of Russia, Central Asia and Mongolia* (Malden: Blackwell, 1998); S. A. M. Adshead, *Central Asia in World History* (New York: St. Martin's Press, 1993); André Gunder Frank, *The Centrality of Central Asia* (Amsterdam: VU University Press, 1992).
12 Charles Tilly, *Coercion, Capital, and European States. AD 990-1992* (Cambridge: Blackwell, 1990).
13 Douglass North, *Structure and Change in Economic History* (New York: Norton 1981); Eric Jones, *Growth Recurring. Economic Change in World History* (Ann Arbor: University of Michigan Press, 1988).
14 Jane Burbank, Fred Cooper, *Empires in World History*. (Princeton: Princeton University Press, 2010).
15 Rossiikii Gosudastvenny Arkhiv Drevnikh Aktov (henceforth: RGADA), *Kholopii prikaz*, fond 210 (Razriadnyi prikaz), fond 396 (*archiv oruzhennoi palaty*, opis'1, chasty *1, 2, 4, 5, 7, 11, 24, 26-33, 35, 36, opis'2, ch. 2*.
16 RGADA, fond 210 and 141, opis'1, Dokumenty tsarskogo arkhiva i posol'skogo prikaza; fond 109 (snosheniia Rossii s Bukharoi), opis'1, 1643; fond 123 (Snosheniia Rossii s Krymom), opis'2 in particular; fond 127 (Snosheniia Rossii s Nogaiskimi Tatarami).
17 Halil Inalcik, *Sources and Studies on the Ottoman Black Sea. The Customs Register of Caffa, 1487-1990* (Cambridge, Mass.: Harvard University Press, 1996).
18 Archivio di stato di Genova (ASG), Massaria Caffae, 1374, fol. 1-354. See G. Bratianu, *Actes des notaires genois de Pira et de Caffa de la fin du XIIIe siècle (1281 1290)* (*Bucharest*: Académie Roumaine, Etudes et Recherches, ii, 1927); Michel Balard, *Gênes et L'Outre Mer, I: Les Actes de Caffa du notaire Lamberto di Sambuceto 1289-1290* (Paris-The Hague: Mouton, 1973). For later testimony, see Giorgio Balbi, 'Atti rogati a Caffa da Nicolo' Beltrame (1343-1344)', in Giorgio Balbi, Stefano Raiteri, *Notai genovesi in Oltremare: Atti rogati a Caffa e a Licostomo (sec. XIV)* (Collana Storica di Fonti e Studi, 14, Genoa, 1973).
19 Giorgio Pistarino, *Notai genovesi in Oltremare. Atti rogati a Chilia da Antonio di Ponzo (1362-1369)*, (Genoa: Collana Storica di Fonti e Studi, I 3, 1971).
20 Marhall Poe, 'What did Russians Mean when They Called Themselves Slaves of the Tsar?', *Slavic Review*, 57, 3 (1998): 585-608.
21 For example: *Russko-dagenstanskie otnosheniia XVII-pervoi chetverti XVIII vv: Dokumenty i materially*, (Russian-Daghestan relations during the seventeenth

22 Aleksandr' I. Iakovlev, *Kholopstvo i kholopy v moskovskom gosudarstve XVII v.* (*kholopstvo* and *kholopy* in the Russian state, Seventeenth century) (Moscow: Nauka, 1943): 16–17.
23 This expression has usually been translated as: any free person marrying a slave becomes a slave (Hellie, *Slavery*: 93). This translation takes for granted that *kholop* meant 'slave' and that *rab* was synonymous with *kholop*. But we have seen that the meaning of *rab* changed over time; also, if both *rab* and *kholop* meant 'slave', then, the quoted expression does not contain any reference to 'free person'; and the proposed interpretation assumes such a reference (except if one argues that a *kholop* was a free person). On the contrary, one overcomes these difficulties by accepting the argument that *kholop* signified a form of bondage, that *rab* expressed a particular bondage, and that, in the case of marriage between a *kholop* and a *rab*, they were jointly responsible for each other's obligation.
24 'Ole strashno ciudo I divno, brat'e, poidosha synove na ottsa, a ottsy na deti, brat nab rata, raby na gospodinu, a gospodin na raby', *Lavrente'eskaia letopis' pod 1216*, izd 1897, p. 419 quoted in Iakovlev, *Kholopstvo*: 29.
25 Mikhail F. Vladimirskii-Budanov, *Obzor istorii russkogo prava* (Summary of the history of Russian law) (6th edn. Kiev: Izdanie knigoprodstva N. Ia. Oglobina, 1909); *Entsiklopedicheskii slovar' Brokgauz-Efron* (Encyclopaedia Brokgauz-Efron), vol. XVI (Saint-Petersburg: Brokgauz, 1895), entry for *krest'ianie* (peasant), 681. See also *Slovar' russkogo iazika XVIII veka* (Dictionary of the Russian language of the eighteenth century), (Saint-Petersburg: Sorokin, 1998) vol. 10, entry for *krepostnoi*. Hellie, *Slavery*; Evgeniia I. Kolycheva, *Kholopstvo i krepostinichestvo, konets XV-XVI vek* (The *kholopy* and enserfment, end of the fifteenth century to sixteenth century), (Moscow: Nauka, 1971); Viktor M. Paneiakh, *Kholopstvo v pervoi polovine XVII veke* (Kholopstvo in the first half of the seventeenth century), (Leningrad: Nauka, 1984).
26 Iakovlev, *Kholopy*: 15.
27 Daniel Kaiser, trans. and ed., *The Russkaia Pravda: The Expanded Redaction* in *The Laws of Russia. Series I: The Laws of Rus'—Tenth to Fifteenth Centuries* (Salt Lake City: Charles Schlacks, 1992): 31–32.
28 Kaiser, *Russkaia Pravda*, article 110.
29 Ibid., articles 117, 119, 120.
30 Nancy Kollmann, *By Honor Bound: State and Society in Early Modern Russia* (Ithaca and London: Cornell University Press, 1999).
31 Out of 2,499 documents containing the word *kholop* or *kholopostvo*, 2,116 refer to the *kabal'noe* variety (Hellie, *Slavery*: 33). Examples of contracts are in the

Saltykov-Shchedrin Library in Saint Petersburg, manuscript section, *Obshchee sobranie gramot*, n. 1727,1937, 1941, 2017, 2019, 2348, 2406, 2635, 2672, 3026, 3081, 3392, 3475, 3486.

32 Hellie, *Slavery*: 15.
33 *Dokumenty i dogorovnye gramoty velikikh i udel'nykh kniazei XIV-XVI vv.* (*Documents and acts decreed by princes, fourteenth-sixteenth centuries*), edited by L. V. Cherepnin and S. V. Bakhrushin (Moscow: Nauka, 1950): 409, document n. 98.
34 Paneiakh, *Kholopstvo*; Viktor Paneiakh, 'Ulozhenie 1597 g. o *kholopstve*' (Ulozhenie of 1597 on *kholopstvo*), *Istoricheskie Zapiski*, 77 (1955): 154–189.
35 In 1609, this was reduced from six to five months, and was further reduced to three months in 1649: *Akty istoricheskie, sobrannye i izdannye arkheograficheskoiu kommissieiu*, 5 vols. (Saint Petersburg, 1841–1843), 2(85).
36 Paneiakh, 'Ulozhenie 1597': 161.
37 Paneiakh, *Kabal'noe kholopstvo na Rusi v XVI veke* (Temporary limited servants in Russia in the sixteenth century), (Leningrad: Nauka, 1967): 127–128.
38 Hellie, *Slavery*: 59.
39 Richard Hellie, *Enserfment and Military Change in Muscovy* (Chicago: University of Chicago Press, 1971).
40 Paneiakh, *Kabal'noe*; Iakovlev, *Kholopstvo*.
41 Hellie, *Slavery*: 9–11.
42 Iakovlev, *Kholopstvo*: 316.
43 *Opisanie dokumentov i bumag, khraniashchikhsia v moskovskom arkhive ministerstva iustitsii* (Inventory of documents and papers kept in the Moscow archives of the Ministry of Justice), vol. 15 (Saint Petersburg, 1908).
44 Arkadii Man'kov, *Ulozhenie 1649. Kodeks feodal'nogo prava Rossii* (The law code of 1649. The code of feudal law in Russia), (Leningrad, Nauka, 1980): 113–114; Petr Ivanovich Ivanov, *Alfavitnyi ukazatel' familii i lits, upominaemykh v boiarkikh knigach, khraniashchikhsia v l-m otdelenii moskovskogo arkhiva ministerstva iustitsii*, (Alphabetical index of families and persons named in the boyari books, conserved in the first section of Moscow's Archives of the Ministry of Justice), (Moscow: Ministerstvo Iustitsii, 1853); Iakovlev, *Kholopstvo*: 496–513.
45 Hellie, *Slavery*: 211.
46 Anne Kussmaul, *Servants in Husbandry* (Cambridge: Cambridge University Press, 1981).
47 Gyan Prakash, 'Terms of Servitude: the Colonial Discourse on Slavery and Bondage in India', in Martin Klein ed., *Breaking the Chains: Slavery, Bondage and Emancipation in Modern Africa and Asia* (Madison: University of Wisconsin Press, 1986): 131–149.
48 Toledano, *Slavery*.
49 Hellie, *Slavery*: 194–198.

50 Aleksei K. Leont'ev, *Obrazovanie prikaznoi sistemy upravleniia v russkom gosudarstve. Iz istorii sozdaniia tsentralizovannogo gosudarstvennogo apparata v kontse XV-pervoi polovine XVI v.* (The formation of chancellery system in the Russian state. History of the formation of the centralized state, fifteenth-sixteenth centuries), (Moscow: Moskovskii Universitet, 1961): 179–192.

51 RGADA, *Kholopii prikaz*, fond 210 (Razriadnyi prikaz), fonds 396 (archiv oruzhenoi palaty, opis'1), chasty *1, 2, 4, 5, 7, 11, 24, 26 - 33, 35, 36, opis'2, ch. 2.*

52 Hellie, *Slavery*: 506.

53 Kolycheva, *Kholopstvo*.

54 Hellie, *Slavery*: 423–424.

55 Iakovlev, *Kholopstvo*: 35.

56 Hellie, *Serfdom*.

57 Hellie, *Slavery*: 84.

58 Jacques Heers, *Esclaves et domestiques au Moyen Age dans le monde méditerranéen* (Paris: Hachette, 1996): 67; Charles Verlinden, 'L'origine de sclavus-esclave', *Bulletin du Cange*, XVII (1942): 97–128; Charles Verlinden, 'L'esclavage du sud-est et de l'est européen en Europe orientale à la fin du moyen-âge', *Revue historique du sud-est européen*, XIX (1942): 18–29; Charles Verlinden, *L'esclavage dans l'Europe médiévale* (Bruges, 1955); Steven Epstein, *Speaking of Slavery* (Ithaca and London: Cornell University Press, 2001).

59 Herman Van der Wee, 'Structural Changes in European Long-Distance Trade, and Particularly in the Re-export Trade from South to the North, 1350–1750', in James Tracy ed., *The Rise of Merchant Empires. Long Distance Trade in the Early Modern World, 1350–1750* (Cambridge: Cambridge University Press, 1990): 14–33.

60 Roberto Sabatino Lopez, *The Commercial Revolution of the Middle Ages, 950–1350* (New York: Cambridge University Press, 1972): 92.

61 Dennis Deletant, 'Genoese, Tatars and Rumanians at the Mouth of the Danube in the Fourteenth Century', *The Slavonic and East European Review*, 62, 4 (1984): 511–530.

62 Domenico Gioffré, *Il mercato degli schiavi a Genova nel secolo XV* (Genoa: Bozzi 1971); Robert Delort, 'Quelques précisions sur le commerce des esclaves à Gênes vers la fin du XIVe siècle', *Mélanges d'archéologie et d'histoire*, 78, 1 (1966): 215–250.

63 Michel Balard, 'Esclavage en Crimée et sources fiscales génoises au XVe siècle', *Byzantinische Forschungen*, 22 (1996): 9–17, Reprinted in: Henri Bresc, ed., *Figures de l'esclave au Moyen-Age et dans le monde moderne. Actes de la table ronde organisée les 27 et 28 octobre 1992 par le Centre d'Histoire sociale et culturelle de l'Occident de l'Université de Paris-X Nanterre* (Paris: Université Paris X, 1996): 77–87.

64 Francesco Panero, *Schiavi, servi e villani nell'Italia medievale* (Turin: Paravia, 1999).

65 Gioffré, *Il mercato*.

66 Mikhail V. Kirilov, 'Slave Trade in Early Modern Crimea from the Perspective of Christian, Muslim and Jewish Sources', *Journal of Early Modern History*, 11, 1 (2007): 1–32.
67 Geoffrey Vaughan Scammell, *The World Encompassed. The First European Maritime Empires, c. 800–1650* (Berkeley: University of California Press, 1981).
68 Fernand Braudel, *Civilisation matérielle, économie et capitalisme* (Paris: Colin, 3 vols. 1977–1979); Immanuel Wallerstein, *The Modern World System* (New York, London: Academic Press, 2 vols., 1974–1980).
69 Morris Rossabi, *China and Inner Asia from 1368 to Present Day* (London: Thames and Hudson, 1975); Niels Steensgaard, *The Asian Trade Revolution of the Seventeenth Century: the East India Company and the Decline of the Caravan Trade* (Chicago: University of Chicago Press, 1973).
70 There is debate whether the caravan trade declined or was simply reshaped. For the former interpretation: Rossabi, *China*; Steensgaard, *The Asian Trade*; A.A. Askarov et al. eds., *Istoriia Uzbekistana* (History of Uzbekistan) vol. II: *Pervaia polovina XIXe veka* (First half of the nineteenth century) (Tashkent: Fan, 1993); Yuri Bregel, 'Central Asia in the Twelfth-Thirteenth/ Eighteenth-Nineteenth centuries', *Encyclopaedia Iranica* 5, fasc. 2 (Costa Mesa: Mazda, 1992): 193–205. Against this interpretation: Scott Levi, 'India, Russia and the Eighteenth Century Transformation of the Central Asian Caravan Trade', *Journal of Economic and Social History of the Orient*, 42, 4 (1999): 519–548.
71 André Wink, *Al-Hind: the Making of the Indo-Islamic World*, vol. 1, *Early Medieval India and the Expansion of Islam, Seventh-Eleventh Centuries* (Leiden: Brill 1991): 45–64.
72 Scott Levi, 'Hindus Beyond the Hindu Kush: Indians in the Central Asian Slave Trade', *Journal of the Royal Asiatic Society*, 12, 3 (2002): 277–288.
73 Levi, 'Hindus Beyond the Hindu Kush'.
74 Muzaffar Alam, 'Trade, State Policy and Regional Change: Aspects of Mughal-Uzbek Commercial Relations, c. 1550–1750', *Journal of Economic and Social History of the Orient*, 37, 3 (1994): 202–227. Surendra Gopal, *Indians in Russia in the Seventeenth and Eighteenth Centuries* (Calcutta: Naya Prokash, 1988).
75 Samuel Adrien. Adshead, *Central Asia in World History* (New York: St. Martin's Press, 1993).
76 Jos Gommans, 'Mughal India and Central Asia in the Eighteenth Century: an Introduction to a Wider Perspective', *Itinerario*, 15, 1 (1991): 51–70; Jos Gommans, 'The Horse Trade in Eighteenth-Century South Asia', *Journal of Economic and Social History of the Orient*, 37, 3 (1994): 228–250; Jos Gommans, *The Rise of the Indo-Afghan Empire, c. 1710–1780* (Leiden: Brill,1995). Islam Riazul, *Indo-Persian Relations* (Teheran: Iranian Culture foundation, 1970); K.A. Antonova, Nikolai M. Goldberg, eds., *Russko-indyskie otnosheniia v XVIII veke: sbornik dokumentov* (Russian-Indian relations in the eighteenth century. Collected documents) (Moscow: Nauka, 1965).

77 Scott Levi, *The Indian Diaspora in Central Asia and Its Trade, 1550-1900* (Leiden: Brill, 2002).
78 Levi, 'India, Russia'.
79 Janet Abu-Lughod, *Before European Hegemony. The World System A.D. 1250-1350* (New York: Oxford University Press, 1989): 178.
80 Alam, 'Trade State Policy'.
81 Oleg. D. Chekhovich, *Bukharkie dokumenty XIV veka* (Documents from Bukhara, Fourteenth century), (Tashkent: Nauka, 1965): 108-110.
82 Levi, *The Indian Diaspora*: 68.
83 Gommans, 'Mughal India and Central Asia'.
84 Audrey Burton, 'Russian Slaves in Seventeenth-Century Bukhara', in Touraj Astabaki, John O'Kane eds., *Post-Soviet Central Asia* (London: Taurus Academic studies, 1998): 345-365. Brian Glyn Williams, *The Crimean Tatars* (Leiden: Brill, 2001).
85 Levi, *Indian Diaspora*: 121-22. Also André Gunder Frank, 'Re*Orient*: From the Centrality of Central Asia to China's Middle Kingdom', in Korkut A. Ertürk ed., *Rethinking Central Asia: Non-Eurocentric Studies in History, Social Structure, and Identity* (Reading, UK: Ithaca Press, 1999): 11-38.
86 Gommans, 'Mughal India'.
87 Marshall Hodgson, *Rethinking World History* (Cambridge: Cambridge University Press, 1993); Christopher Bayly, *The Imperial Meridian* (London: Longman, Pearson Education, 1989).
88 Kirti N. Chaudhuri, *The Trading World of Asia and the English East India Company, 1660-1760* (Cambridge: Cambridge University Press, 1978).
89 Gommans, 'Mughal India'.
90 Muzzafar Alam, 'Trade, State Policy and Regional Change', in Scott Levi ed., *India and Central Asia. Commerce and Culture, 1500-1800* (Oxford: Oxford University Press, 2007); Stephen Dale, *Indian Merchants and Eurasian Trade, 1600-1750* (Cambridge: Cambridge University Press, 1994).
91 Khodarkovsky, Russia's *Steppe Frontier*: 102-103.
92 *Prodolzhenie drevnei Rossiksoi bibliofiki*, 11 vols. Saint Petersburg, Imper. Akad. Nauk, 1786-1801; reprint, C.H. van Schooneved, ed. *Slavic Printings and Reprintings*, 251 (The Hague-Paris: Mouton, 1970), vol. 8: 219-223.
93 Khodarkovsky, Russia's *Steppe Frontier*: 27.
94 Steensgaard, *The Asian Trade*.
95 Edmund Herzig, 'The Volume of Iranian Raw Silk Exports in the Safavid Period', *Iranian Studies*, 25, 1-2 (1992): 61-79. Nina G. Kukanova, *Ocherki po istorii russko-iranskikh torgovykh otnoshenii v XVII-pervoi polovine XIXev veka* (Studies on Russian-Iranian relations from the seventeenth to the first half of the Nineteenth century), (Saransk: Mordovskoe knizhnoe izd-vo, 1977).

96 Khodarkovsky, Russia's *Steppe Frontier*: 29.
97 Fernand Braudel, *La Méditerranée et le monde méditerranéen à l'époque de Philippe II* (Paris: Colin, 1949); Janice E. Thomson, *Mercenaries, Pirates and Sovereign: State-Building and Extraterritorial Violence in Early Modern Europe* (Princeton: Princeton University Press, 1994); Wolfgang Kaiser, ed., *Négociations et transferts. Les intermédiaires dans l'échange et le rachat des captifs en Méditerranée, XVIe-XVIIe siècles* (Rome: Ecole française de Rome, 2008).
98 Perdue, *China Marches West*: 39.
99 Donald Ostrowski, *Muscovy and the Mongols. Cross-Cultural Influences on the Steppe Frontier, 1304–1589* (Cambridge: Cambridge University Press, 1998); John Fennell, *Ivan the Great of Moscow* (London: MacMillan, 1961); John Fennell, *The Crisis of Medieval Russia, 1200–1304* (New York: Longman, 1983); John L. Fennell, 'The Dynastic Crisis, 1497–1502', *Slavonic and East European Studies*, 39, 92 (1960): 1–23.
100 Brian Davis, *State, Power and Community in Early Modern Russia: the Case of Kozlov, 1635–1649* (Basingstoke, New York: Palgrave, Macmillan, 2004).
101 Elena N. Shipova, *Slovar' turkizmov v russkom iazyke* (Dictionary of Turkish into Russian language) (Alma-Ata: Nauka, 1976): 442.
102 Alan Fisher, 'Muscovy and the Black Sea Trade', *Canadian-American Slavic Studies*, 6, 4 (1972): 582–593.
103 Aleksei A. Novosel'skii, *Bor'ba Moskovskogo gosudarstva s tatarami v pervoi polovine 17 veka* (The fight of the Muscovite state against the Tatars during the first half of the seventeenth century) (Moscow, Leningrad: Nauka, 1948).
104 Norman Davies, *God's Playground: a History of Poland*, 2 vols., (New York: Columbia University Press, 1982), vol. 1: 139–141; Khodarkovsky, *Russia's Steppe Frontier*: 21–22.
105 *Materialy po istorii Uzbeskoi, Tadzhikskoi I* (Materials for the history of Uzbekistan, Tajikistan, and Turkmenistan), part 1 (Leningrad: AN SSSR, 1932): 386–397, quoted in Hellie, *Slavery*: 25, note 43.
106 Hellie, Slavery.
107 William Gervase Clarence-Smith, *Islam and the Abolition of Slavery* (Oxford: Oxford University Press, 2006): 118–119.
108 Richard Hellie, ed., *The Muscovite Law Code (Ulozhenie) of 1649*, part. I (Irvine California: Charles Schlacks, 1988), Chapter 8: 17–18.
109 Rossiiskaia Akademiia nauk. Arkhiv, fond 1714, op. 1 (A.A. Novosel'skii), delo 66, l. 123; RGADA, fond 123, opis' 3, delo 13.
110 RGADA, fond 123, Krymskie dela 13, l. 53; *Materialy po istorii Uzbeksoi, Tadzhiskoi i Turkmenskoi SSR*, vol. 1 (Leningrad, Moscow: Nauka, 1932): 386–387.
111 RGADA, fond 109, opis'1, delo 1643.

112 Hellie, *Slavery*: 68–69.
113 Paul of Aleppo, *The Travels of Macarius; Extracts From the Diary of the Travels of Macarius, Patriarch of Antioch* (London: Oxford University Press, 1936, ed. by Lady Laura Ridding): 28, 76.
114 Aleksandr' L. Khoroshkevich, *Russkoe gosudarstvo v sisteme mezhdunarodnykh otnoshenii kontsa XV-nachala XVI v.* (The Russian state in the system of international relations towards the end of the fifteenth and beginning of the sixteenth century), (Moscow: Nauka, 1980): 30–32.
115 Khodarkovsky, *Russia's Steppe Frontier*: 24.
116 RGADA, fond 89, *Turetskie dela*, delo 3.
117 David Christian, *Inner Eurasia from Prehistory to the Mongol Empire* (Oxford: Blackwell, 1998).
118 Ronald Drew, 'The Siberian Fair: 1600–1750', *The Slavonic and East European Review*, 39, 93 (1961): 423–439.
119 Morris Rossabi, 'The Decline of the Central Asian Caravan Trade', in James Tracy ed., *The Rise of Merchant Empires* (Cambridge: Cambridge University Press: 1990): 351–370.
120 Antonova, Goldberg, *Russkoe-Indiiskie*.
121 Gommans, 'Mughal India'.
122 *Kazakhsko-russkie otnosheniia v 16–18 vekakh, Sbornik dokumentov i materialov* (Russian-Kazakh relations during the Sixteenth-Eighteenth centuries. Collected documents and materials), (Alma-Ata: Akademia nauk Kazakhskoi SSSR, 1961 and 1964), n. 88: 209, n. 33: 64, n. 76: 181,184. Also: *Mezhdunarodnye otnosheniia v Tsentral'noi Azii: 17–18vv. Dokumenty I materialy*, (International relations in central Asia: Seventeenth-Eighteenth centuries), 2 vols. (Moscow: Nauka, 1989).
123 After the disbanding of what the Russians called 'the Golden Horde', Mongol power fractured into several khanates in Inner and Central Asia. The Small, Middle, and Great Hordes were each ruled by a khan; they called themselves Kazakhs and were descended from Mongol and Turkic clans. They spoke Turkic and were Sunni Muslims Martha Brill-Olcott, *The Kazakhs* (Stanford: Hoover Institutions Press, 1987).
124 Clarence-Smith, *Islam*: 13.
125 Alan Fisher, 'The Ottoman Crimea in the Sixteeenth Century', *Harvard Ukrainian studies*, 2 (1981): 141–142.
126 Halil Inalcik, 'Servile Labor in Ottoman Empire', in Abraham Ascher, Tibor Halasi-Kun, and Bela Kiraly eds., *The Mutual Effects of the Islamic and Judeo-Christian Worlds: the East European Patterns* (New York, Brooklyn: College Press, 1979): 39–40; Yvonne Seng, 'Fugitives and Factotums: Slaves in Early Sixteenth-Century Istanbul', *Journal of the Economic and Social History of the Orient*, 39, 2 (1996): 136–169.

127 Fisher, 'Muscovy and the Black Sea'.
128 Halil Inalcik, 'The Custom Register of Caffa, 1487-1490', in Victor Ostapchuk ed., *Sources and Studies on the Ottoman Black Sea* (Cambridge, MA: Harvard University Press, 1996) vol. 1: 93, 145-146.
129 *Sbornik Imperatorskogo Russkogo Istoricheskogo Obshchestvo* (Collected works of the Imperial Russian historical society), vol. 41 (Saint Petersburg, 1884): 42-43, 52-53, 104-107, 115-121, 146-157.
130 Toledano, *Slavery*: 8.
131 Thomas Barrett, 'Lines of Uncertainty: the Frontier of the North Caucasus', *Slavic Review*, 54, 3 (1995): 578-601; Clarence-Smith, *Islam*: 13-14.
132 Toledano, *Slavery*: 81.
133 David Brion Davis, *Slavery and Human Progress* (New York: Oxford University Press, 1984); Robert Crummey, *The Formation of Muscovy, 1304-1614* (London: Longman, 1987).
134 *Rospisnoi spisok goroda Moskvy 1638 goda* (Lists of the town of Moscow in 1638) (Moscow: Tipografiia Moskovskogo Universiteta, 1911).
135 Ia. E. Vodarskii, *Naselenie Rossii v kontse XVII-nachale XVIII veka* (The population of Russia during the Seventeenth-early Eighteenth centuries) (Moscow: Nauka, 1977).
136 Annika Stello, 'La traite d'esclaves en Mer Noire au début du XVe siècle', paper at the international conference on: *Esclavages en Méditerranée et en Europe Centrale. Espaces de traite et dynamiques économiques (Moyen Âge et temps modernes)*, Casa de Velázquez, Madrid, 26-27 March 2009.
137 Fisher, 'Muscovy and the Black Sea': 755-583.
138 Halil Inalcik, *An Economic and Social History of the Ottoman Empire, vol. 1, 1300-1600* (Cambridge: Cambridge University Press, 1997): 285.
139 Ehud Toledano, *The Ottoman Slave Trade and its Suppression* (Princeton: Princeton University Press, 1982): 82, 90.
140 On Africa and the Indian Ocean: Lovejoy, *Transformations*; on the volume of transatlantic slaves: David Eltis, Stephen Behrendt, David Richardson, Herbert Klein, *The Trans-Atlantic Slave Trade. A Database on CD-Rom* (Cambridge: Cambridge University Press, 2000).
141 Steensgaard, *The Asian Trade*.
142 Kirti N. Chaudhuri, *Asia Before Europe. Economy and Civilization of the Indian Ocean from the Rise of Islam to 1750* (Cambridge: Cambridge University Press, 1990).
143 Gunder Frank, 'Re-Orient'; Scott Levi, *India and Central Asia*; Dale, *Indian Merchants*.
144 Levi, 'India, Russia': 528.
145 Gommans, *The Rise*.

146 Sevket Pamuk, 'The Black Death and the Origin of the Great Divergence across Europe, 1300–1600', *European Review of Economic History*, II (2007): 289–317.
147 Gillian Weiss, *Captives and Corsairs. France and Slavery in the Early Mediterranean World* (Stanford: Stanford University Press, 2011); Robert Davis, *Christian Slaves, Muslim Masters. White Slavery in the Mediterranean, the Barbary Coast, and Italy, 1500–1800* (Basingstoke: Mac Millan, 2003).
148 Paul Lovejoy, *Transformations of Slavery* (Cambridge: Cambridge University Press, 2000).

Chapter 5

1 Immanuel Wallerstein, *The Modern World-System: Capitalist Agriculture and the Origins of the European World-Economy in the Sixteenth Century* (New York, London: Atheneum, 1974, 1976); Witold Kula, *An Economic Theory of the Feudal System* (London: New Left Books, 1976); Douglass North, *Structure and Change in Economic History* (New York: Norton, 1981).
2 Kenneth Pomeranz, *The Great Divergence* (Princeton: Princeton University Press, 2000).
3 Marc Bloch, 'Serf de la glèbe. Histoire d'une expression toute faite', *Revue historique*, 36 (1921): 220–242.
4 Guy Bois, *La crise du féodalisme* (Paris: Presses de Sciences-Po, EHESS, 1976); Georges Duby, *Les trois ordres ou l'imaginaire du féodalisme*, (Paris: Gallimard, 1978); Pierre Bonnassie, *From Slavery to Feudalism* (Cambridge: Cambridge University Press, 1991); Tom Scott, ed., *The Peasantries of Europe. From the Fourteenth to the Eighteenth Centuries* (London: Longman, 1998); Paul Freedman, Monique Bourin, eds., *Forms of Servitude in Northern and Central Europe* (Turnhout: Brepols, 2005).
5 Robert Brenner, 'Agrarian Class Structure and Economic Development in Pre-Industrial Europe', *Past and Present*, 70 (1976): 30–74; Trevor Aston, Charles Philpin, eds., *The Brenner Debate: Agrarian Class Structure and Economic Development in Pre-industrial Europe* (Cambridge, Cambridge University Press, 1985); Michael North, *From the North Sea to the Baltic: Essays in Commercial, Monetary and Agrarian History, 1500–1800* (Aldershot: Ashgate, 1996); Marc Raeff, *The Well-Ordered Police State: Social and Institutional Change Through Law in the German States and Russia, 1600–1800* (New Haven: Yale University Press, 1983); William Hagen, *Ordinary Prussians: Brandenburg Junkers and Villagers, 1500–1840* (Cambridge: Cambridge University Press, 2002).
6 Jerome Blum, *Lord and Peasant in Russian from the Ninth to the Nineteenth Century* (New York: Atheneum, 1964); Alexander Gershenkron, *Economic Backwardness in*

Historical Perspective (Cambridge, MA: Harvard University Press, 1962); Richard Hellie, *Enserfment and Military Change in Muscovy* (Chicago: University of Chicago Press, 1971); Peter Kolchin, *Unfree Labor: American Slavery and Russian Serfdom*, (Cambridge: Cambridge University Press, 1987); Daniel Field, *The End of Serfdom: Nobility and Bureaucracy in Russia, 1855-1861* (Cambridge, Mass.: Harvard University Press, 1976).

7 Steven Hoch, *Serfdom and Social Control in Russia: Petrovskoe, a Village in Tambov* (Chicago: University of Chicago Press, 1986).

8 Ivan D. Koval'chenko, *Russkoe krepostnoe krest'ianstvo v pervoi polovine XIX v.* (The Russian serf economy during the first half of the nineteenth century), (Moscow: Nauka, 1967); See also Evsey Domar, M. Machina, 'On the Profitability of Russian Serfdom', *The Journal of Economic History*, 44, 4 (1984): 919–955.

9 Michael Confino, *Domaines et seigneurs en Russie vers la fin du XVIIIe siècle: Étude de structures agraires et de mentalités économiques* (Paris: Mouton, 1963); *Systèmes agraires et progrès agricole en Russie aux XVIIIe–XIXe siècles: Étude d' économie et de sociologie rurales* (Paris: Mouton, 1969); David Moon, *The Abolition of Serfdom in Russia, 1762-1907* (London: Pearson, 2001); David Moon, *The Russian Peasantry, 1600-1930* (London: Longman, 1996); Elise Kimerling Wirtschafter, *Structures of Society: Imperial Russia's 'People of various ranks'* (Dekalb: Northern Illinois University Press, 1994); Elise Kimerling Wirtschafter, *Social Identity in Imperial Russia* (Dekalb: Northern Illinois University Press, 1997).

10 Roger Bartlett, 'Serfdom and State Power in Imperial Russia', *European History Quarterly*, 33, 1 (2003): 29–64; David Moon, 'Reassessing Russian serfdom', *European History Quarterly*, 26, 1 (1996): 483–526.

11 Tracy Dennison, *The Institutional Framework of Russian Serfdom* (Cambridge: Cambridge University Press, 2011).

12 Ian Blanchard, *Russia's Age of Silver: Precious Metal Production and Economic Growth in the Eighteenth Century* (New York and London: Routledge, 1989).

13 Alessandro Stanziani, *Bondage: Labor and Rights in Eurasia, Seventeenth-early Twentieth Century* (New York: Berghahn Press, 2014).

14 Robert Crummey, 'Sources of Boyar Power in the Seventeenth Century', *Cahiers du Monde Russe et soviétique*, 34, 1–2 (1993): 107–118.

15 Edgar Melton, 'The Russian Peasantries, 1450–1860," In Tom Scott ed., *The Peasantries of Europe* (London Longman, 1998), 227–268.

16 Arcadius Kahan, *The Plow, the Hammer and the Knout: An Economic History of Eighteenth-Century Russia* (Chicago: University of Chicago Press, 1985): 76–77.

17 Melton, 'The Russian Peasantries, 1450–1860', 227–268.

18 David Moon, 'Peasant Migration and the Settlement of Russian Frontiers, 1550–1897', *The Historical Journal*, 40, 4, 1997: 859–893; Williard Sunderland, 'Peasants on the Move: State Peasant Resettlement in Imperial Russia, 1805–1830',

Russian Review, 52, 4 (1993): 472–485; Serguei I. Bruk, Vladimir M. Kabuzan, 'Dinamika chislennosti i rasselenie russkogo etnosa, 1678–1917' (La dynamique du nombre et de l'établissement des ethnies russes, 1678–1917), *Sovetskaya istoriografiya* (1982), 4: 9–25.

19 Moon, *The Russian Peasantry*: 20–21.
20 The High Chamber (senate) records several such cases in 1816. *Arkhiv gosudarstvennogo soveta*, 5 vols. (Saint Petersburg, 1869–1904), vol. 4, vyp. 1, ch. 2: 253–258.
21 Alexander Gershenkron, *Economic Backwardness in Historical Perspective: A Book of Essays* (Cambridge, Mass.: Harvard University Press 1962). Olga Crisp, 'Labor and Industrialization in Russia,' in *The Cambridge Economic History of Europe*, vol. 7, pt. 2, ed. Peter Mathias and Michael Postan (Cambridge: Cambridge University Press 1978), 308–415.
22 Bonnassie, *From Slavery*.
23 Aston and Philpin, eds., *The Brenner Debate*.
24 Blanchard, *Russia's Age of Silver*; Dennison, *The Institutional*.
25 Hoch, *Serfdom and Social Control in Russia*.
26 Vasilii I. Semevskii, *Krest'ianskii vopros v Rossii v XVIII i pervoi polovine XIX veka* (The peasant question in Russia in the eighteenth to the first half of the nineteenth century), 2 vols. (Saint Petersburg, 1888); idem, *Krest'iane v tsarstvovanie Imperatritsy Ekateriny II* (The peasantry under the reign of Catherine II), Vol. 1, 2nd ed.. (1881; Saint Petersburg, 1903), Vol. 2 (St. Petersburg, 1901).
27 Koval'chenko, *Russkoe*.
28 Peter Czap, 'The Perennial Multiple-Family Household, Mishino, Russia, 1782–1858', *Journal of Family History* (Spring, 1982): 5–26.
29 Carol Leonard, *Agrarian Reforms in Russia* (Cambridge: Cambridge University Press, 2011).
30 For a synthesis and a discussion: Sheilagh Ogilvie, Markus Cerman, eds., *European Proto-Industrialization* (Cambridge, Cambridge University Press, 1996); Pierre Jeannin, 'La proto-industrialization: développement ou impasse?', *Annales ESC*, 35 (1980): 52–65.
31 Jan De Vries, *The Industrious Revolution* (Cambridge: Cambridge University Press, 2008).
32 Sheilagh Ogilvie, 'The Economic World of the Bohemian Serf', *Economic History Review*, LIV (2001): 430–453.
33 Sheilagh Ogilvie, 'Guild, Efficiency, and Social Capital', *Economic History Review*, LVII (2004): 286–333; Carlo Poni, 'Per la storia del distretto serico di Bologna, secoli XVI-XIX', *Quaderni storici*, 73 (1990): 93–167; Gérard Gayot, *De la pluralité des mondes industriels. La manufacture royale des draps de Sedan, 1646–1870* (Paris: EHESS, 1995).

34 Boris Mironov, *The Social History of the Russian Empire*, 2 vols. (Boulder, CO: Westview, 1999).
35 *Mironov, The Social History of the Russian Empire*
36 Boris Mironov and Carol S. Leonard, 'In Search of Hidden Information: Some Issues in the Socio-Economic History of Russia in the Eighteenth and Nineteenth Centuries', *Social Science History*, 9 (Autumn 1985): 339–359; Boris Mironov, *Vnytrennii rynok Rossii vo vtoroi polovine XVIII-pervoi po-lovine XIX v.* (The domestic market in Russia during the second half of the eighteenth-first half of the nineteenth century), (Leningrad: Nauka, 1981).
37 Mironov, *Vnutrennyi rynok*: 153–154.
38 Koval'chenko, *Russkoe*.
39 Klaus Gestwa, *Protoindustrialisierung in Russland* (Göttingen: Vandenhoeck and Ruprecht, 1999); Ksenia N. Serbina, *Krest'ianskaia zhelezodelatel'naia promyshlennost' tsentral'noi Rossii XVI-pervoi poloviny XIXe vekoi* (The peasant metallurgic home industry in Central Russia, from the Sixteenth to the first half of the Nineteenth century), (Leningrad: Nauka, 1978). For the Demydov estate in Tula: RGADA, fond 271, delo 1061.
40 Tatiana F. Izmes'eva, *Rossiia v sisteme evropeiskogo rynka. Konets XIXe-nachalo XX v.* (Russia in the system of the European market. End of the nineteenth to the early twentieth century), (Moscow: Nauka, 1991).
41 Sergei Strumilin, *Ocherki ekonomicheskoi istorii Rossii i SSSR* (Studies in the economic history of Russia and the USSR) (Moscow: Nauka, 1966): 330–333; RGADA, fond 199 (G. F. Miller); Emilia I. Indova, 'O rossiskikh manufakturakh vtoroi poloviny XVIII v'. (On the Russian manufactures during the second half of the eighteenth century), *Istoricheskaia geografiia Rossii: XIX-nachalo XX v.* (Moscow: Nauka, 1975): 248–345; Emilia I. Indova, *Dvortsovoe khoziaistvo v Rossii* (The palace economy in Russia), (Moscow: Nauka, 1964).
42 Boris Mironov, 'Consequences of the Price Revolution in Eighteenth-Century Russia', *The Economic History Review*, 45 (1992): 457–478.
43 Mironov, 'Consequences': 465.
44 Lidia S. Prokov'eva, *Krest'ianskaia obshchina v Rossii vo vtoroi polovine XVIII-pervoi polovine XIX v* (The peasant commune in Russia during the second half of the eighteenth to the first half of the nineteenth centuries) (Leningrad: Nauka, 1981); Iurii A. Tikhonov, *Pomeshchic'i krest'iane v rossii: feodal'naia renta v XVII-nachale XVIII v* (The private estates' peasants in Russia: the feudal rent in the seventeenth to early eighteenth century) (Moscow: Nauka, 1974). On the urban activity of private peasants, I have consulted the following archives: RGADA, fond 294, opis' 2 and 3; fond 1287, opis' 3. TsGIAM, opis' 2, dela 31, 40, 82, 124, 146; RGADA, fond 210: razriadnyi prikaz; fond 248, Senat I senatskie uchrezhdeniia; fond 350: revizkie skazki po nizhegorodskoi gubernii, opis' 2, dela 1975 and 2056;

fonds 615, krepostnye knigi, dela 526, 528, 529, 4753, 6654; fond 1209 (pomestnyi prikaz), opis' 1, delo 292; fond 1287 (Sheremetev), opis' 5 and 6; RGIA, fond 1088 (Sheremetev, opis' 3, 5, 10). See also Gestwa, *Proto-Industrialisierung*.

45 Serbina, *Krest'ianskaia*, 37.
46 Edgar Melton, 'Proto-industrialization, Serf Agriculture and Agrarian Social Structure. Two Estates in Nineteenth-Century Russia', *Past and Present*, 115 (May 1987): 73–81.
47 RGIA, fond 1088, opis' 10, dela 616 and 618.
48 RGIA, fond 1088, opis' 10, dela 616 and 618.
49 RGIA, fond 1088, opis' 10, delo 611.
50 Sheremetev published instruktsiia in 1802 and 1832. RGIA, fond 1088, opis' 10, delo 607.
51 Robert Rudolph, 'Agricultural Structure and Proto-Industrialization in Russia: Economic Development with Unfree Labor', *The Journal of Economic History*, 45 (1985): 47–69.
52 Serbina, *Krest'ianaskaia*: 100–101; Gestwa, *Proto-industrialisierung*.
53 RGIA, fond 1088, opis' 10, delo 524. On this, see also Boris N. Kashin, *Kres'ianskaia promyshlennost'* (The peasant rural industry), 2 vols. (Moscow and Leningrad, 1935), Vol. I: 215, 347–349.
54 Domar and Machina, 'On the Profitability of Russian Serfdom'.
55 RGADA, fond 1252, opis' 1:Abamelek-Lazarevy's estate, province of Tula; fond 1282, Tolstye-Kristi's estate, province of Riazan; fond 1262, opis' 1, Prince Gagarin's estates in Saratov and Tambov provinces; fond 1287, Sheremetev's estate.
56 Aleksandr' Troinitskii, *Krepostnoe naselenie v Rossii po 10 narodnoi perepisi* (The Russian serf population according to the tenth census) (Saint Petersburg: Wulf, 1861): 45.
57 Irina V. Ledovskaia, 'Biudzhet russkogo pomeshchika v 40–60kh godakh XIX v' (Estate owners' budgets in the 1840s-60s), in Akademiia Nauk SSSR, *Materialy po istorii sel'skogo khoziaistva i krest'ianstva SSSR*, vol. 8 (Moscow: Nauka, 1974): 240–245.
58 Boris. Mironov, Carol Leonard, 'In Search of the Hidden Information: Some Issues in the Socio-Economic History of Russia in the Eighteenth Century and Nineteenth Centuries', *Social Science History*, 9, 4 (1985): 339–359; Ivan D. Koval'nchenko, L.V. Milov, *Vserossiskii agrarnyi rynok XVIII-nachala XXv*. (The all-Russian agrarian market, eighteenth century-early twentieth centuries), (Moscow: Nauka, 1974).
59 Koval'chenko, *Krepost'noe*: 394; Boris Gorshkov, 'Serfs on the Move: Peasant Seasonal Migration in Pre-reform Russia, 1800–1860', *Kritika. Explorations in Russian history*, 1, 4 (2000): 627–656.
60 Nikolai M. Druzhinin, *Gosudarstvennye krest'iane i reforma P.D. Kiseleva* (the state peasants and the reforms of Kiselev), (Moscow: AN SSSR), vol. 2: 296–390.

61 Dave Pretty, *Neither Peasant nor Proletarian: The Workers of the Ivanovo-Voznesensk Region, 1885–1905* (Ph.D. diss.: Brown University, 1997).
62 Olga Crisp, 'Labor and Industrialization in Russia', in Peter Mathias and Michael Postan eds., *The Cambridge Economic History of Europe*, vol. 7, pt. 2 (Cambridge: Cambridge University Press, 1978): 308–415, 337–339.
63 For the Sheremetevs' estates in Pavlovo and Vors'mo: TsGIA fond 1088; opis' 3, delo 626, 974, 440, 370, 417.
64 RGIA, fond 1088, opis' 10 delo 642. (ukaz 11 Sept. 1802).
65 RGIA, fond 18, opis' 2, delo 1927, ll. 1, 3, 212–213; TsGIAM fond 14, opis' 1, delo 3266, ll. 2–38 and TsIAM fond 2354, opis' 1, delo 41, ll. 197a–99, 228.
66 For a deep revision of second serfdom in Central and Eastern Europe, see Markus Cerman, 'Social Structure and Land Markets in Late Medieval Central and Eastern Europe', *Continuity and Change*, 23, 1 (2008): 55–100.
67 Hartmut Harnisch, 'Bäuerliche Ökonomie und Mentalität unter den Bedingungen der ostelbischen Gutsherrschaft in den letzten Jahrzehnten vor Beginn der Agrarreformen', *Jahrbuch für Wirtschaftsgeschichte*, 24 (1989): 87–108.
68 Hagen, *Ordinary*.
69 Robert Frost, 'The Nobility of Poland-Lithuania, 1569–1795', in Hamish Scott ed., *The European Nobilities in the Seventeenth and Eighteenth Centuries*, Vol. II, Northern, Central and Eastern Europe (London: Routledge, 1994).
70 Edgar Melton, 'Population Structure, the Market Economy, and the Transformation of Gutscherrschaft in East Central Europe, 1650–1800: The Case of Brandenburg and Bohemia', *German History* 16, 3 (1998): 297–324.
71 Tracy Dennison and Sheilagh Ogilvie, 'Serfdom and Social Capital in Bohemia and Russia', *Economic History Review*, 60 (2007): 513–544.
72 Jan de Vries, *European Urbanization, 1500–1800* (London: Meuthen, 1984).
73 Alessandro Stanziani, 'Les statistiques des récoltes en Russie, 1905–1928', *Histoire et mesure*, vol. VII, nr. 1/2 (1992): 73–98.
74 Alessandro Stanziani, 'Les enquêtes orales en Russie, 1861–1914', *Annales ESC* (2000), 1: 219–241.
75 For a full discussion of these materials, see Blanchard, *Russia's Age of Silver*, Chapter 5 and appendix 2, revised in Ian Blanchard, 'Le développement économique en perspective historique: l'avenir de la Russie à la lumière de son évolution à l époque moderene (1700–1914)', in Michèle Merger et Dominique Barjot eds., *Les enterprises et leurs réseaux: hommes, capitaux, techniques et pouvoirs xixe-xxe siècles. Mèlanges en l honneur de François Caron* (Paris: Presse de l Université de Paris-Sorbonne, 1998): 381–392.
76 Leonard, *Agrarian Reform in Russia*, in particular figure 8.1: 258.
77 Blanchard, 'Russian and Soviet'.
78 Moon, *The Russian Peasantry*: 27.

79 Koval'chenko, *Russkoe*; Dennison, *The Institutions*; Hoch, *Serfdom and Social Control in Russia*.
80 Vladimir M. Kabuzan, *Izmeneniia v razmeshchenii naseleniia Rossii v XVIII-pervoi polovine XIX v.* (Changes in the rate of growth of the Russian population during the Eighteenth and the first half of the Nineteenth centuries), (Moscow: Nauka, 1971); Alain Blum, Irina Troitskaia, 'La mortalité en Russie au XVIIIe et XIXe siècles. Estimations locales à partir des Revizii', *Population*, 51 (1996): 303–328; Steven Hoch, 'Famine, Disease, and Mortality Patterns in the Parish of Borshevka, 1830–1912', *Population Studies*, 52, 3 (1998): 357–368.

Chapter 6

1 Steven Hoch, *Serfdom and Social Control in Russia: Petrovskoe, a Village in Tambov* (Chicago: University of Chicago Press, 1986); David Moon, *The Russian Peasantry, 1600–1930: The World the Peasants Made* (London and New York: Addison Wesley Longman, 1999).
2 Steven Hoch, 'Famine, Disease and Mortality Patterns in the Parish of Boshervka, Russia, 1830–1932', *Population Studies*, 52, 3 (1998): 357–368. Steven Hoch, 'On Good Numbers and Bad: Malthus, Population Trend and Peasant Standard of Living in Late Imperial Russia', *Slavic Review*, 53, 1 (1994): 41–75. Steven Hoch, 'Serfs in Imperial Russia: Demographic Insights', *Journal of Interdisciplinary History*, 13, 2 (1982): 221–246.
3 Stephen Wheatcroft, 'Crisis and Condition of the Peasantry in Late Imperial Russia', in Esther Kingston-Mann, Timothy Mixter eds., *Peasant Economy, Culture and Politics of European Russia, 1800–1921* (Princeton: Princeton University Press, 1991): 101–127.
4 Elvira M. Wilbur, 'Was Russian Peasant Agriculture Really That Impoverished? New Evidence From a Case Study From the "Impoverished Center" at the End of the Nineteenth Century', *Journal of Economic History*, 43 (March 1983): 137–144; Esther Kingston-Mann, 'Marxism and Russian Rural Development: Problems of Evidence, Experience and Culture', *American Historical Review*, 84 (October 1981): 731–752; James Y. Simms, Jr., 'The Crisis in Russian Agriculture at the End of the Nineteenth Century: A Different View', *Slavic Review*, 36 (September 1977): 377–398; James Simms, 'The Crop Failure of 1891: Soil Exhaustion, Technological Backwardness, and Russia's "Agrarian Crisis"', *Slavic Review*, 41 (Summer 1982): 236–250.
5 Paul Gregory, *Russian National Income 1885–1913* (Cambridge: Cambridge University Press, 1982), paperback 2004; Alessandro Stanziani, *L'économie en revolution. Le cas russe, 1870–1930* (Paris: Albin Michel, 1998); Peter Gatrell, *The Tsarist Economy, 1850–1917* (London: Batsford, 1986).

6 Ivan Koval'chenko, L. Milov, *Vserossiiskii agrarnyi rynok, XVIII – nachalo XX v.* (The Russian agrarian market, eighteenth-nineteenth centuries), (Moscow: Nauka, 1974).
7 Barry K. Goodwin and Thomas J. Grennes, 'Tsarist Russia and the World Wheat Market', *Explorations in Economic History*, 35 (1998): 405–430.
8 Gregory, *Russian*: 126–130; 168–194.
9 Robert Allen, *Farm to Factory: A Reinterpretation of the Soviet Industrial Revolution* (Princeton: Princeton University Press, 2003).
10 Gregory, *Russian*, Table 6.3.
11 Serguei N. Prokopovich, *Opyt ischsleniia narodonogo dokhoda 50 gubernii Evropeiskoi Rossii v 1900–1913 gg* (Study of the national income of 50 provinces of European Russia, 1900–1913) (Moscow: Sovet Vserossiikikh kooperatvinikh S'ezdov, 1918): 67.
12 Donald McCloskey, 'The Open Fields of England: Rent, Risk, and the Rate of Interest, 1300–1815', in David Galenson ed., *Markets in History: Economic Studies of the Past* (Cambridge: Cambridge University Press, 1989): 5–51.
13 Esther Kingston-Mann, 'Peasant Communes and Economic Innovation: A Preliminary Inquiry', in Esther Kingston-Mann and Timothy Mixter eds., *Peasant Economy, Culture, and Politics of European Russia, 1800–1921* (Princeton: Princeton University Press, 1991): 23–51; Pavel' N Zyrianov, *Krest'ianskaia obshchina Evropeiskoi Rossii 1907–1914 gg.* (The peasant commune in European Russia, 1907–1914), (Moscow: Nauka, 1992); Judith Pallot, *Land Reform in Russia 1906–1917: Peasant Responses to Stolypin's Project of Rural Transformation* (Oxford: Clarendon Press, 1999).
14 Steven Nafziger, *Communal Institutions, Resource Allocation, and Russian Economic Development* (Yale University, unpublished Ph.D. dissertation, 2006).
15 Pallot, Land Reform in Russia 1906–1917: 81.
16 G.Y. Z. i Z., *Ezhegodnik*, 1907–1916 (Yearbook) (Saint Petersburg, 1908–1916, 10 volumes); G.Y.Z.i Z., *Obzor dejatel'nosti za…*, 1908–1914.
17 Gregory, *Russian*: 132.
18 Gatrell, *The Tsarist*.
19 Dave Pretty, *Neither Peasant nor Proletarian: The Workers of the Ivanovo-Voznesensk Region, 1885–1905* (Brown University: 1997).
20 Gatrell, *The Tsarist*.
21 Carol Leonard, *Agrarian Reform in Russia* (Cambridge: Cambridge University Press, 2011).
22 Alessandro Stanziani, *L'économie en revolution, 1870–1914* (Paris: Albin Michel, 1998); Alessandro Stanziani, 'The First World War and the Disintegration of Economic Spaces in Russia', in Judith Pallot ed., *Transforming Peasants. Society, State, and the Peasantry, 1861–1930*, (London: MacMillan 1998): 174–194.

23 Details on conflicts in the province of Vladimir, close to Moscow, in REM (Rossiiskoi etnograficheskii musei), fond 7, opis' 1.
24 REM, fonds 7, opis' 1; TsSK (Tsentral'nyi Statisticheskii Komitet, *Statisticheskiya dannyya o razvodakh i nedeistvitel'nykh brakakh za 1867–1886* (Statistical data on marriages and separations, 1867–1886) (Saint Petersburg, 1893): 16–21.
25 Robert Allen, *Enclosures and the Yeoman. The Agricultural Development of the South Midlands, 1450–1850* (Oxford: Clarendon Press, 1992).
26 Kenneth Pomeranz, *The Great Divergence* (Berkeley: University of California Press, 2000).
27 Robert Allen, 'Tracking the Agricultural Revolution in England', *The Economic History Review*, 52, 2 (1999): 209–235.
28 Patrick O' Brien 'Agriculture and the Industrial Revolution', *The Economic History Review*, 30, 1 (1977): 166–181.
29 O' Brien, 'Agriculture'.
30 George Grantham, 'Agricultural Supply during the Industrial Revolution: French Evidence and European Implications', *The Journal of Economic History*, 49, 1 (1989): 43–72.
31 Giovanni Federico, *Feeding the World. An Economic History of Agriculture, 1800–2000* (Princeton: Princeton University press, 2008).
32 Patrick O'Brien, 'Path Dependency, or Why Britain Became an Industrialized and Urbanized Economy Long Before France', *Economic History Review*, 49, 2 (1996): 213–249.
33 Gregory Clark, 'Productivity Growth Without Technical Change in European Agriculture Before 1850', *The Journal of Economic History*, 47, 2 (1987): 419–432.
34 Grantham, 'Agricultural Supply'; O'Brien, 'Agriculture'.
35 F.M.L. Thompson, 'The Second Agricultural Revolution, 1815–1880', *Economic History Review*, 21 (1968): 62–77.
36 Franklin Mendels, 'Proto-industrialization: the First Phase of the Industrialization Process', *Journal of economic history*, 32 (1972): 241–261; Franklin Mendels, 'Des industries rurales à la proto-industrialisation: historique d'un changement de perspective', *Annales ESC*, 39 (1984): 977–1008; Peter Kriedte, Hans Medick, and Jürgen Schlumbhom, *Industrilization Before Industrialization. Rural Industry in the Genesis of Capitalism* (Cambridge: Cambridge University Press, 1982).
37 William Hagen, 'Capitalism in the Countryside in Early Modern Europe: Interpretations, Models, Debates', *Agricultural History*, 62, 1 (1988): 13–47.
38 Ogilvie, Cerman, *European proto-Industrialization*.
39 Charles Sabel and Jonhatan Zeitlin eds., *Worlds of Possibilities. Flexibility and Mass Production in Western Industrialization* (Cambridge, Paris: Maison des Sciences de l'Homme, Cambridge University Press, 1997).
40 Jan De Vries, 'The Industrial Revolution and the Industrious Revolution', *Journal of Economic History*, 54, 2 (1994): 249–270.

41 Kaouro Sugihara, 'Labour-Intensive Industrialisation in Global History', *Australian Economic History*, 47, 2 (2007): 121–154; John Lee, 'Trade and Economy in Preindustrial East Asia, c. 1500–1800: East Asia in the Age of Global Integration', *The Journal of Asian Studies*, 58, 1 (1999): 2–26.
42 Penelope Franck, *Rural Economic Development in Japan: from the Nineteenth Century to the Pacific War* (London, New York: Routledge, 2006).
43 Sugihara, 'Labour-Intensive'.
44 Osamu Saito, 'The Labour Market in Tokugawa Japan: Wage Differentials and the Real Wage Level, 1727, 1830', *Explorations in Economic History*, 15, 1 (1978): 84–100.
45 Tirthankar Roy, *The Economic History of India, 1857–1947* (New York: Oxford University Press, 2001); Frank Perlin, 'Proto-Industrialization and Pre-Colonial South Asia', *Past and Present*, 98, (February 1983): 30–95.
46 Gilles Postel-Vinay, 'The Di-integration of Traditional Labour Markets in France. From Agriculture and Industry to Agriculture or Industry', in George Grantham and Mary MacKinnon eds., *Labor Market Evolution: The Economic History of Market Integration, Wage Flexibility and the Employment Relation* (London and New York: Routledge, 1994): 64–83.
47 Paul Lindert and Geoffrey Williamson, 'English Workers Living Standards During the Industrial Revolution: A New Look', *Economic History Review*, XXXIV (1983): 1–25; Paul Lindert and Geoffrey Williamson, 'Revising England's Social Tables, 1688–1812', *Explorations in Economic History*, XIX (1982): 385–408.
48 E. J. T. Collins, 'Migrant Labour in British Agriculture in Nineteenth Century', *Economic History Review*, 29, 1 (1976): 38–59; Edgar Melton, 'Population Structure, the Market Economy, and the Transformation of Gutsherrschaft in East Central Europe, 1650–1800: The Cases of Brandenburg and Bohemia', *German History*, 16, 3 (1998): 297–324.
49 George Grantham, 'Divisions of Labour: Agricultural Productivity and Occupational Specialization in Pre-Industrial France', *The Economic History Review*, 46, 3 (1993): 478–502.
50 Charles Feinstein, 'Capital Formation in Great Britain', in: Peter Mathias and Michael Postan eds., *The Cambridge Economic History of Europe, vol. VII: The industrial Economies: Capital, Labor and Enterprise* (Cambridge: Cambridge University Press, 1978): 28–94.
51 Nicolas Crafts, *British Economic Growth During the Industrial Revolution* (Oxford: Clarendon Press, 1985); Knick Harley, 'British Industrialization before 1841: Evidence of Slower Growth During the Industrial Revolution', *The Journal of Economic History*, 42, 2 (1982): 267–289; Jeoffrey Williamson, 'Why Was British Growth So Slow During the Industrial Revolution?', *The Journal of Economic History*, 44, 3 (1984): 687–712; Phyllis Deane, 'Capital Formation in Britain Before

the Railway Age', *Economic Development and Cultural Change*, 9, 3 (1961): 352–368; Charles Feinstein, and Sidney Pollard, eds., *Studies in Capital Formation in the United Kingdom, 1750–1920* (Oxford: Clarendon Press, 1988).

52 Simon Deakin, and Frank Wilkinson, *The Law of the Labour Market: Industrialization, Employment, and Legal Evolution* (Oxford: Oxford University Press, 2005).

53 François Crouzet, *British Ascendant: Comparative Studies in Franco-British Economic History* (Cambridge: Cambridge University Press, 1990); Maurice Lévy-Leboyer, and François Bourguignon, *L'économie française au XIXe siècle* (Paris: Economica, 1985).

54 Patrick O'Brien, *Economic Growth in Britain and France, 1780–1914. Two Paths to the Twentieth Century* (London: Unwin, 1987).

55 Nicolas Crafts, *British Economic Growth during the Industrial Revolution* (Oxford: Clarendon Press, 1985).

56 Clark, 'Productivity Growth'.

57 Christine Mac Leod, *Inventing the Industrial Revolution. The English Patent System, 1660–1800* (Cambridge: Cambridge University Press, 1988).

58 Hans-Joachim Voth, 'Time and Work in Eighteenth Century London', *The Journal of Economic History*, 58, 1 (1998): 29–58.

59 Edward P. Thompson, 'Time, Work-Discipline and Industrial Capitalism', *Past and Present*, 38 (1967): 56–97.

60 Joel Mokyred, *The Economics of the Industrial Revolution* (Totowa: Rowman and Allanheld, 1985).

61 Gary Cross, *A Quest for Time. The Reduction of Work in Britain and France, 1840–1940* (Berkeley: University of California Press, 1989); Gary Cross ed., *Worktime and Industrialization: An International History* (Philadelphia: Temple University Press, 1988); James Schmiechen, *Sweated Industries and Sweated Labour: The London Clothing Trades, 1860–1914* (Urbana: University of Illinois Press, 1982).

Conclusion

1 On this comparison, cf. Alessandro Stanziani, *Bâtisseurs d'Empires. Russia, Inde et Chine à la croisée des mondes* (Paris: Liber, 2012).

2 Jeremy Black, *European Warfare, 1600–1815* (New Haven: Yale University Press, 1994).

3 Bartolomé Yun-Casalilla, Patrick O'Brien, Francisco Comin, *The Rise of the Fiscal States. A Global History 1500–1914* (Cambridge: Cambridge University Press, 2012).

4 Arno Mayer, *The Persistence of the Old Regime. Europe from 1848 to the Great War* (New York: Pantheon, 1981).

5 Carol Leonard, *Agrarian Reform in Russia* (Cambridge: Cambridge University Press, 2011), in particular figure 8.1: 258.

References

Archives

Archivio di stato di Genova (ASG), Massaria Caffae, 1374, fol. 1–354.
Arkhiv gosudarstvennogo soveta, 5 vols (Saint Petersburg, 1869–1904), vol. 4, vyp. 1, ch. 2: 253–258.
REM (Rossiiskoi etnograficheskii musei), fond 7, opis' 1.
Russian State Archive of Ancien Act (RGADA):
fond 89, *Turetskie dela*, delo 3.
fond 109 Snosheniia Rossii s Bukharoi, opis'1, delo 1643.
fond 123, Krymskie dela, opis'2, 13, l. 53.
fond 127 (Snosheniia Rossii s Nogaiskimi Tatarami).
fond 141, opis'1, Dokumenty tsarskogo arkhiva i posol'skogo prikaza.
fond 210 (Razriadnyi prikaz), Belgorodskii stol, knigi 118, 152, 156643, 772.
fond 248, Senat i senatskie uchrezhdeniia.
fond 294, Manufaktor-Kontora opis' 2 and 3; fond 1287, opis' 3.
fond 350, Revizkie skazki po nizhegorodskoi gubernii, opis' 2, dela 1975 and 2056.
fond 396 Archiv oruzhennoi palaty, opis'1, chasty *1, 2, 4, 5, 7, 11, 24, 26–33, 35, 36, opis'2, ch. 2*.
fond 615, Krepostnye knigi, dela 526, 528, 529, 4753, 6654.
fond 1209 Pomestnyi prikaz, opis' 1, delo 292; fond 1287 (Sheremetev), opis' 5 and 6.
fond 1252, opis' 1:Abamelek-Lazarevy's estate, province of Tula
fond 1282, Tolstye-Kristi's estate, province of Riazan
fond 1262, opis' 1, Prince Gagarin's estates in Saratov and Tambov provinces
fond 1287, Sheremetev's estate.
fond 199 (G. F. Miller).

Russian State Historical Archive (RGIA):
fond 379 opis'1.
fond 1088, Sheremetev opisi 3, 5, 10, in particular opis'10, dela 524, 607, 611, 616, 618, 642.

Rossiiskaia Akademiia nauk. Arkhiv, fond 1714, op. 1 (A.A. Novosel'skii), delo 66, l. 123.
Saltykov-Shchedrin Library in Saint Petersburg, manuscript section, *Obshchee sobranie gramot*, n. 1727,1937, 1941, 2017, 2019, 2348, 2406, 2635, 2672, 3026, 3081, 3392, 3475, 3486.
Central State Imperial Moscow Archives (TsGIAM):
fond 14, opis' 1, delo 3266, ll. 2–38, opis' 2, dela 31, 40, 82, 124, 146
fond 2354, opis' 1, delo 41, ll. 197a–99, 228.

Sources

Akty istoricheskie, sobrannye i izdannye arkheograficheskoiu kommissieiu (Historical acts collected and published by the commission of archeo-geography) 5 vols. vol. 2, n. 85 (Saint Petersburg, 1841–1843).

Akty, sobrannye v bibliothekakh i arkivakh Rossiskoi Imperii arkheograficheskii ekspeditsieiu imperatoskoi akademiia nauk (Acts collected in the libraries and archives of the Russian Empire by the archeographical expeditions of the Imperial Academy of Sciences), 4 vol. (Saint Petersburg, 1836, 1858).

Chekhovich Oleg, D. *Bukharkie dokumenty XIV veka* (Documents from Bukhara, Fourteenth century) (Tashkent: Nauka, 1965), 108–110.

———. *Samarkandie dokumenty, XV–XVI vv* (Documents on Samarkand, 15th-16th centuries) (Moscow, 1974, in Persian with Russian translation).

Demidova Natalia F. (ed.). *Materialy po istorii russko-mongol'skikh otnoshenii: Russko-mongol'skie otnosheniia, 1654–1685 sbornik dokumentov* (Materials for the history of Russian-Mongol relations: Russian-Mongol Relations, 1654–1685, collection of documents) (Moscow: Izdatel'skaia Firma Vostochnaia Lietartura, 1995, 1996, 2000).

———. and Viktor S. Miasnikov (eds). *Russko-kitaiskie otnosheniia v xvii veke: Materialy i dokumenty* (Russian-Chinese relations in the 17th century: materials and documents) (2 vv, Moscow: Nauka, 1969–1972).

Dokumenty i dogorovnye gramoty velikikh i udel'nykh kniazei XIV–XVI vv (Documents and acts decreed by princes, fourteenth–sixteenth centuries), ed. L. V. Cherepnin and S. V. Bakhrushin (Moscow: Nauka, 1950): 409, document n. 98.

Kazakhsko-russkie otnosheniia v 16–18 vekakh, Sbornik dokumentov i materialov (Russian-Kazak relations in the 18th century. Collection of materials and documents) (Alma-Ata: Akademia nauk Kazakhskoi SSSR, 1961 and 1964).

Kazakhsko-russkie otnosheniia v 16–18 vekakh, Sbornik dokumentov i materialov (Russian-Kazakh relations during the Sixteenth-Eighteenth centuries. Collected documents and materials) (Alma-Ata: Akademia nauk Kazakhskoi SSSR, 1961 and 1964).

Materialy po istorii Uzbeskoi, Tadzhikskoi I (Materials for the history of Uzbekistan, Tajikistan, and Turkmenistan) (Leningrad: AN SSSR, 1932).

Mezhdunarodnye otnosheniia v Tsentral'noi Azii: 17–18vv. Dokumenty I materialy (International relations in Central Asia, 17th–18th centuries. Documents and materials), 2 vol. (Moscow: Nauka, 1989).

Opisanie dokumentov i bumag, khraniashchikhsia v moskovskom arkhive ministerstva iustitsii (Inventory of documents and papers kept in the Moscow archives of the Ministry of Justice), vol. 15 (Saint Petersburg, 1908).

Russko-dagenstanskie otnosheniia XVII-pervoi chetverti XVIII vv: Dokumenty i materially (Russian-Daghestan relations during the seventeenth and the first quarter of the eighteenth century. Documents and materials), vol. 79 (Makhachkala: Dagenstanskoe kn. Izd., 1958).

Printed documents

Abu-Lughod, Janet. *Before European Hegemony. The World System A.D. 1250-1350* (New York: Oxford University Press, 1989).

Adshead, Samuel Adrien. *Central Asia in World History* (New York: St. Martin's Press, 1993).

Alam, Muzaffar. 'Trade, State Policy and Regional Change: Aspects of Mughal-Uzbek Commercial Relations, c. 1550-1750', *Journal of Economic and Social History of the Orient*, 37, 3 (1994): 202-227.

———. *The Languages of Political Islam. India 1200-1800* (Chicago: The University of Chicago Press, 2004).

———. 'Trade, State Policy and Regional Change', in Scott Levi (ed.), *India and Central Asia. Commerce and Culture, 1500-1800* (Oxford: Oxford University Press, 2007)

Aleppo, Paul of. *The Travels of Macarius: Extracts From the Diary of the Travels of Macarius, Patriarch of Antioch* ed. Lady Laura Ridding (London: Oxford University Press, 1936).

Allen, Robert. *Enclosures and the Yeoman: The Agricultural Development of the South Midlands, 1450-1850* (Oxford: Clarendon Press, 1992).

———. 'Tracking the Agricultural Revolution in England', *The Economic History Review*, 52, 2 (1999): 209-235.

———. *Farm to Factory: A Reinterpretation of the Soviet Industrial Revolution* (Princeton: Princeton University Press, 2003).

———. *The British Industrial Revolution in Global Perspective* (Cambridge: Cambridge University Press, 2009).

Anderson, J. L. 'Piracy and World History: An Economic Perspective on Maritime Predation', *Journal of World History*, 6 (1995): 175-199.

André, Gunder Frank. *The Centrality of Central Asia* (Amsterdam: VU University Press, 1992).

———. 'ReOrient: From the Centrality of Central Asia to China's Middle Kingdom', in Korkut A. Ertürk (ed.), *Rethinking Central Asia: Non-Eurocentric Studies in History, Social Structure, and Identity* (Reading, UK: Ithaca Press, 1999): 11-38.

Anisimov, Evgenii V. *Podatnaia reforma Petra I: Vvedenie podushnoi podati v Rossii 1719-1728 gg* (Tax reform under Pierre I: the introduction of per capita taxation in Russia, 1719-1728) (Moscow: Nauka, 1982).

———. 'Remarks on the Fiscal Policy of Russian Absolutism During the First Quarter of the Eighteenth Century', *Soviet Studies in History*, 28, 1 (1989): 10-32.

Antonova, Katarina, A. Nikolai, and M. Goldberg (eds). *Russko-indyiskie otnosheniia v XVIII veke: Sbornik dokumentov* (Russian-Indian relations in the eighteenth century. Collected documents) (Moscow: Nauka, 1965).

Appadurai, Arjun. *The Social Life of Things. Commodities in Cultural Perspective* (Cambridge: Cambridge University Press, 1986).

Arndt, Par. *Economic Development. The History of an Idea* (Chicago: the University of Chicago Press, 1987).

Askarov, A. A. *Istoriia Uzbekistana (History of Uzbekistan) vol. II: Pervaia polovina XIXe veka* (First half of the nineteenth century) (Tashkent: Fan, 1993).
Aston, Trevor and Charles Philpin (eds). *The Brenner Debate: Agrarian Class Structure and Economic Development in Pre-industrial Europe* (Cambridge: Cambridge University Press, 1985).
Austin, Gareth. 'Reciprocal Comparison and African History: Tackling Conceptual Eurocentrism in the Study of Africa's Economic Past', *African Studies Review*, 50, 3 (2007): 1–28.
Balard, Michel. *Gênes et L'Outre-Mer, I: Les Actes de Caffa du notaire Lamberto di Sambuceto 1289– 1290* (Paris-The Hague: Mouton, 1973).
———. 'Esclavage en Crimée et sources fiscales génoises au XVe siècle', *Byzantinische Forschungen*, 22 (1996): 9–17, Reprinted in Henri Bresc, ed., *Figures de l'esclave au Moyen-Age et dans le monde moderne. Actes de la table ronde organisée les 27 et 28 octobre 1992 par le Centre d'Histoire sociale et culturelle de l'Occident de l'Université de Paris-X Nanterre* (Paris: Université Paris X, 1996): 77–87.
Balbi, Giorgio. 'Atti rogati a Caffa da Nicolo' Beltrame (1343–44)', in Giorgio Balbi and Stefano Raiteri (eds), *Notai genovesi in Oltremare: Atti rogati a Caffa e a Licostomo (sec. XIV)* (Collana Storica di Fonti e Studi, 14, Università degli studi di Genova, 1973).
Barnier, François. *Un libertin dans l'Inde moghole (1656–1669)* (Paris: Chandeigne, 2008).
Bartlett, Roger. 'Serfdom and State Power in Imperial Russia', *European History Quarterly* 33, 1 (2003): 29–64.
Barrett, Thomas. 'Lines of Uncertainty: The Frontier of the North Caucasus', *Slavic Review*, 54, 3 (1995): 578–601.
Bayly, Christopher Alan. *The Imperial Meridian* (London: Longman, Pearson Education, 1989).
Beaujard, Philippe. 'The Indian Ocean in Eurasian and African World-Systems before the Sixteenth Century', *Journal of World History*, 16, 4 (2005): 411–465.
Benot, Yves. 'Condorcet journaliste et le combat anti-esclavagiste', in Equipe Rehseis (ed.) *Condorcet mathématicien, économiste, philosophe et homme politique* (Paris: Minerve, 1989): 376–384.
Bernand, Lepetit. 'Une logique du raisonnement historique', *Annale ESC*, 5 (1993): 1209–1219, special issue 'Histoire et sciences sociales', *Annales ESC*, 38, 6 (1983).
Black, Jeremy. *European Warfare, 1600–1815* (New Haven: Yale University Press, 1994).
Blakely, Allison. 'American Influences on Russian Reformists in the Era of the French Revolution', *Russian Review*, 52, 4 (1993): 451–471.
Blanchard, Ian. *Russia's Age of Silver: Precious Metal Production and Economic Growth in the Eighteenth Century* (New York and London: Routledge, 1989).
———. 'Le développement économique en perspective historique: L'avenir de la Russie à la lumière de son évolution à l époque moderne (1700–1914)', in Michèle Merger and Dominique Barjot (eds), *Les entreprises et leurs réseaux: Hommes, capitaux, techniques et pouvoirs xixe-xxe siècles. Mèlanges en l honneur de François Caron* (Paris: Presse de l'Université de Paris-Sorbonne, 1998): 381–392.

Bloch, Marc. 'Serf de la glèbe. Histoire d'une expression toute faite', *Revue Historique*, 36 (1921): 220–242.
———. *Apologie pour l'histoire ou métier d'historien* (orig. 1949) (Paris: Colin, 1993).
Blum, Alain and Troitskaia, Irina. 'La mortalité en Russie au XVIIIe et XIXe siècles. Estimations locales à partir des Revizii', *Population*, 51 (1996): 303–328.
Blum, Jerome. *Lord and Peasant in Russian from the Ninth to the Nineteenth Century* (New York: Atheneum, 1964).
Bois, Guy. *La crise du féodalisme* (Paris: Presses de Sciences-Po, EHESS, 1976).
Bonnassie, Pierre. *From Slavery to Feudalism* (Cambridge: Cambridge University Press, 1991).
Bratianu, G. *Actes des notaires genois de Pira et de Caffa de la fin du XIIIe siècle (1281–1290)* (Bucharest: Académie Roumaine, Etudes et Recherches, ii, 1927).
Braudel, Fernand. *La Méditerranée à l'époque de Philippe II* (Paris: Armand Colin, 1949).
———. *Civilisation matérielle, économie et capitalisme* 3 vols (Paris: Colin, 1977–1979).
Bregel, Yuri. 'Central Asia in the Twelfth-Thirteenth/ Eighteenth-Nineteenth Centuries', *Encyclopaedia Iranica*, 5, fasc. 2 (Costa Mesa: Mazda, 1992): 193–205.
Brenner, Robert. 'Agrarian Class Structure and Economic Development in Pre-industrial Europe', *Past and Present*, 70 (1976): 30–74.
Brill-Olcott, Martha. *The Kazakhs* (Stanford: Hoover Institutions Press, 1987).
Bruk, Serguei I. and Kabuzan, Vladimir M. 'Dinamika chislennosti i rasselenie russkogo etnosa, 1678–1917' (La dynamique du nombre et de l'établissement des ethnies russes, 1678–1917), *Sovetskaya istoriografiya*, 4 (1982): 9–25.
Burbank, Jane and Cooper, Frederick. *Empires in World History: Power and the Politics of Difference* (Princeton: Princeton University Press, 2010).
Burton, Audrey. 'Russian Slaves in Seventeenth-Century Bukhara', in Touraj Astabaki and O'Kane John (eds.), *Post-Soviet Central Asia* (London: Taurus Academic studies, 1998): 345–365.
Bush, Michael (ed.). *Serfdom and Slavery: Studies in Legal Bondage* (Manchester: Manchester University Press, 1996).
Bushkovitch, Paul. 'Taxation, Tax Farming and Merchants in Sixteenth-Century Russia', *Slavic Review*, 37, 3 (1978): 381–398.
Carole, Steven Balkins. *Soldiers of the Steppe: Army Reform and Social Change in Early Modern Russia* (Dekalb, Illinois: Northern Illinois University Press, 1995).
Cerman, Markus. 'Social Structure and Land Markets in Late Medieval Central and Eastern Europe', *Continuity and Change*, 23, 1 (2008): 55–100.
Chakrabarty, Dipesh. *Provincializing Europe* (Princeton: Princeton University Press, 2000).
Chaudhuri, Kirti N. *The Trading World of Asia and the English East India Company, 1660–1760* (Cambridge: Cambridge University Press, 1978).
———. *Asia Before Europe: Economy and Civilization in the Indian Ocean from the rise of Islam to 1750* (Cambridge: Cambridge University Press, 1990).

Chernov, Aleksandr'V. *Vooruzhennye sily Russkogo gosudarstva v XV–XVI vv* (The defence forces of the Muscovite estate in the 15th and 16th centuries) (Moscow: Ministerstvo Oborony, 1954).

Chimitdorzhiev, Sh. B. *Vzaimootnosheniia Mongolii i Rossii v 17–18 vekakh* (Relations between Mongolia and Russian in the 17th and 18th centuries) (Moscow: Nauka, 1978).

Christian, David. *A History of Russia, Central Asia and Mongolia* (Malden: Blackwell, 1998)

Clarence-Smith, William Gervase. *Islam and the Abolition of Slavery* (Oxford: Oxford University Press, 2006).

Clark, Gregory. 'Productivity Growth Without Technical Change in European Agriculture Before 1850', *The Journal of Economic History*, 47, 2 (1987): 419–432.

Collins, E. J. T. 'Migrant Labour in British Agriculture in Nineteenth Century', *Economic History Review*, 29, 1 (1976): 38–59.

Condillac, Bonnot-Etienne. *Œuvres complètes* vol. XX (original published in 1798) (Paris: PUF, 1947).

Confino, Michael. *Domaines et seigneurs en Russie vers la fin du XVIIIe siècle: Étude de structures agraires et de mentalités économiques* (Paris: Mouton, 1963).

———. *Systèmes graires et progrès agricole en Russie aux XVIIIe–XIXe siècles: Étude d' économie et de sociologie rurales* (Paris: Mouton, 1969).

———. 'Reinventing the Enlightenment: Western Images of Eastern Realities in the Eighteenth Century', *Canadian Slavonic Papers*, 36, 3–4 (1994): 505–522.

Cooper, Frederick. *Colonialism in Question. Theory, Knowledge, History* (Berkeley: University of California Press, 2005).

Crafts, Nicolas. *British Economic Growth During the Industrial Revolution* (Oxford: Clarendon Press, 1985).

Crisp, Olga. 'Labor and Industrialization in Russia', in Peter Mathias and Michael Postan (eds), *The Cambridge Economic History of Europe*, vol. 7, pt. 2 (Cambridge: Cambridge University Press, 1978): 308–415.

Cross, Gary (ed.). *Worktime and Industrialization: An International History* (Philadelphia: Temple University Press, 1988).

———. *A Quest for Time. The Reduction of Work in Britain and France, 1840–1940* (Berkeley: University of California Press, 1989).

Crouzet, François. *British Ascendant: Comparative Studies in Franco-British Economic History* (Cambridge: Cambridge University Press, 1990).

Crummey, Robert. 'Sources of Boyar Power in the Seventeenth Century', *Cahiers du Monde Russe et soviétique*, 34, 1–2 (1993): 107–118.

———. *The Formation of Muscovy, 1304–1614* (London: Longman, 1987).

Curtin, Philip. *Cross-Cultural Trade in World History* (Cambridge: Cambridge University Press, 1984).

Czap, Peter. 'The Perennial Multiple-Family Household, Mishino, Russia, 1782–1858', *Journal of Family History* 7, 1 (Spring, 1982): 5–26.

Dale, Stephen. *Indian Merchants and Eurasian Trade, 1600–1750* (Cambridge: Cambridge University Press, 1994).

———. *The Muslim Empires of the Ottoman, Safavids, and Mughal* (Cambridge: Cambridge University Press, 2009).
Dalton, George (ed.). *Research in Economic Anthropology* (Greenwich, Connecticut: JAI Press, 1983).
Davies, Brian. *Warfare, State and Society on the Black Sea Steppe, 1500–1700* (London: Routledge, 2007).
Davies, Norman. *God's Playground: A History of Poland, 2 vols* (New York: Columbia University Press, 1982).
Davis, Brian. *State, Power and Community in Early Modern Russia: The Case of Kozlov, 1635–1649* (Basingstoke, New York: Palgrave, Macmillan, 2004).
Davis, David Brion. *Slavery and Human Progress* (New York: Oxford University Press, 1984).
Davis, Robert. *Christian Slaves, Muslim Masters. White Slavery in the Mediterranean, the Barbary Coast, and Italy, 1500–1800* (Basingstoke: Mac Millan, 2003).
Deakin, Simon and Wilkinson, Frank. *The Law of the Labour Market: Industrialization, Employment, and Legal Evolution* (Oxford: Oxford University Press, 2005).
Deane, Phyllis. 'Capital Formation in Britain Before the Railway Age', *Economic Development and Cultural Change*, 9, 3 (1961): 352–368.
Deletant, Dennis. 'Genoese, Tatars and Rumanians at the Mouth of the Danube in the Fourteenth Century', *The Slavonic and East European Review*, 62, 4 (1984): 511–530.
Delort, Robert. 'Quelques précisions sur le commerce des esclaves à Gênes vers la fin du XIVe siècle', *Mélanges d'archéologie et d'histoire*, 78, 1 (1966): 215–250.
Dennison, Tracy K. 'Did Serfdom Matter? Russian Rural Society, 1750–1860', *Historical Research*, 79 (2003): 74–89.
———. *The Institutional Framework of Russian Serfdom* (Cambridge: Cambridge University Press, 2011).
Dennison, Tracy K. and Sheilagh Ogilvie. 'Serfdom and Social Capital in Bohemia and Russia', *Economic History Review*, 60 (2007): 513–544.
De Vries, Jan. *European Urbanization, 1500–1800* (London: Meuthen, 1984).
———. 'The Industrial Revolution and the Industrious Revolution', *Journal of Economic History* 54, 2 (1994): 249–270.
———. *The Industrious Revolution* (Cambridge: Cambridge University Press, 2008).
Di Cosmo, Nicola. 'Ancient Inner Asian Nomads: Their Economic Basis and Its Significance in Chinese History', *Journal of Asian Studies*, 53 (1993): 1092–1126.
Diamond, Jared. *Guns, Germs, and Steel: The Fates of Human Societies* (New York: Norton, 1999).
Diderot, Denis. 'Questions à Catherine II sur la situation économique de l'Empire de Russie', in Tourneux Michel (ed.), *Diderot et Catherine II* (Paris: Calmann-Lévy, 1899), reproduced in 'Mémoires pour Catherine II', vol. 11: 813–817.
———. 'Observations sur le Nakaz de Catherine II', in Paul Vernière (ed.) *Œuvres politiques* (Paris: Garnier, 1963).
Dixon, Simon. *The Modernization of Russia, 1676–1825* (Cambridge: Cambridge University Press, 1999).

Domar, Evsey and Machina, M. 'On the Profitability of Russian Serfdom', *The Journal of Economic History*, 44, 4 (1984): 919–955.
Drew, Ronald. 'The Siberian Fair: 1600–1750', *The Slavonic and East European Review*, 39, 93 (1961): 423–439.
Druzhinin, Nikolai M. *Gosudarstvennye krest'iane i reforma P.D. Kiseleva* (Moscow: AN SSSR, 1958), the state peasants and the reforms of Kiselev, vol. 2, 296–390.
D'souza, Rohan. 'Crisis Before the Fall: Some Speculations on the Decline of the Ottomans, Safavids and Mughals', *Social Scientist*, 30 (September–October 2002): 3–30.
Duby, Georges. *Les trois ordres ou l'imaginaire du féodalisme* (Paris: Gallimard, 1978).
Duchet, Michèle. *Anthropologie et histoire au siècle des Lumières* (Paris: Albin Michel, 1971).
Duffy, Christopher. *Russia's Military Way to the West: Origins and Nature of Russian Military Power, 1700–1800* (London: Routledge, 1981).
Eltis, David, Behrendt, Stephen, Richardson, David and Klein, Herbert. *The Trans-Atlantic Slave Trade. A Database on CD-Rom* (Cambridge: Cambridge University Press, 2000).
Engerman, Stanley (ed.). *Terms of Labor. Slavery, Freedom and Free Labor* (Stanford: Stanford University Press, 1999).
Entsiklopedicheskii slovar' Brokgauz-Efron (Encyclopaedia Brokgauz-Efron), vol. XVI (Saint-Petersburg: Brokgauz, 1895).
Epstein, Steven. *Speaking of Slavery* (Ithaca and London: Cornell University Press, 2001)
Esper, Thomas. 'The Odnodvortsy and the Russian Nobility', *Slavonic and East European Review*, 45 (1967): 124–135.
Feinstein, Charles. 'Capital Formation in Great Britain', in Peter Mathias and Michael Postan (eds), *The Cambridge Economic History of Europe, vol. VII: The Industrial Economies: Capital, Labor and Enterprise* (Cambridge: Cambridge University Press, 1978): 28–94.
——— and Sidney Pollard (eds). *Studies in Capital Formation in the United Kingdom, 1750–1920* (Oxford: Clarendon Press, 1988).
Federico, Giovanni. *Feeding the World. An Economic History of Agriculture, 1800–2000* (Princeton: Princeton University Press, 2008).
Fennell, John. 'The Dynastic Crisis, 1497–1502', *Slavonic and East European Studies*, 39, 92 (1960): 1–23.
———. *Ivan the Great of Moscow* (London: MacMillan, 1961).
———. *The Crisis of Medieval Russia, 1200–1304* (New York: Longman, 1983).
Field, Daniel. *The End of Serfdom: Nobility and Bureaucracy in Russia, 1855–1861* (Cambridge, MA: Harvard University Press, 1976).
Finley, Moses. *Esclavage moderne et idéologie antique* (Paris: Editions de minuit, 1981).
Fisher, Alan. 'Muscovy and the Black Sea Trade', *Canadian-American Slavic Studies*, 6, 4 (1972): 582–593.
———. 'The Ottoman Crimea in the Sixteeenth Century', *Harvard Ukrainian studies*, 2 (1981): 141–142.

Franck, Penelope. *Rural Economic Development in Japan: From the Nineteenth Century to the Pacific War* (London, New York: Routledge, 2006).

Freedman, Paul and Monique Bourin (eds). *Forms of Servitude in Northern and Central Europe* (Turnhout: Brepols, 2005).

Frost, Robert. 'The Nobility of Poland-Lithuania, 1569-1795', in Scott Hamish (ed.), *The European Nobilities in the Seventeenth and Eighteenth Centuries* Vol. II, Northern, Central and Eastern Europe (London: Routledge, 1994).

Gayot, Gérard. *De la pluralité des mondes industriels. La manufacture royale des draps de Sedan, 1646-1870* (Paris: EHESS, 1995).

Geertz, Clifford. *The Interpretation of Culture* (New York: Basic Book, 1973).

Genicot, Léopold. *Rural Communities in the Medieval West* (Baltimore: John Hopkins University, 1990).

Gershenkron, Alexander. *Economic Backwardness in Historical Perspective* (Cambridge, Mass: Harvard University Press, 1962).

Gestwa, Klaus. *Protoindustrialisierung in Russland* (Göttingen: Vandenhoeck and Ruprecht, 1999).

Gioffré, Domenico. *Il mercato degli schiavi a Genova nel secolo XV* (Genoa: Bozzi, 1971).

Goldstone, Jack. 'The Rise of the West or Not? A Revision to Socio-economic History', *Sociological Theory*, 18, 2 (2000): 175-194.

Gommans, Jos. 'Mughal India and Central Asia in the Eighteenth Century: An Introduction to a Wider Perspective', *Itinerario*, 15, 1 (1991): 51-70.

——. 'The Horse Trade in Eighteenth-Century South Asia', *Journal of Economic and Social History of the Orient*, 37, 3 (1994): 228-250.

——. *The Rise of the Indo-Afghan Empire, c. 1710-1780* (Leiden: Brill, 1995).

Goodwin, Barry K. and Grennes, Thomas J. 'Tsarist Russia and the World Wheat Market', *Explorations in Economic History*, 35 (1998): 405-430.

Gopal, Surendra. *Indians in Russia in the Seventeenth and Eighteenth Centuries* (Calcutta: Naya Prokash, 1988).

Gorshkov, Boris. 'Serfs on the Move: Peasant Seasonal Migration in Pre-reform Russia, 1800-1860', *Kritika. Explorations in Russian History*, 1, 4 (2000): 627-656.

Grantham, George. 'Agricultural Supply during the Industrial Revolution: French Evidence and European Implications', *The Journal of Economic History*, 49, 1 (1989): 43-72.

——. 'Divisions of Labour: Agricultural Productivity and Occupational Specialization in Pre-Industrial France', *The Economic History Review*, 46, 3 (1993): 478-502.

—— and Mary MacKinnon (ed.). *Labor Market Evolution: The Economic History of Market Integration, Wage Flexibility and the Employment Relation* (London-New York: Routledge, 1994).

Green, Marcus (ed.). *Rethinking Gramsci* (New York: Routledge, 2011).

Gregory, Paul. *Russian National Income 1885-1913* (paperback 2004) (Cambridge: Cambridge University Press, 1982).

Grève, Claude de. *Le Voyage en Russie* (Paris: Laffont, 1990).

Griffith, Paul. 'Ethnocentrism as Act of Kidnapping. The Procrustean Complex in the West', *American International Journal of Social Science*, 1, 2 (2012): 59–70.

G.Y. Z. i Z., Ezhegodnik, 1907–1916 (Yearbook) (Saint Petersburg, 1908–1916, 10 volumes); G.Y.Z.i Z., Obzor dejatel'nosti za..., 1908–1914.

Hagen, William. 'Capitalism in the Countryside in Early Modern Europe: Interpretations, Models, Debates', *Agricultural History*, 62, 1 (1988): 13–47.

———. *Ordinary Prussians: Brandenburg Junkers and Villagers, 1500–1840* (Cambridge: Cambridge University Press, 2002).

Hansson, Anders. *Chinese Outcast. Discrimination and Emancipation in Late Imperial China* (Leiden: Brill, 1996).

Harley, Knick. 'British Industrialization before 1841: Evidence of Slower Growth During the Industrial Revolution', *The Journal of Economic History*, 42, 2 (1982): 267–289.

Harnisch, Hartmut. 'Bäuerliche Ökonomie und Mentalität unter den Bedingungen der ostelbischen Gutsherrschaft in den letzten Jahrzehnten vor Beginn der Agrarreformen', *Jahrbuch für Wirtschaftsgeschichte*, 24 (1989): 87–108.

Heers, Jacques. *Esclaves et domestiques au Moyen Age dans le monde méditerranéen* (Paris: Hachette, 1996).

Hellie, Richard (ed.). *The Muscovite Law Code (Ulozhenie) of 1649, part. I* (Irvine California: Charles Schlacks, 1988).

———. 'Recent Soviet Historiography on Medieval and Early Modern Russian Slavery', *Russian Review*, 35, 1 (1976): 1–36.

———. *Enserfment and Military Change in Muscovy* (Chicago: University of Chicago Press, 1971).

———. *Slavery in Russia, 1450–1725* (Chicago: University of Chicago Press, 1982).

Herzig, Edmund. 'The Volume of Iranian Raw Silk Exports in the Safavid Period', *Iranian Studies*, 25, 1–2 (1992): 61–79.

Hirsch, Francine. *Empire of Nations. Ethnographic Knowledge and the Making of the Soviet Empire* (Ithaca: Cornell University Press, 2005).

Hobsbawn, Eric. 'The General Crisis of the European Economy in the 17th Century', *Past and Present*, 6, 1 (1954): 33–53.

———. *The Age of Empire* (New York: Vintage Books, 1987).

———. *The Age of Extremes: A History of the World, 1914–1991* (London: Vintage, 1996).

———. *On History* (New York: New Press, 1997).

Hoch, Steven. 'Serfs in Imperial Russia: Demographic Insights', *Journal of Interdisciplinary History*, 13, 2 (1982): 221–246.

———. *Serfdom and Social Control in Russia. Petrovskoe, a Village in Tambov* (Chicago: University of Chicago Press, 1986).

———. 'On Good Numbers and Bad: Malthus, Population Trend and Peasant Standard of Living in Late Imperial Russia', *Slavic Review*, 53, 1 (1994): 41–75.

———. 'Famine, Disease and Mortality Patterns in the Parish of Boshervka, Russia, 1830–1932', *Population Studies*, 52, 3 (1998): 357–368.

Hodgson, Marshall. *Rethinking World History* (Cambridge: Cambridge University Press, 1993).

Hoffman, Philip. *Growth in a Traditional Society. The French Countryside, 1450–1815* (Princeton: Princeton University Press, 1996).

Holloway, David. *Stalin and the Bomb: The Soviet Union and the Atomic Energy, 1939–1956* (New Haven: Yale University Press, 1994).

Hrushevsky, Mykhailo. *History of Ukraine-Rus', vol. 7 and 8* (The Cossack Age to 1625 and from 1626 to 1650) (Edmonton: Canadian Institute of Ukrainian Studies, 2002).

Iakovlev, Aleksandr' I. *Kholopstvo i kholopy v moskovskom gosudarstve XVII v kholopstvo* and *kholopy* (In the Russian state, seventeenth century) (Moscow: Nauka, 1943).

———. *Zasechnaia cherta Moskovskogo gosudarstva v XVII veka* (The limits of the defences of Muscovy in the 17th century) (Moscow: tipografiia Lissner, 1916).

ILO. *International Labor Conference, Papers and Proceedings* (Geneva, 2001).

Inalcik, Halil. 'Servile Labor in Ottoman Empire', in Abraham Ascher Tibor Halasi-Kun and Bela Kiraly (eds), *The Mutual Effects of the Islamic and Judeo-Christian Worlds: The East European Patterns* (New York, Brooklyn: College Press, 1979): 39–40.

———. 'The Custom Register of Caffa, 1487–1490', in Victor Ostapchuk (ed.), *Sources and Studies on the Ottoman Black Sea* (Cambridge, Mass: Harvard University Press, 1996) vol. 1: 93, 145–146.

———. *Sources and Studies on the Ottoman Black Sea. The Customs Register of Caffa, 1487–1990* (Cambridge, Mass: Harvard University Press, 1996).

———. *An Economic and Social History of the Ottoman Empire, vol. 1, 1300–1600* (Cambridge: Cambridge University Press, 1997).

Indova, Emilia I. 'Rol' dvortsovoi derevni pervoi poloviny XVIII v. v formirovanii russkogo kupechestva' (The role of the village court during the first half of the eighteenth century in the formation of a Russian bourgeoisie). *Istoricheskie Zapiski*, 68 (1961): 189–210.

———. *Dvortsovoe khoziaistvo v Rossii* (The palace economy in Russia) (Moscow: Nauka, 1964).

———. 'O rossiskikh manufakturakh vtoroi poloviny XVIII v' (On the Russian manufactures during the second half of the eighteenth century) in *Istoricheskaia geografiia Rossii: XIX–nachalo XX v* (Moscow: Nauka, 1975): 248–345.

IPEC. *Every Child Counts: New Global Estimates on Child Labor* (Geneva: BIT, 2002).

Islam, Shafiqul and Michael Mandelbaum, (eds). *Making Markets Economic Transformations in Eastern Europe and the Post-Soviet States* (New York: Council of Foreign Relations, 1993).

Ivanov, Petr Ivanovich. *Alfavitnyi ukazatel' familii i lits, upominaemykh v boiarkikh knigach, khraniashchikhsia v l-m otdelenii moskovskogo arkhiva ministerstva iustitsii* (Alphabetical index of families and persons named in the boyari books, conserved in the first section of Moscow's Archives of the Ministry of Justice) (Moscow: Ministerstvo Iustitsii, 1853).

Izmes'eva, Tatiana F. *Rossiia v sisteme evropeiskogo rynka. Konets XIXe-nachalo XX v* (Russia in the system of the European market. End of the nineteenth to the early twentieth century) (Moscow: Nauka, 1991).

Jeannin, Pierre. 'La proto-industrialization: Développement ou impasse?', *Annales ESC*, 35 (1980): 52–65.

Jones, Eric. *Growth Recurring. Economic Change in World History* (Ann Arbor: University of Michigan Press, 1988).

Jurt, Joseph. 'Condorcert: L'idée de progrès et l'opposition à l'esclavage' in Equipe Rehseis (ed.) *Condorcet mathématicien, économiste, philosophe et homme politique* (Paris: Minerve, 1989): 385–395.

Kablukov, Nikolai. *Posobie pri mestnykh statistichekikh obsledovaniiakh* (Remarks for local statistical surveys) (Moscow: Leman, 1910): 8–10.

Kabuzan, Vladimir M. *Izmeneniia v razmeshchenii naseleniia Rossii v XVIII-pervoi polovine XIX v* (Changes in the rate of growth of the Russian population during the Eighteenth and the first half of the Nineteenth centuries) (Moscow: Nauka, 1971).

Kahan, Arcadius. *The Plow, the Hammer and the Knout: An Economic History of Eighteenth-Century Russia* (Chicago: University of Chicago Press, 1985): 76–77.

Kaiser, Daniel (trans. and ed.). *The Russkaia Pravda: The Expanded Redaction* in *The Laws of Russia*. Series I: *The Laws of Rus' – Tenth to Fifteenth Centuries* (Salt Lake City: Charles Schlacks, 1992).

Kaiser, Wolfgang (ed.). *Négociations et transferts. Les intermédiaires dans l'échange et le rachat des captifs en Méditerranée, XVIe–XVIIe siècles* (Rome: Ecole française de Rome, 2008).

Kappeler, Andreas. *The Russian Empire. A Multiethnic History* (London: Pearson, 2001).

Kashin, Boris N. *Kres'ianskaia promyshlennost* (Moscow and Leningrad: Gosizdat, 1935), The peasant rural industry, 2 vols, Vol. I: 215, 347–349.

Keep, John. *Soldiers of the Tsar: Army and Society in Russia, 1462–1874* (Oxford: Clarendon Press, 1985).

Khodarkovsky, Michael. *Russia's Steppe Frontier. The Making of a Colonial Empire, 1500–1800* (Bloomington and Indianapolis: Indiana University Press, 2002).

Khoroshkevich, Aleksandr' L. *Russkoe gosudarstvo v sisteme mezhdunarodnykh otnoshenii kontsa XV-nachala XVI v* (The Russian state in the system of international relations towards the end of the fifteenth and beginning of the sixteenth century) (Moscow: Nauka, 1980).

Kingston-Mann, Esther. 'Marxism and Russian Rural Development: Problems of Evidence, Experience and Culture', *American Historical Review*, 84 (October 1981): 731–752.

———. 'Peasant Communes and Economic Innovation: A Preliminary Inquiry, in Esther Kingston-Mann and Timothy Mixter (eds), *Peasant Economy, Culture, and Politics of European Russia, 1800–1921* (Princeton: Princeton University Press, 1991): 23–51.

——— and Timothy Mixter (eds). *Peasant Economy, Culture and Politics of European Russia, 1800–1921* (Princeton: Princeton University Press, 1991).

Kirilov, Mikhail V. 'Slave Trade in Early Modern Crimea from the Perspective of Christian, Muslim and Jewish Sources', *Journal of Early Modern History*, 11, 1 (2007): 1–32.

Klein, Martin (ed.). *Breaking the Chains. Slavery, Bondage and Emancipation in Modern Africa and Asia* (Madison: University of Wisconsin Press, 1993).

Kolchin, Peter. *Unfree Labour: American Slavery and Russian Serfdom* (Cambridge, Mass: Harvard University Press, 1987).

Kollmann, Nancy. *By Honor Bound: State and Society in Early Modern Russia* (Ithaca and London: Cornell University Press, 1999).

Kolycheva, Evgeniia I. *Kholopstvo i krepostinichestvo, konets XV–XVI vek* (The kholopy and enserfment, end of the fifteenth century to sixteenth century) (Moscow: Nauka, 1971).

Kondrateva, Tamara. *Gouverner et nourrir. Du pouvoir en Russie, xvie-xxe siècles* (Paris: Les Belles Lettres, 2002).

Koselleck, Reinhart. *Le Futur passé. Contribution à la sémantique des temps historiques* (Paris: EHESS, 1990).

Kostomarov, Nikolai. *Smutnoe vremia Moskovskogo gosudarstva v nachale XVII stoletiia, 1604–1613* (The Time of Troubles in the State of Muscovy at the early 17th century, 1604–1613) (Moscow: Charli, 1994).

Koval'chenko, Ivan D. *Russkoe krepostnoe krest'ianstvo v pervoi polovine XIX v* (The Russian serf economy during the first half of the nineteenth century) (Moscow: Nauka, 1967).

—— and Milov, L.V. *Vserossiskii agrarnyi rynok XVIII-nachala XXv* (The all-Russian agrarian market, eighteenth century-early twentieth centuries) (Moscow: Nauka, 1974).

Kriedte, Peter, Medick, Hans and Schlumbhom, Jürgen. *Industrilization Before Industrialization. Rural Industry in the Genesis of Capitalism* (Cambridge: Cambridge University Press, 1982).

Kukanova, Nina G. *Ocherki po istorii russko-iranskikh torgovykh otnoshenii v XVII-pervoi polovine XIXev veka* (Studies on Russian-Iranian relations from the seventeenth to the first half of the nineteenth century) (Saransk: Mordovskoe knizhnoe izd-vo, 1977).

Kula, Witold. *An Economic Theory of the Feudal System* (London: New Left Books, 1976).

Kussmaul, Anne. *Servants in Husbandry* (Cambridge: Cambridge University Press, 1981).

Lal, Deepak. *The Poverty of Development Economics* (Boston: MIT Press, 2000).

Le Donne, John. *Absolutims and Ruling Class: The Formation of the Russian Political Order, 1700–1825* (Oxford: Oxford University Press, 1991).

Ledovskaia, Irina V. 'Biudzhet russkogo pomeshchika v 40–60kh godakh XIX v' (Estate owners' budgets in the 1840s–60s) in Akademiia Nauk SSSR (ed.), *Materialy po istorii sel'skogo khoziaistva i krest'ianstva SSSR, vol. 8* (Moscow: Nauka, 1974): 240–245.

Lee, John. 'Trade and Economy in Preindustrial East Asia, c. 1500–1800: East Asia in the Age of Global Integration', *The Journal of Asian Studies*, 58, 1 (1999): 2–26.

Leonard, Carol. *Agrarian Reforms in Russia* (Cambridge: Cambridge University Press, 2011).

Leont'ev, Aleksei K. *Obrazovanie prikaznoi sistemy upravleniia v russkom gosudarstve. Iz istorii sozdaniia tsentralizovannogo gosudarstvennogo apparata v kontse XV-pervoi polovine XVI v* (The formation of chancellery system in the Russian state. History of the formation of the centralized state, fifteenth-sixteenth centuries) (Moscow: Moskovskii Universitet, 1961), 179–192.

Leventer, Herbert. 'Comments on Richard Hellie', *Russian Review*, 36, 1 (1977): 64–67.

Levi, Scott. 'India, Russia and the Eighteenth Century Transformation of the Central Asian Caravan Trade', *Journal of Economic and Social History of the Orient*, 42, 4 (1999): 519–548.

———. 'Hindus Beyond the Hindu Kush: Indians in the Central Asian Slave Trade', *Journal of the Royal Asiatic Society*, 12, 3 (2002): 277–288.

———. *The Indian Diaspora in Central Asia and Its Trade, 1550–1900* (Leiden: Brill, 2002).

———. *India and Central Asia. Commerce and Culture* (Oxford–Delhi: Oxford University Press, 2007).

Lévy-Leboyer, Maurice and Bourguignon, François. *L'économie française au XIXe siècle* (Paris: Economica, 1985).

Lieven, Dominic. *Empire, The Russian Empire and its Rivals from the Sixteenth Century to the Present* (London: Pimlico, 2003).

Lindert, Paul and Williamson, Geoffrey. 'Revising England's social tables, 1688–1812', *Explorations in Economic History*, XIX (1982): 385–408.

———. 'English Workers Living Standards During the Industrial Revolution: A New Look', *Economic History Review*, XXXIV (1983): 1–25.

Lloyd, Christopher. *The Structures of History* (Oxford: Blackwell, 1993).

Lombard, Denys *Le Carrefour javanais* (Paris: EHESS, 1990), 3 volre-edited in 2004.

Lopez, Roberto Sabatino. *The Commercial Revolution of the Middle Ages, 950–1350* (New York: Cambridge University Press, 1972).

Lortholary, Albert. *Le mirage russe en France au XVIII siècle* (Paris: Éditions contemporaines, 1948).

Lovejoy, Paul. *The Ideology of Slavery in Africa* (Beverly Hills: Sage, 1981).

———. *Transformations in Slavery: A History of Slavery in Africa* (2nd edn, 2000) (Cambridge: Cambridge University Press,1983).

Lovejoy, Paul and Fayola, Toyin. *Pawnship, Slavery and Colonialism in Africa* (Asmara: Africa World Press, 2003).

Mac Leod, Christine. *Inventing the Industrial Revolution. The English Patent System, 1660–1800* (Cambridge: Cambridge University Press, 1988).

Maddison, Angus. *Contours of the World Economy, 1–2030 AD* (Oxford: Oxford University Press, 2007).

Man'kov, Arkadii. *Ulozhenie 1649. Kodeks feodal'nogo prava Rossii* (The law code of 1649. The code of feudal law in Russia) (Leningrad: Nauka, 1980).

Martinière, Pierre de la. *Voyage des païs septentrionaux* (Paris: L. Vendame, 1671).

Mayer, Arno. *The Persistence of the Old Regime. Europe from 1848 to the Great War* (New York: Pantheon, 1981).

McCloskey, Donald. 'The Open Fields of England: Rent, Risk, and the Rate of Interest, 1300–1815', in David Galenson (ed.), *Markets in History: Economic Studies of the Past* (Cambridge: Cambridge University Press, 1989): 5–51.

Meier, Gerald and Rauch, James. *Leading Issues in Development Economics* (Oxford: Oxford University Press, 2000).

Meillassoux, Claude. *Anthropologie de l'esclavage* (Paris: PUF, 1986).

Melton, Edgar. 'Proto-industrialization, Serf Agriculture and Agrarian Social Structure. Two Estates in Nineteenth-Century Russia', *Past and Present*, 115, 1 (May 1987): 73–81.

———. 'Enlightened Seignorialism and its Dilemmas in Serf Russia, 1750–1830', *The Journal of Modern History*, 62, 4 (1990): 675–708.

———. 'Population Structure, the Market Economy, and the Transformation of Gutsherrschaft in East Central Europe, 1650–1800: The Cases of Brandenburg and Bohemia', *German History*, 16, 3 (1998): 297–324.

———. 'The Russian Peasantries, 1450–1860' in Tom Scott (ed.), *The Peasantries of Europe* (London: Longman, 1998): 227–268.

Mendel, Alexander. *Dilemmas of Progress in Tsarist Russia. Legal Marxism and Legal Populism* (Cambridge, Mass.: Harvard University Press, 1961).

Mendels, Franklin. 'Proto-industrialization: The First Phase of the Industrialization Process', *Journal of Economic History*, 32 (1972): 241–261.

———. 'Des industries rurales à la proto-industrialisation: Historique d'un changement de perspective', *Annales ESC*, 39 (1984): 977–1008.

Miers, Suzanne. 'Contemporary Forms of Slavery', in Richard Roberts and Philip Zachuernuk (eds), *Canadian Journal of African Studies*. 34, 3 (Special issue: On slavery and Islam in African History: a tribute to Martin Klein (2000): 714–747.

——— and Igor Kopytoff (eds). *Slavery in Africa: Historical and Anthropological Perspectives* (Madison: University of Wisconsin Press, 1977).

Mironov, Boris. *Vnytrennii rynok Rossii vo vtoroi polovine XVIII-pervoi po-lovine XIX v* (The domestic market in Russia during the second half of the eighteenth-first half of the nineteenth century) (Leningrad: Nauka, 1981).

———. 'Consequences of the Price Revolution in Eighteenth-Century Russia', *The Economic History Review*, 45 (1992): 457–478.

———. *The Social History of the Russian Empire*, 2 vols (Boulder, CO: Westview, 1999).

——— and Leonard, Carol S. 'In Search of Hidden Information: Some Issues in the Socio-Economic History of Russia in the Eighteenth and Nineteenth Centuries', *Social Science History*, 9 (Autumn 1985): 339–359.

Mokyr, Joel (ed.). *The Economics of the Industrial Revolution* (Totowa: Rowman and Allanheld, 1985).

Momigliano, Arnaldo. *Problèmes d'historiographie ancienne et moderne* (Paris: Gallimard, 1983).

Moon, David. *The Russian Peasantry, 1600–1930* (London and New York: Longman, 1996).

———. 'Reassessing Russian Serfdom', *European History Quarterly*, 26, 1 (1996): 483–526.

——. 'Peasant Migration and the Settlement of Russian Frontiers, 1550–1897', *The Historical Journal*, 40, 4 (1997): 859–893.

——. *The Abolition of Serfdom in Russia, 1762–1907* (London: Pearson, 2001).

Moore, Barrington Jr. *The Social Origins of Dictatorship and Democracy* (Boston: Beacon Press, 1966).

Morgan, David. *The Mongols* (2nd edn), (Malden: Blackwell, 2007).

Moriakov, Vladimir I. *Iz istorii evoliutsii obshchstvenno-politiceheskikh vzgliadov prosvetitelei kontsa XVIII veka: Reinal' i Radishchev* (On the history of the evolution of the socio-political orientations of the Enlightenment in the eighteenth century) (Moscow: Nauka, 1981).

Mukminova, Rozia G. *Sotsial'naia differentiatiia naseleniia gorodov Uzbekistana v XV–XVIe vv* (The social differentiation of the population of the cities in Uzbekistan in the 15th and 16th centuries) (Tashkent: Nauka, 1985).

Munro, John. 'Crisis and Change in Late Medieval English Economy', *Journal of Economic History*, 58, 1 (1998): 215–219.

Myrdal, Gunner. *Economic Theory and Underdeveloped Regions* (London: Duckworth, 1956).

Myshlaevskii, Aleksandr' Z. *Ofitserskii vopros v XVII veke* (The officer problem in the 17th century) (Sankt-Saint-Petersburg: tipografiia Glavnoe upravlenie udelov, 1899).

Nafziger, Steven. *Communal Institutions, Resource Allocation, and Russian Economic Development* (Yale University, unpublished Ph.D. dissertation, 2006).

Nicola, Di Cosmo. 'State Formation and Periodization in Inner Asian History', *Journal of World History*, 10, 1 (1999): 1–40.

——. *Ancient China and Its Ennemies. The Rise of Nomadic Power in East Asian History* (Cambridge: Cambridge University Press, 2002).

Nielsen, Randall. 'Storage and English Government Intervention in Early Modern Grain Markets', *The Journal of Economic History*, 57, 1 (1997): 1–33.

North, Douglass. *Structure and Change in Economic History* (New York: Norton, 1981).

—— and Thomas, Robert. *The Rise of Western Civilization: A New Economic History* (Cambridge: Cambridge University Press, 1973).

North, Michael. *From the North Sea to the Baltic: Essays in Commercial, Monetary and Agrarian History, 1500–1800* (Aldershot: Ashgate, 1996).

Novosel'skii, Aleksei A. *Bor'ba Moskovskogo gosudarstva s tatarami v pervoi polovine 17 veka* (The fight of the Muscovite state against the Tatars during the first half of the seventeenth century) (Moscow, Leningrad: Nauka, 1948).

O' Brien, Patrick. 'Agriculture and the Industrial Revolution', *The Economic History Review*, 30, 1 (1977): 166–181.

——. *Economic Growth in Britain and France, 1780–1914. Two Paths to the Twentieth Century* (London: Unwin, 1987).

——. 'Path Dependency, or Why Britain Became an Industrialized and Urbanized Economy Long Before France', *Economic History Review*, 49, 2 (1996): 213–249.

Ogilvie, Sheilagh. 'The Economic World of the Bohemian Serf', *Economic History Review*, LIV, 3 (2001): 430–453.

———. 'Guild, Efficiency, and Social Capital', *Economic History Review*, LVII, 2 (2004): 286–333.

———. and Markus Cerman (eds). *European Proto-industrialisation* (Cambridge: Cambridge University Press, 1996).

Ostrowki, Donald. *Muscovy and the Mongols: Cross-Cultural Influences on the Steppe Frontier, 1304–1589* (Cambridge: Cambridge University Press, 1998).

Pallot, Judith. *Land Reform in Russia 1906–1917: Peasant Responses to Stolypin's Project of Rural Transformation* (Oxford: Clarendon Press, 1999).

Pamuk, Sevket. 'The Black Death and the Origin of the Great Divergence across Europe, 1300–1600', *European Review of Economic History*, II (2007): 289–317.

Paneiakh, Viktor. 'Ulozhenie 1597 g. o *kholopstve*' (Ulozhenie of 1597 on *kholopstvo*), *Istoricheskie Zapiski*, 77 (1955): 154–189.

———. *Kabal'noe kholopstvo na Rusi v XVI veke* (Temporary limited servants in Russia in the sixteenth century) (Leningrad: Nauka, 1967).

———. *Kholopstvo v pervoi polovine XVII veke Kholopstvo* (In the first half of the seventeenth century) (Leningrad: Nauka, 1984).

Panero, Francesco. *Schiavi, servi e villani nell'Italia medievale* (Turin: Paravia, 1999).

Parker, Geoffrey. *The Military Revolution and the Rise of the West, 1500–1800* (Cambridge: Cambridge University Press, 1988).

Passeron, Jean-Claude. *Le raisonnement sociologique* (Paris: Nathan, 1991).

Patterson, Orlando. *Slavery and Social Death: A Comparative Study* (Cambridge: Cambridge University Press, 1982).

Pearsons, Michael. *The Indian Ocean* (London: Routledge, 2003).

Perdue, Peter. *China Marches West. The Qing Conquest of Central Eurasia* (Harvard, Mass.: Belknap Press, 2005).

Perlin, Frank. 'Proto-Industrialization and Pre-Colonial South Asia', *Past and Present*, 98 (February, 1983): 30–95.

Perry, John. *État présent de la grande Russie* (La Haye: H. Dusanzet, 1717).

Peter, Gatrell. *The Tsarist Economy, 1850–1917* (London: Batsford, 1986).

Pistarino, Giorgio. *Notai genovesi in Oltremare. Atti rogati a Chilia da Antonio di Ponzo (1362–1969)* (Genoa: Collana Storica di Fonti e Studi, I 3, 1971).

Poe, Marhall. 'What did Russians Mean when They Called Themselves Slaves of the Tsar?', *Slavic Review*, 57, 3 (1998): 585–608.

Pomeranz, Kenneth. *The Great Divergence* (Princeton: Princeton University Press, 2000).

Poni, Carlo, 'Per la storia del distretto serico di Bologna, secoli XVI–XIX', *Quaderni storici*, 73 (1990): 93–167.

Postel-Vinay, Gilles. 'The Disintegration of Traditional Labour Markets in France: From Agriculture and Industry to Agriculture or Industry' in George Grantham and Mary MacKinnon (ed.), *Labor Market Evolution: The Economic History of Market Integration, Wage Flexibility and the Employment Relation* (London-New York: Routledge, 1994): 64–84.

Prakash, Gyan. 'Terms of Servitude: The Colonial Discourse on Slavery and Bondage in India', in Martin Klein (ed.), *Breaking the Chains: Slavery, Bondage and Emancipation in Modern Africa and Asia* (Madison: University of Wisconsin Press, 1986): 131–149.

——. *Bonded Histories: Genealogies of Labor Servitude in Colonial India* (Cambridge: Cambridge University Press, 1990).

Preiswerk, Roy and Perrot, Dominique. *Ethnocentrism and History: Africa, Asia and Indian America in Western textbooks* (New York: Nok. Print, 1978).

Pretty, Dave. *Neither Peasant nor Proletarian: The Workers of the Ivanovo-Voznesensk Region, 1885–1905* (Brown University, Ph.D. diss, 1997).

Prodolzhenie drevnei rossiskoi bibliofiki (Continuation of the ancient Russian bibliophiles) 11 vol. (Saint Petersburg: Imperator. Akademiia Nauk, 1786–1801).

Prokopovich, Serguei N. *Opyt ischsleniia narodonogo dokhoda 50 gubernii Evropeiskoi Rossii v 1900–1913 gg* (Study of the national income of 50 provinces of European Russia, 1900–1913) (Moscow: Sovet Vserossiikikh kooperatvinikh S'ezdov, 1918).

Prokov'eva, Lidia S. *Krest'ianskaia obshchina v Rossii vo vtoroi polovine XVIII-pervoi polovine XIX v* (The peasant commune in Russia during the second half of the eighteenth to the first half of the nineteenth centuries) (Leningrad: Nauka, 1981).

Raeff, Marc. *The Well-Ordered Police State: Social and Institutional Change Through Law in the German States and Russia, 1600–1800* (New Haven: Yale University Press, 1983).

Ralston, David B. *Importing the European Army. The Introduction of European Military Techniques and Institutions into the Extra-European World, 1600–1914* (Chicago: University of Chicago Press, 1990).

Razin, E. A. *Istoriia voennogo iskusstva, XVI–XVII vv* (Military history 16th–17th centuries) (Saint Petersburg: Poligon, 1994).

Reuvan, Amitai and Michal Biran (eds). *Mongols, Turks, and Others: Eurasian Nomads and the Sedentary World* (Boston: Brill, 2005).

Riazul, Islam. *Indo-Persian Relations* (Teheran: Iranian Culture foundation, 1970).

Rosenstein-Rodan, Paul. 'Problems of Industrialization of Eastern and Southeastern Europe', *Economic Journal*, June–September, 53 (1943): 202–211.

Rospisnoi spisok goroda Moskvy 1638 goda (Lists of the town of Moscow in 1638) (Moscow: Tipografiia Moskovskogo Universiteta, 1911).

Rossabi, Morris. *China and Inner Asia from 1368 to Present Day* (London: Thames and Hudson, 1975).

Roy, Tirthankar. *The Economic History of India, 1857–1947* (New York: Oxford University Press, 2001).

Rudolph, Robert. 'Agricultural Structure and Proto-Industrialization in Russia: Economic Development with Unfree Labor', *The Journal of Economic History*, 45 (1985): 47–69.

Sabel, Charles and Jonhatan Zeitlin (eds). *Worlds of Possibilities. Flexibility and Mass Production in Western Industrialization* (Cambridge; Paris: Maison des Sciences de l'Homme, Cambridge University Press, 1997).

Said, Edward. *Orientalism* (London: Penguin, 1977).

Saito, Osamu. 'The Labour Market in Tokugawa Japan: Wage Differentials and the Real Wage Level, 1727, 1830', *Explorations in Economic History*, 15, 1 (1978): 84–100.

Sbornik Imperatorskogo Russkogo Istoricheskogo Obshchestvo (Collected works of the Imperial Russian historical society), vol. 41 (Saint Petersburg, 1884).

Scammell, Geoffrey Vaughan. *The World Encompassed. The First European Maritime Empires, c. 800–1650* (Berkeley: University of California Press, 1981).

Schmiechen, James. *Sweated Industries and Sweated Labour: The London Clothing Trades, 1860–1914* (Urbana: University of Illinois Press, 1982).

Scott, Tom (ed.). *The Peasantries of Europe. From the 14th to the 18th Centuries* (London: Longman, 1998).

Semevskii, Vasilii I. *Krest'iane v tsarstvovanie Imperatritsy Ekateriny II* Vol. 1 (2nd edn. 1881; Saint Petersburg, 1903), Vol. 2 (The peasantry under the reign of Catherine II) (Tipografiia F. S. Sushchinskago: St. Petersburg, 1901).

Seng, Yvonne. 'Fugitives and Factotums: Slaves in Early Sixteenth-Century Istanbul', *Journal of the Economic and Social History of the Orient*, 39, 2 (1996): 136–169.

Serbina, Ksenia N. *Krest'ianskaia zhelezodelatel'naia promyshlennost' tsentral'noi Rossii XVI-pervoi poloviny XIXe vekoi* (The peasant metallurgic home industry in Central Russia, from the sixteenth to the first half of the nineteenth century) (Leningrad: Nauka, 1978).

Shipova, Elena N. *Slovar' turkizmov v russkom iazyke* (Dictionary of Turkish into Russian language) (Alma-Ata: Nauka, 1976): 442.

Simms, James Y. Jr. 'The Crisis in Russian Agriculture at the End of the Nineteenth Century: A Different View', *Slavic Review*, 36 (September 1977): 377–398.

——. 'The Crop Failure of 1891: Soil Exhaustion, Technological Backwardness, and Russia's 'Agrarian Crisis', *Slavic Review*, 41 (Summer 1982): 236–250.

Slovar' russkogo iazika XVIII veka (Dictionary of the Russian language of the eighteenth century) (Saint-Petersburg: Sorokin, 1998) vol. 10, entry for *krepostnoi*.

Smith, Dianne I. 'Muscovite Logistics 1462–1598', *Slavonic and East European Review*, 71, 1 (January 1993): 35–65.

Stanziani, Alessandro. 'Les statistiques des récoltes en Russie, 1905–1928', *Histoire et mesure*, VII, nr. 1/2 (1992): 73–98.

——. *L'économie en revolution. Le cas russe, 1870–1930* (Paris: Albin Michel, 1998).

——. 'The First World War and the Disintegration of Economic Spaces in Russia', in Judith Pallot (ed.), *Transforming Peasants. Society, State, and the Peasantry, 1861–1930* (London: MacMillan, 1998): 174–194.

——. 'Information, institutions et temporalités. Quelques remarques critiques sur l'usage de la nouvelle économie de l'information en histoire', *Revue de synthèse*, 1–2 (2000): 117–155.

——. 'Les enquêtes orales en Russie,1861–1914', *Annales ESC*, 1 (2000): 219–241.

——. 'Serfs, Slaves, or Wage Earners? The Legal Status of Labour in Russia from a Comparative Perspective, from the 16th to the 19th Century', *Journal of Global History*, 3, 2 (2008): 183–202.

———. 'Free Labor-Forced Labor: An Uncertain Boundary? The Circulation of Economic Ideas between Russia and Europe from the 18th to the Mid-19th Century', *Kritika. Explorations in Russian and Eurasian History*, 9, 1 (2008): 1–27.

———. 'The Legal Statute of Labour in the Seventeenth to the Nineteenth Century: Russia in a Comparative European Perspective', *International Review of Social History*, 54 (2009): 359–389.

———. 'Revisiting Russian Serfdom: Bonded Peasants and Market Dynamics, 1600–1800', *International Labor and Working Class History*, 78, 1 (2010): 12–27.

———. *Bâtisseurs d'Empires. Russia, Inde et Chine à la croisée des mondes* (Paris: Liber, 2012).

———. *Bondage. Labor and Rights in Eurasia, Seventeenth-early Twentieth Century* (New York: Berghahn Press, 2014).

Steensgaard, Niels. *The Asian Trade Revolution of the 17th Century: The East India Company and the Decline of the Caravan Trade* (Chicago: University of Chicago Press, 1975).

Stello, Annika. 'La traite d'esclaves en Mer Noire au début du XVe siècle', paper at the international conference on: *Esclavages en Méditerranée et en Europe Centrale. Espaces de traite et dynamiques économiques (Moyen Âge et temps modernes)*, Casa de Velázquez, Madrid, 26–27 March 2009.

Stiglitz, Joseph. *Whither Socialism?* (Harvard: MIT Press, 1994).

Strumilin, Sergei. *Ocherki ekonomicheskoi istorii Rossii i SSSR* (Studies in the economic history of Russia and the USSR) (Moscow: Nauka, 1966), 330–333.

Struys, Jan. *Les voyages en Moscovie, en Tartarie, Perse, aux Indes et en plusieurs pays étrangers* (Amsterdam: Van Meers, 1681).

Sugihara, Kaouro. 'Labour-Intensive Industrialisation in Global History', *Australian Economic History*, 47, 2 (2007): 121–154.

Sunderland, Williard. 'Peasants on the Move: State Peasant Resettlement in Imperial Russia, 1805–1830', *Russian Review*, 52, 4 (1993): 472–485.

———. *Taming the Wild Field. Colonization and Empire on the Russian Steppe* (Ithaca: Cornell University Press, 2004).

Temin, Peter. 'Two Views of the British Industrial Revolution', *The Journal of Economic History*, 57, 1 (1997): 63–82.

Thompson, Edward P. 'Time, Work-Discipline and Industrial Capitalism', *Past and Present*, 38 (1967): 56–97.

Thompson, F.M.L. 'The Second Agricultural Revolution, 1815–1880', *Economic History Review*, 21 (1968): 62–77.

Thomson, Janice. *Mercenaries, Pirates and Sovereigns* (Princeton: Princeton University Press, 1994).

Tikhonov, Iurii A. *Pomeshchic'i krest'iane v rossii: Feodal'naia renta v XVII-nachale XVIII v* (The private estates' peasants in Russia: the feudal rent in the seventeenth to early eighteenth century) (Moscow: Nauka, 1974).

Tilly, Charles. *Coercion, Capital, and European States. AD 990–1992* (Cambridge: Blackwell, 1990).

Toledano, Ehud. *The Ottoman Slave Trade and its Suppression* (Princeton: Princeton University Press, 1982).

Toledano, Ehud. *Slavery and Abolition in the Ottoman Middle East* (Seattle and London: University of Washington Press, 1998).

Tracy, James (ed.). *The Rise of Merchant Empires. Long Distance Trade in the Early Modern World, 1350–1750* (Cambridge: Cambridge University Press, 1990).

Troinitskii, Aleksandr. *Krepostnoe naselenie v Rossii po 10 narodnoi perepisi* (The Russian serf population according to the tenth census) (Saint Petersburg: Wulf, 1861).

TsSK (Tsentral'nyi Statisticheskii Komitet, *Statisticheskiya dannyya o razvodakh i nedeistvitel'nykh brakakh za 1867–1886* (Statistical data on marriages and separations, 1867–1886) (Saint Petersburg, 1893): 16–21.

UNICEF. *The State of the World's Children* (Oxford: Oxford University. Press, 1991).

Van der Wee, Herman. 'Structural Changes in European Long-distance Trade, and particularly in the Re-export Trade from South to the North, 1350–1750', in James Tracy (ed.), *The Rise of Merchant Empires. Long Distance Trade in the Early Modern World, 1350–1750* (Cambridge: Cambridge University Press, 1990): 14–33.

van Schoonveld, C. H. (ed.). *Slavic printings and reprinting*, 251 (The Hague-Paris: Mouton, 1970).

Vazhinskii, Viktor M. 'Vvedenie podushnogo oblozheniia na iuge Rossii v 90-kh godov XVII veka' (The introduction of per capita taxation in the south of Russia during the 1690s of the 17th century) *Izvestiia Voronzhskogo gospedinstituta*, 127 (1973): 88–103.

Verlinden, Charles. 'L'esclavage du sud-est et de l'est européen en Europe orientale à la fin du moyen-âge', *Revue historique du sud-est européen*, XIX (1942): 18–29.

———. 'L'origine de sclavus=esclave', *Bulletin du Cange*, XVII (1942): 97–128.

———. *L'esclavage dans l'Europe médiévale* (Bruges: De Temple, 1955).

Vladimirskii-Budanov, Mikhail F. *Obzor istorii russkogo prava* (Summary of the history of Russian law) (6th edn) (Kiev: Izdanie knigoprodstva N. Ia. Oglobina, 1909).

Vodarskii, Ia. E. *Naselenie Rossii v kontse XVII-nachale XVIII veka* (The population of Russia during the seventeenth-early eighteenth centuries) (Moscow: Nauka, 1977).

Voltaire, François-Marie. *Histoire de l'Empire de Russie sous Pierre le Grand* (Paris: 1763) reproduced in Oeuvres historiques (Paris: Pléiade, 1957).

Voltaire, François-Marie. 'Lettres à Catherine II en 1762, 1765, 1766, in Theodore Besterman (ed.), *Correspondance* (Institut et musée Voltaire: Genève, 1953–1965).

Voth, Hans-Joachim. 'Time and Work in Eighteenth Century London, *The Journal of Economic History*, 58, 1 (1998): 29–58.

Wallerstein, Immanuel. *The Modern World System* 2 vols (New York, London: Academic Press, 1974–1980).

Weiss, Gillian. *Captives and Corsairs. France and Slavery in the Early Mediterranean World* (Stanford: Stanford University Press, 2011).

Wheatcroft, Stephen. 'Crisis and Condition of the Peasantry in Late Imperial Russia, in Esther Kingston-Mann and Timothy Mixter (eds), *Peasant Economy, Culture and Politics of European Russia, 1800–1921* (Princeton: Princeton University Press, 1991): 101–127.

Wilbur, Chris M. *Slavery in China During the Former Han Dynasty* (Chicago: Field Museum of Natural History, 1943).

Wilbur, Elvira M. 'Was Russian Peasant Agriculture Really That Impoverished? New Evidence From a Case Study From the 'Impoverished Center' at the End of the Nineteenth Century', *Journal of Economic History*, 43 (March 1983): 137–144.

Williams, Brian Glyn. *The Crimean Tatars* (Leiden: Brill, 2001).

Williams, Eric. *Capitalism and Slavery* (Chapel Hill: University Of North Carolina Press, 1944).

Williamson, Jeoffrey. 'Why Was British Growth So Slow During the Industrial Revolution?', *The Journal of Economic History*, 44, 3 (1984): 687–712.

Wink, André. *Al-Hind: The Making of the Indo-Islamic World, vol. 1, Early Medieval India and the Expansion of Islam, Seventh-Eleventh Centuries* (Leiden: Brill, 1991), 45–64.

Wirtschafter, Elise Kimerling. *Structures of Society: Imperial Russia's "People of various ranks"* (Dekalb: Northern Illinois University Press, 1994).

———. *Social Identity in Imperial Russia* (Dekalb: Northern Illinois University Press, 1997).

Wittfogel, Karl. *Oriental Despotism. A Comparative Study of Total Power* (New Haven: Yale University Press, 1957).

Wolff, Larry. *Inventing Eastern Europe, The Map of Civilization on the Mind of Enlightenment* (Stanford: Stanford University Press, 1994).

Wong, Bin. 'Entre monde et nation: Les régions braudeliennes en Asie', *Annales HSC*, 56, 1 (2001): 5–41.

Yavlinsky, Gregory. *Laissez Faire versus Policy-Led Transformation, Lessons of the Economic Reforms in Russia* (Moscow: Center for Economic and Political Research, 1996).

Yun-Casalilla, Bartolomé Patrick O'Brien and Francisco, Comin Comin. *The Rise of the Fiscal States. A Global History 1500–1914* (Cambridge: Cambridge University Press, 2012).

Zagorovskii, Viktor P. *Belgorodskaia cherta* (The Belgorod line of defence) (Voronezh: Voronezhskii Gosudarstvennui Universitet, 1969).

Zlatkin, Igor Ia. and Nikolai V. Ustiugov (eds). *Materialy po Istorii russko-mongolskikh otnoshenii: Russko-mongol'skie otnosheniia 1607–1636, sbornik dokumentov* (Materials for the history of Russian-Mongol relations: Russian-Mongol Relations 1607–1636, collection of documents) (Moscow: Izdatel'estvo vostochnoi literatury, 1959).

Zurndorfer, Harriet. *Change and Continuity in Chinese Local History* (Leiden: Brill, 1989).

Zyrianov, Pavel' N. *Krest'ianskaia obshchina Evropeiskoi Rossii 1907–1914 gg* (The peasant commune in European Russia, 1907–1914) (Moscow: Nauka, 1992).

Index

Abkhazian 73
abolition 4, 8, 16, 72, 104, 106, 108, 120, 122
absolutism 13, 23, 59, 123
Afghanistan 23, 34, 76, 77
Africa/African 9, 10, 11, 14, 15, 22, 25, 61, 62, 64, 66, 75, 77, 86, 90, 91, 120, 122
Anatolia 85
apprentice/apprenticeship 70
aristocracy 107, 120
artillery 22, 25, 40, 41, 42, 69
artisan 30, 69, 72, 76, 97
Astrakhan 36, 37, 38, 42, 76, 77, 79, 80, 84

bad harvest 72, 99
bailiff 3, 4
Balkans 73, 87
barshchina 96, 98
  see also corvée; labour service
Bashkir 36, 78, 84
birth rate 103, 104, 108
black earth 37, 94, 99
Black Sea 37, 73, 74, 75, 79, 82, 85, 88
Bohemia 95, 102
bondage 2, 3, 56, 61–70, 86–90, 102, 104, 108, 116, 122
boyari 54, 92, 139n. 44
Brandenburg 101, 102, 114
Bukhara 76, 77, 83, 84, 88
Bulgarian 73
bureaucracy 10, 25, 37, 43, 44, 58
Byzantium/byzantine empire 33, 38, 65, 74, 75, 89, 90

cadastre 55, 92, 93
Caffa 37, 65, 73, 74, 75, 85, 87
canon 22, 38, 40, 42, 133n. 14
capital 2, 7, 18, 19, 20, 29, 58, 59, 76, 99, 100, 108, 110, 111, 112, 114, 115, 117, 120

capitalism 4, 7, 9, 10, 14, 15, 16, 17, 19, 30, 59, 62, 94, 104, 108, 111, 115, 117, 123
capitalist 12, 20, 22, 25, 59, 104, 119, 122
captive 2, 3, 61–7, 68, 73–76, 78, 80, 81–86, 87, 89, 90
caravan trade 75, 76, 84, 88, 89
Caspian Sea 73, 84
Catherine II 12, 97, 120
Caucasus 76, 79, 85, 88
cavalry 22, 23, 26, 33, 41, 42, 47, 48, 49, 53, 67, 68, 72
cavalrymen 33, 40, 44, 47, 50, 53, 72
census 87, 103, 110, 113
Central Asia 2, 3, 19, 20, 21, 22, 29, 32, 33, 34, 36, 37, 39, 42, 53, 59, 61, 62, 73–89
Central industrial region (of Russia) 100
centralization (administration, military, state) 32, 35, 43, 44, 45, 78
child 14, 61, 63, 64, 66, 67, 70, 71, 83, 84, 85, 104, 110, 114
China 4, 9, 10, 11, 18, 19, 21, 22, 24, 25, 27, 29, 31, 32, 33, 34, 39, 45, 46, 47, 58, 59, 61, 62, 64, 70, 75, 76, 80, 81, 83, 91, 113, 114, 117, 118, 119
Circassian 73, 85, 88
city-state 18, 36, 77, 78
civil right 5, 19
clan 19, 22, 52, 62, 144 n. 123
code (legal) 67, 69
  see also Sudebnik; Ulozhenie
coercion 18, 19, 20, 29, 32, 58, 59, 91–7, 117, 121, 122
colon/colonized 9, 10, 13, 15, 28, 29, 47, 56, 59, 74
colonial/colony (ies) 3, 12, 13, 14, 15, 28, 29, 37, 61, 69, 73, 74, 84, 88
colonialism (historiography) 9, 10, 90, 117
colonization 2, 14, 37, 47, 50–6, 57, 59, 80, 90, 93
commerce 78, 84, 113

commercialization 95–7, 101–3, 108, 113, 121
common lands (commons) 8, 9, 108, 121
commons 8, 9, 121
commune *see* peasant commune
compensation (after emancipation) 83
competition
   among estate owners 3, 83, 84, 97, 98, 105, 114
   on the labour market 84, 97, 98, 105, 114, 115, 116
   in the slave trade 84
   between states 3, 36
concentration (economic size) 99, 111, 114
Condillac, abbé de 13
conscription 2, 19, 22, 23, 27, 29, 33, 39, 41, 49, 50, 51, 52, 57, 92, 117, 118
consumption 7, 119, 120
corvée 15, 91, 93, 94, 96, 98, 99, 104
Cossack 20, 22, 40, 50, 51, 52, 57, 81, 85, 109
cottage industry 97, 98, 110, 113, 115
cotton 84, 89, 98, 100, 114, 119
court (legal) 71, 87, 97, 110
craftsmen 69, 82, 97, 102
Crimea 36, 37, 38, 42, 45, 52, 54, 65, 73, 78, 79, 81, 82, 85, 88
Crimean Khanate 3, 36, 37, 38, 39, 41, 42, 43, 44, 45, 51, 79
Crimean war 1, 85
customary law 70

debt 45, 61, 67, 69, 70, 99
debt bondage 61, 62, 63, 66, 67, 69, 70, 72, 90
defence line 42–4
Demidov (estate) 97, 98
desertion (desertor) 45, 50, 51, 54
Diderot, Denis 1, 12, 13, 25
domestic service 68, 70, 72, 74, 82, 87, 101
domestic slave 62, 63, 72, 87

economic rationality 7–9, 94–101, 107–11
Egypt 74, 75, 85, 87
Elbian 102, 105
emancipation 99, 120
enclosure 109
English Muscovy Company 79

estate 3, 15, 16, 23, 53, 54, 55, 56, 66, 67, 68, 71, 90–104, 111–14
   owner 3, 23, 54–5, 71, 92–4, 97–9, 105, 111
export (products) 15, 80, 96, 98
export (slave) 76, 77, 85, 88

fairs 10, 84, 96
family 8, 14, 22, 27, 54, 69, 98, 105, 110, 113
famine 4, 30, 48, 104, 108
Fergana 84
finance 40, 43–6, 52
firearm 22, 23, 25, 39, 40, 41, 48, 49, 51, 53, 54, 68, 79
flax 98
fortification 42, 43, 44, 52, 80
fortress 41, 42, 44, 54
frontier 29–35, 37, 50–8, 84, 85, 108
fur 74, 80, 119

Geertz, Clifford 11
Genoa 65, 73, 74, 75, 87, 88, 89
Gershenkron, Alexander 4, 7, 8, 15, 16, 107
Golden Horde 36, 75, 78, 144n. 123
grain reserve 24, 42, 47, 48
growth (economic) 15, 16, 18, 24, 26, 27, 28, 30, 31, 33, 36, 44, 56, 58, 78, 81, 89, 90, 93, 94, 95, 96, 99–107, 109–17, 118–23
guild 12, 58, 95, 112

harvest 9, 26, 47, 49, 51, 72, 95, 99, 101, 102, 112, 114
horse 23, 41, 42, 45, 47, 52, 76, 80
horse trade 33, 77, 80, 84, 89, 90
household 56, 67, 72, 87, 94, 98, 109, 110, 113, 115

immigration/immigrants 56, 93, 119–20
income 4, 14, 16, 74, 92, 96, 97, 98, 103, 104, 108, 109, 110, 113, 120, 121, 122
indentured 65, 66, 70, 90, 119
India 3, 9, 14, 15, 18, 21, 22, 23, 25, 27, 31, 32, 34, 52, 61, 62, 70, 73, 75, 76–8, 80, 81, 84, 86, 87–90, 113, 115, 118, 119, 123
Indian Ocean 88, 89, 90, 119

industrial revolution 8, 18, 111, 114, 115, 122, 126n. 3
industrialization 7, 8, 15, 28, 30, 31, 95, 107, 109, 111
industrious revolution 113, 115
Inner Asia 2, 3, 59, 78, 87, 88, 89, 90, 119
innovation 23, 26, 27, 56, 94, 105, 115, 118
Iran 3, 73, 76, 77, 80, 84, 88, 89
Islam 21, 22, 62, 69, 70, 75, 76, 77, 83, 85, 90
Islamic law 83
Istanbul 77, 79, 80, 89
Ivan IV 38, 42, 64
Ivanovo 96, 100

Kalmyk 38, 39, 52, 78, 80, 82
Karakalpak 84
Kazakh 32, 34, 36, 75, 78, 79, 84
Kazan 36, 37, 38, 40, 51, 54, 78, 79, 81
Khan/Khanate 3, 20, 21, 35, 36, 37, 38, 39, 41, 43, 44, 45, 51,57, 73, 78–82, 144n. 123
 see also Crimean Khanate
Khiva 77
Kilia 74
Kipchak 36
Kokand 84
kormlenie 47
Kostroma 100
Krepost' 69

labour mobility 50–2, 94–101, 102, 104
labour service 15, 69, 94–6, 101, 102, 104, 114, 118
 see also corvée; domestic service
labour-intensification 101–17
landlord 3, 4, 54, 55, 93, 94, 96–107, 110, 113, 118
 see also estate, owner; noble/nobility
liberalism 13
Lithuania 20, 35, 36, 37, 38, 39, 40, 41, 43, 50, 51, 76, 78, 79, 81, 83, 85, 102
livestock 111, 112
 see also horse
living condition 108
 see also standard of living
luxury 4, 75, 76, 84

Manchu 21, 22, 49, 52, 118
manufacture 77, 95, 97, 99, 101, 112, 113, 114, 115
manumission 83
 see also emancipation
marriage 3, 138n. 23
Maurocastro 73, 74
mechanization 112, 121, 122
Mediterranean 3, 21, 73–8, 81, 86, 88, 89, 90, 119
mercenaries 40, 41, 50, 51, 57
merchant 4, 16, 28, 31, 46, 47, 48, 54, 55, 58, 73, 75, 76, 77, 80, 81, 84, 87, 89, 92, 96, 97, 98, 99, 111, 118
migrant/migration 3, 54, 55, 56, 57, 93, 102, 109, 110, 114, 115, 119, 120
 see also colon/colonized; colonization
military chancellery 42, 44, 49
military revolution 22, 23, 40, 57
mine 40, 74
mobility 54, 55, 57, 70, 92, 98, 102, 104, 110, 116, 119, 121, 135n. 51
 see also colonization; immigration/immigrants; labour mobility
Mongol 2, 17, 19, 21, 23, 24, 29, 35, 38, 40, 42, 43, 44, 45, 50, 52, 53, 57, 63, 64, 67, 73, 74, 78, 82, 89, 117, 118
mortality 16, 104, 108
mortgage 53
Moscow 8, 23, 24, 29, 37, 38, 39, 40, 41, 42, 43, 44, 45, 46, 49, 51, 53, 54, 57, 58, 79, 80, 81, 82, 83, 87, 96, 97, 98, 109, 110
Mughal 14, 18, 21, 22, 31, 52, 77, 89, 130n. 24
musket 22
musketeer 40, 48, 49, 54, 69
Muslim 22, 53, 66, 76, 77, 80, 82, 83, 85, 90

Nizhegorod 97, 149n. 44
Nizhnyi–Novgorod 97
noble/nobility 16, 37, 53, 54, 93, 96, 104, 106, 120
 see also estate, owner, landlord
Nogay 36, 38, 39, 43, 52, 54, 78, 79, 80, 82, 83, 84
nomad 19, 20, 29, 31, 32, 36, 37, 39, 52, 58, 62, 64, 65, 76, 78–86, 117

odnodvortsy 53, 54
Orenburg 34, 84
orientalism 2, 12, 14, 117
Ottoman Empire 3, 22, 35, 37, 38, 39, 41, 43, 44, 51, 57, 61, 65, 75, 76, 78, 80, 81, 82, 85, 88, 89, 90, 118, 119
ownership 16, 25, 53, 54, 64, 93, 94, 109

passport 100, 101, 110
pavlovo 97, 151n. 63
pawnship 62, 64
peasant commune 98, 107, 109
　see also commons, ownership
peasant mobility see colonization; labour mobility; migrant/migration
peasant-soldier see colon/colonized
peasant-worker 97, 100, 110
Persia/Persian merchants 34, 35, 37, 75, 76, 77, 79, 80, 84, 87, 88, 89
Peter the Great 1, 12, 39, 40, 46, 50, 51, 56, 65, 67, 71, 72, 87, 118
petition 54, 55, 69, 92, 100
pishchal'niki 40
plantation 116
Poland 24, 35, 37, 38, 39, 40, 41, 43, 50, 51, 75, 78, 79, 102, 105
Polanyi, Karl 8
police 40, 70
pomest'e 53, 54
　see also estate
Pontic Steppe 79
population 14, 17, 18, 19, 24, 27, 31, 33, 35, 36, 38, 42, 47, 48, 50, 51, 52, 53, 55, 56, 57, 64, 68, 70, 71, 72, 74, 85, 87, 93, 96, 100, 102, 103, 104, 108, 110, 111, 115, 120
price 10, 95, 101, 111, 112, 114, 120, 122
　grain prices 46–8, 96, 99, 100
productivity 94, 99, 101, 102, 103, 104, 108, 109, 111, 112, 115, 122
profit/profitability 3, 10, 20, 21, 74, 92, 95, 104, 105, 110, 122
proto-industry 16, 30, 95–101, 102, 105, 110, 111, 112, 113
Prussia 7, 12, 30, 44, 50, 101, 102, 112, 119, 120
putting-out 101, 113

Qing 22, 47, 49
quitrent 94–5, 99

rank 50, 51, 57, 69, 70, 82, 94
ransom (captives) 61, 73, 80, 81, 82, 85
reform 4, 8, 12, 13, 15, 16, 21, 25, 59, 65, 72, 94, 107
refugee 85
regiment 41, 49
rifle 22, 40, 133n. 14
rights 3, 4, 5, 18, 19, 44, 54, 63, 66, 68, 71, 86, 104, 106, 109, 118, 119, 121, 122, 123
runaway 55, 92, 93, 97

Saint-Petersburg 23, 29, 96
Samarkand 34, 76, 77
seasonal (labour, worker) 110, 113, 114
servant 45, 63, 66, 69, 70, 72, 82, 84, 87, 121
service see labour service
settlement 9, 56, 93, 103
Sheremetev, Count 82, 97, 100, 101
Siberia 24, 56, 79, 81, 83, 84, 93, 110
siege 38, 40, 41, 42
silk 79, 80, 84, 89, 98, 119
silk road 3, 73
silver 46, 82
skilled labour 76
Slavery Chancellery 83
Smolensk 37, 41, 50, 83
social status 13, 53, 56, 57, 110
soldier 22, 23, 24, 26, 27, 29, 39, 40, 41, 42, 44, 46, 47, 49, 50, 51, 54, 58, 59, 61, 69, 117, 118, 119
soul tax 72, 120
Spain 27, 74, 75, 118, 119
spice 79, 119
standard of living 53, 99
state peasant 54, 100
statistics 8, 87, 88, 89, 95, 103
steam 112, 114
strel'tsy 40
Sudebnik of 1550 71, 82
supplies (military) 2, 24, 36, 38, 43, 44, 45, 47, 48, 49, 58, 90

tactic (military) 40–3, 53, 117
Tashkent 34, 76, 84
Tatar 18, 34, 36, 40, 42, 43, 44, 45, 51, 52, 54, 66, 73, 74, 75, 78, 79, 81, 82, 85, 88
tax/taxation 14, 19, 20, 22, 24, 25, 27, 28, 29, 37, 39, 46, 47, 48, 49, 51, 52, 53, 54, 56, 61, 63, 68, 69, 72, 82, 85, 92, 119, 120, 121
Thirteen Years War 41, 46, 49, 50, 51
Time of trouble 38, 42, 64
transaction cost 9, 10, 27, 74
transports 41, 45, 47, 49, 58, 85, 88, 97, 114
Tula 38, 98, 149n. 39
Turkistan 82
Turkmen 77
Tver' 37, 81

Ukraine 24, 36, 37, 41, 42, 45, 51, 82, 85
Ulozhenie 1649 55, 69, 71, 72, 82
Urals 41, 56, 84, 93

urbanization 18, 29, 30, 31, 107, 109, 110, 113
Uzbek 75, 77, 78, 84

Venice 18, 65, 73, 74, 75, 80, 87, 88, 89
Vladimir (province) 79, 100, 110
Volga 37, 42, 56, 79, 80, 83, 84, 93
Voltaire, François–Marie 1, 12, 25
Voronezh 43
votchina 53
  see also estate

wage 15, 16, 25, 27, 46, 59, 70, 89, 91, 100, 102, 112, 122
wage labour 15, 16, 25, 59, 91, 122
war captive *see* captive
Wittfogel, Karl 17, 59
woman/women 71, 74, 84, 85, 110
worker booklet 116
working time 98, 115, 122

zemstvo 8
Zunghar 21, 39

www.ingramcontent.com/pod-product-compliance
Lightning Source LLC
Chambersburg PA
CBHW052046300426
44117CB00012B/1997